ADVANCE PRAISE FOR

Elemental: A Collection of Michigan Creative Nonfiction

"Michigan's population surpasses Jamaica and Ireland combined, and Anne-Marie Oomen showcases the Marlon Jameses and James Joyces of this land by gifting readers with stunning pieces by the likes of Ari L. Mokdad and Rochelle Riley—two names that should be household and heartheld, just like this collection. In the anthology, Michigan is described as two gloves, but unmentioned is what those two gloves are holding: the answer is literary talent."

— Ron Riekki, editor of *The Way North: Collected Upper Peninsula New Works* (Wayne State University Press, 2013)

"This collection is not a love letter to Michigan. The writers are not sparing in their complaints of the brutal winters, the bad deeds of their neighbors, or the potential isolation of deeply rural living, but they also warmly and generously sing the praises of Michigan's natural beauty, its striving toward diversity, and its residents' tenacity and goodness. Oftentimes, Michigan is a backdrop to these essays, and its presence—like the slant of autumn light over the woods—throws light and shadow through the leaves."

— Patricia Ann McNair, author of *And These Are the Good Times*

"I found this collection to be stunning and broadly illustrative of what I believe is the great theme of Midwestern literature: namely the drama one feels between believing you are in the heart of the country while feeling that you are in the middle of nowhere. This book collects the suppressed angst of the lake effect and the subtle sublime ecstasy of the island of the inland sea."

— Michael Martone, author of *Brooding* and *The Moon Over Wapakoneta*

"The magic of this anthology—aside from the quality of each essay—is the way in which these distinct and individual voices coalesce, montage-like, into a single defining declaration of what it means to fully embrace and celebrate a place and its inhabitants—human and nonhuman—in such a reckless and troubled time. The spirit of this book resonated days later, like pure song."

—Jack Driscoll, author of *The Goat Fish and the Lover's Knot* (Wayne State University Press, 2017) and *The World of a Few Minutes Ago* (Wayne State University Press, 2012)

"The essays in *Elemental*—full of the form's associative genius—are rooted in the ways of Michigan, the physical and emotional geography, approached from a remarkable array of angles. The reader comes to see Michigan as an unrepentant gateway to all manner of universes—ecological, personal, political, and geological, among others. All the writing sparkles and engages; all the writing evokes actualities that, as the title indicates, emanate from the dearly prized earth."

—Baron Wormser, author of *The Road Washes Out in Spring: A Poet's Memoir of Living Off the Grid*

"Loren Eisley was surely right when he said, 'If there is magic on this planet, it is contained in water'—and ditto for the magic that inheres in these pages of *Elemental* that explores, contemplates, and celebrates the great freshwater state of Michigan that is utterly like no other place on earth. In a time of drought and mayhem, what a gift and reminder that this beautiful place surrounded by water gives voice to such powerful writers."

—Robert Vivian, author of *Cold Snap as Yearning, The Mover of Bones,* and *Immortal Soft-Spoken*

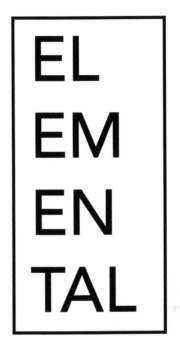

Made in Michigan Writers Series

General Editors

Michael Delp, Interlochen Center for the Arts

M. L. Liebler, Wayne State University

A complete listing of the books in this series can be found online at wsupress.wayne.edu

EL EM EN TAL

A Collection of Michigan Creative Nonfiction

Edited by Anne-Marie Oomen

WAYNE STATE UNIVERSITY PRESS

DETROIT

© 2018 by Wayne State University Press. All rights reserved.
No part of this book may be reproduced without formal permission.
Manufactured in the United States of America.

ISBN 978-0-8143-4567-2 (paperback)
ISBN 978-0-8143-4568-9 (e-book)
Library of Congress Control Number: 2018943987

Publication of this book was made possible by
a generous gift from The Meijer Foundation.
This work is supported in part by an award from
the Michigan Council for Arts and Cultural Affairs.

Wayne State University Press
Leonard N. Simons Building
4809 Woodward Avenue
Detroit, Michigan 48201–1309

Visit us online at wsupress.wayne.edu

CONTENTS

Anne-Marie Oomen

My friend Norm lifts the bucket of lake water over the dying embers, tips and pours it on the still abundant coals of an enormous bonfire. An explosion of sizzling, zinging vapor and the rush of steam-smoke. A shift of light. The cloud pushes upward, shapes itself according to the westerlies of Lake Michigan, to the contours of the dune and shore. It almost hovers, then dissipates in the night air. Sometimes, as our eyes follow it upward, we see stars through that cloud, light shaped by these elements.

Each Friday evening of summer, the Beach Bards, a storytelling group I belong to, closes down our storytelling session with that ritual dousing. For almost thirty summers, after the poems, stories, silly jokes (that's how kids become initiates to storytelling), and folk songs, after all the families have bundled the guitars, kazoos, and marshmallows, and trundled home, my cohort Norm Wheeler drags that bucket of lake water up from the shore and dumps it on the smoldering fire pit. We are required by law to put out the embers, but this gesture is also a respectful adaptation of practices of ancient peoples. Wind, earth, fire, water—all of it simultaneous in that one gesture—and the steam-smoke that rises remind us to send our words to the skies, some would say to muses, or god, however we interpret that word. In that moment we are bound together with these elements and with this place, the circle around the fire on the shores of a Great Lake closes, complete.

I am of Michigan. This place. If place reflects some inner psyche, some interior map of being, then perhaps it is fair to claim the best writing is influenced, down to its breath, by its source, its place. Michigan is a complex place, a coming together of many forces; it makes the writing complex, also a coming together. When I read these essays for the first time, I felt Michigan, especially its complexity, even when the pieces were not about Michigan. What does that mean? I felt *its complexity*? If writing reflects place, imagine this: flying over this "flyover state." Yup, "two states and a bridge," our lower and upper peninsulas separated by water, but joined by a bridge. That metaphor. Add other dualities: industrial-rural, urban-agricultural, interior-coastal, wilderness-tourist—all influence identity, perception, social consciousness, even prejudices. Couple that with interstitials we do not see from the airplane window: interconnected economies, cultures and subcultures, even spiritual ideologies. Geologically we are surrounded by the millennia-old Niagara Escarpment, a buried and timeworn rock shield that encompasses much of the Great Lakes Basin and has shaped our development and industry (think silver, copper, iron), though its presence is so old it defies the clock. A "cradle" of rock? And Michigan is not limited to, but also includes bioregions of flora and fauna, watersheds, weather patterns, economic cycles. And from our airplane window, we don't even see the complexity of history: diverse communities from ancient First Nations who followed rivers through the peninsula to nineteenth-century Dutch settlers in the flatlands of Zeeland, from Finnish miners of Iron Mountain to black Americans of the Southern diaspora, from Hmong to Arabic immigrants—each story unique and all too often complicated. I suspect other places have these complexities in microcosm. Do I dare say we are a macrocosm?

But what of our unity? What prevents our complicated dualities, contradictions, diverse complexities from being merely a Michigan kaleidoscope of tumbling images? Or from skittering us off the page into such free-form individuality that we can claim nothing in common at all?

Look at our map. We are also an enormous peninsula. Surrounded by water. Yes, to paraphrase Whitman's claim, *we are multitudes,* but I suspect those particular multitudes are influenced by our subtle perception of isolation, an isolation created by the extraordinary presence of one particular element, a liquid boundary in every direction but south. I'll hazard a guess we get a not-so-secret ego boost knowing we live in the midst of 20 percent of the world's freshwater. We are surrounded by it *and* isolated by it. What if that element shapes a deeply interior, often unseen unity? We live on land, but we're surrounded by the most stunning natural resource that exists, one that will become the most important commodity of the future. It becomes an unconscious force—from the three-thousand-plus-mile coasts, some still pristine, to our most abused rivers and stolen aquifers. Is it water that molds our self-perception, our consciousness? How many of us orient ourselves to the Great Lakes shorelines, our rivers or inland bodies of water, their nearness embedded in our sense of where we are? Farmers particularly think about the *whereness* of water, organizing their fields according to the nearest pond, river, or subterranean source, seeking the richness of the aquifer itself that feeds the fields. And so water was the first commonality I found in many of these essays, and as such, it is perhaps a prediction of who we are in this changing world, not as something set, but as a people in motion—like water, constantly shifting.

But how does this awareness exhibit in the writing? And how does it influence this collection? When I started writing this introduction, I had hoped to comment on a Michigan literature, the characteristics that might rise, like those we note in Southern Gothic or Western literature. But by definition, our complexity defies easy criteria. However, if the essay is, as Phillip Lopate explains in his now seminal introduction to *The Art of the Personal Essay,* a way "to attempt, to test, to make a run at something without knowing if you are going to succeed," then I may start with water as the defining ur element for us Michiganders. Water as attempt. As essential.

What other forces might spring forth?

On a cold spring morning, Annie Martin, acquisitions editor, and I walked around my dining room table, essays spread over the dark wood. Our goal: how to organize these beautiful manuscripts into something that would introduce readers to some Michigan essayists, and give them a way to understand the nature of the personal essay as it is being played out here, in this place of complex motion.

As we drank our tea, we read and reread these essays, shuffling them into piles. As expected, the subjects of these personal essays encompassed a vigorous and complex range. In addition to water, we discovered family, friends, snow, seasons, creatures, rocks, breathing, death, and imagination—each exhibiting a particular association. How would we help readers see? Dividing the manuscript according to *land, ideas, and creatures* held sway for at least fifteen minutes. *Weathers?* I grew up rural, a farmer's daughter, a field worker, so I grew up with a super consciousness about weather. I always thought of it as a Michigan thing, related to winter, so I wondered if we could associate the essays with types of weather. Or seasons? Another ten minutes. In the end, Annie and I came back to where I had started, four stacks that encompassed something essential—a four-way stop, four metaphorical directions, four sides to the square: water, air, earth, and fire. Elements.

As I thought about those categories, I found many of the essays looking back at me with an interior light associated with those elements—a phenomenon Lopate calls, "surrounding a something." Elements connect to this Michigan. I began with water, water that surrounds the land that nurtures the air that feeds the fires. That elemental, that linked. Thus, rather than offering any insight or criteria about what makes a Michigan essay, this collection is a way *to see* Michigan's essays through the lens of the elements we are shaped by. This elemental intimacy touches on related themes in Michigan literature: survival, transformation, tenacity, grit, a sometimes grueling independence. It is a voicing and a spotlighting—the way a hunter follows a sound in the woods at night and shines the light on it. Oh, there is the beautiful creature with that call, there now, in the light.

Thus, in this deeply troubled time, this collection is an act of ecocomposition, and these writers become, as an organism in this anthology, ecocomposers of breadth and complexity, combining these old forces as they reflect the spiritual *weathers* here in Michigan. In that literary gesture, that layered interconnection, I find a rising hope that marks our being, our identity, what we claim about ourselves through these essays. Though this selection of essays is certainly not comprehensive of writers of the personal essay in Michigan—and for that I am sorry—it is, to the degree I could make it, a representative look through a four-sided lens at our complexity. It is most of all a "futuring" of our literature, what we are becoming; it may even be an anticipation.

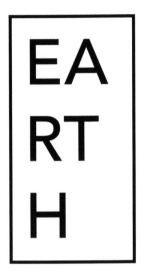

Teresa Scollon

EARTH

THERE IS A SILENCE IN IT. There is a silence and also motion.

Imagine being a tree, with one hand plunged deep into the earth and the other flung up into the sky. The hand in the earth both grasps and is free, free to let its fingers stretch, because the earth also holds. It holds you fast, as when you stand at the edge of the big lake and let your feet sink into the sand. With each wave, your feet sink deeper. It is the water pulling you and the earth into a new combined shape; it is the earth receiving you.

At the end of his life my father was trying to remember a poem he had once learned as a boy in the one-room country schoolhouse he attended with his cousins. In the poem, a farmer is plowing and speaking of the smell of newly turned earth. It was the last year of my father's life and he was turning over memories in his mind. He wanted the smell of earth to be among them. He remembered riding on the back of the draft horse, Sailor, holding tight to the harness as Sailor and his father walked out to the fields. There would have been the smell of horse, of a horse at work, of the leather harness, of sun-warmed air, of trees and their profligate blossom, and under it all, the smell of earth.

I knew a woman who had lost her little daughter; the woman told me in a quiet moment that she was merely waiting out the remainder of her own life; she only wanted to be reunited with her child. I knew another woman who, in her illness and old age, decided it was time to die and did. My father did not want to die; even as his body weakened, his mind was alive with story. It was the heart of a fierce winter. There were heaps of snow. The hospital sent him home for his last days. The Irish say the dying rouse themselves to take a last look, to make a final rounds of their territory and dear ones. The ambulance pulled into the driveway, and the EMTs pulled out the bed with my father in it. He wore a knitted hat over his bare skull. They trundled the bed up to the house and brought him in. His eyes were open and bright. He greeted each of us with his bright blue eyes, and then he rested. My brother could not bear to stay. He breathed into my father's ear: "I'll see you in green fields, Dad."

There is a shed of bent red metal in the backyard. The partly opened door will not close. Inside the partly opened door there is a jewel: the yellow eye of a cat, the cat motionless, the eye unblinking. I am too small to open the door; I look through the crack the door makes and watch the eye. When I run by the shed, the eye is there. My mother says don't look. She says to my father bury that cat. He has put it there to lie quietly until he can put it gently into the ground. I am not afraid. The cat is there when it was not there before. And then it is gone.

They say the body holds memory in its tissue, in its cells. The body is a map of time, a map of feeling. Sometimes we forget the body, cannot read its language, don't hear or heed the body's knottings and exclamations. Sometimes we think of the earth around our houses as something to be decorated, something as flat and inert as a painted wall.

But once a farmer showed me how a plant grows, standing at the edge of a field and curling his tall body down into a ball, slowly unfolding to demonstrate how the seed opens and sends out a spear of life, letting his plaid-shirted torso be the seedling. He was passing on the dance-story that another old farmer had showed him. The old one had stopped his truck and gotten out to counsel the young one against overtilling the ground. They were like bees, these two, passing on the story of joy and survival.

In this story the ground is a living tissue, threaded with rivulets and roots, inhabited and responsive. It is a culture, piled up in layers, one city built on the remains of another. It is a church, peopled with the tiniest of souls, busy in its commerce, the continuous exchange of material: molecules and minerals passed from body to body. The earthworm moves by mouthfuls through the soil, chewing and mixing: leaves and roots and minerals broken down and joined together.

The body has layers like the ground. We are made of layers. I watched my father open the bodies of animals. He held a thin sharp blade to the skin and drew a line down the center of the belly. The line grew dark, and the skin opened to another layer. Open that layer and there was another: luminous, thin, and strong. Open that and there was the inner sanctum, the organs resting in their places. The smell of the body. My father motioned for silence. It was a moment fitted for silence, in the presence of what is holy, of what has been created, of what has been created whole.

The Thumb of Michigan is flat. It was once under the lake, we say. You can drive along the road of an evening and see the lights of a farmhouse several miles away. In places the old lakeshore shows itself running a ridge across the ground. In places the ground swells or falls away, and in places it is full of stones. The Thumb is flat, except where it is not, where the glaciers skidded or slowed and dumped their weighty loads. The trees were burned off in the great Thumb Fire of 1881, when people jumped into creeks and lowered themselves into wells to survive. The ash from the fire darkened and yellowed the skies as far away as New England. There are now trees again in the Thumb, but not the old souls of other parts of the state. The Thumb is rural, often overlooked, settled with farms and small villages. Farms produce dry beans, sugar beets, and dairy. The Thumb is a real place with a real name. To strangers you can demonstrate how Michigan's lower peninsula is shaped like a mitten by lifting one hand into the air. The thumb is the Thumb. People don't believe this is a name until you tell them you have an account at Thumb National Bank or that you played ball in the Thumb B League. Then they laugh.

There is no point in trying to explain. Driving those long ditch-lined roads into the Thumb is a kind of passage into another world. Once, driving a pickup across the Thumb, newly returned home after living in the piled-up narrow slices of room shimmed in among the mountains of Japan, I had to stop. I felt the space around me could not be real. I felt I was driving between two backdrops on which were painted these vast planes—the rows of beans receding into the far distance, the theater of the wide sky and its impossible clouds. I got out of the pickup and walked along the shoulder of the road in the summer heat; the smell of soil and living things revived me, returned me to the world.

The ditches that run along the road are virtual canyons, running deep enough in places to sink a house trailer. In fall, when the beet trucks track heavy clay from the fields onto the roads, a little rain creates a glaze so slick it can send cars spinning like toys into the ditches. In spring, the field tiles pour fast-running water into the ditches. You can see how a life could be swallowed up.

■ ■
■ ■

I am from the village of Cass City, in the center of the Thumb, and my people were from somewhere else. My father grew up on a farm near Laingsburg, near Owosso, and his mother grew up on a farm within two miles of that place, and her parents grew up in Ontario, Canada, in a rocky place, and their parents grew up in Ireland, and before they came here there was little thought of leaving that green and lovely island, where the old spirit gods, the Sidhe, traveled in the wind. But they did leave, every generation, no matter their love of a particular spot of ground. What they carried with them was the connection to earth wherever they found it, to farming, to growing one's food, to living in the company of animals, who pulled and bore and fed.

My mother came from a farm near Grass Lake, where her parents moved from the city of Chicago in 1944. Her father was perhaps seeking refuge from a city that disappointed him, seeking the farm life of his own boyhood. He'd been a soldier, a butcher, a storekeeper, a barkeep. He married my grandmother, who was the third of nine children of Polish immigrants. Her parents had come from Łęki Dolne, near Tarnów. Her mother, Josefina, was pulled out of school as a girl by her new stepfather. He rode his horse into town for tobacco while his stepchildren worked in the fields. On Sundays they walked a few miles and when they were in sight of the church they put on their shoes. Her grandmother sent her off to seek a better life in the New World and gave her a few gold coins and a featherbed for the journey. The teenaged Josefina made her way through partitioned Poland to the free port of Gdánsk, sailed to Baltimore, and then traveled to Chicago, where she lived for the rest of her life. What did she think when her own daughter moved to a Michigan farm and took up that difficult life? But I don't know what she thought. Only small details of Josefina's life survive, weave a loose shawl of story around her epic journey.

I can tell you I grew up in the Thumb, but that does not say anything about the quality of the light over that land, or how clouds hang over Lake Huron far to the east, and how we noticed the clouds in the mornings when we stepped outside to pick up the morning paper. Round a certain bend in M-81 on your way from Caro to Cass City and suddenly the land unfolds to your right: the occasional house or barn punctuates the swells of gently rolling ground. See, said my father, how the road follows the high ground? This was an old stagecoach road, and before that, perhaps a trail.

In the Thumb, people might ask, "Who are you from home?" meaning, who are your people? People marry and have children, who marry, and the web of relationships is embedded in place, in particular farms, in community memory—a historical compost that enriches our understanding of each other.

The ground of my childhood home was hard clay. Digging was hard. In fall the fields around the house were harvested, then tilled, and the up-churned rows made a frozen corduroy all winter. I clambered across the fields clumsily, my legs not quite long enough to stretch from one ridge to the next as I made my way home for supper. I had been grooming our pony, Molly, who we kept in a barn a little way down the road, and sitting in the hayloft with an older friend, a girl who taught me how to eat Jell-O powder straight from the box. Moisten your finger and put it into the Jell-O box and then lick the fruity sour.

One autumn a hunter came to my grandparents' farm. He dragged his kill, a whitetail deer, up to the house and hung it from the old maple in the yard to dress it out. My grandparents sent me out to speak to him; he asked if they would like the heart. Older people know about these things, he said. It was November and cold. The day had light in it and no snow. All around were the listening fields. In the kitchen my grandmother handed me a metal bowl, and I took it out to the man. He made quick work of it and gave me back the bowl, weighted with its soft jewel. I carried it back to the house with both hands. The heart clouded the bowl with steam.

Some people turn away from the ground and others turn toward it. My father's people, the Irish, were driven from their small plots of homeland by forced starvation. They shipped to Canada and settled in a corner of Ontario, choosing, went the joke, the rockiest ground they could find, choosing the familiar in what must have seemed a riotous ocean of forest and ground. Person by person they made their way across Lake St. Clair to mid-Michigan, that flattish and waterless expanse. They farmed in close clusters; several homesteads of cousins settled within a small area, and built a one-room schoolhouse for the children. My grandmother lived nearly her entire long life planted within four square miles. On Friday nights the families gathered at one house and rolled up the rug to dance or sat at the table to play Pedro. My father and his two brothers had one bicycle between them, and they leapfrogged to school. One would ride a way down the road, then get off, lay down the bike, and keep walking. The next brother along would pick up the bike and ride it, then do the same.

They saw their cousins every weekday at the Doyle School, and every Sunday at St. Paul's. My father's best friends were his cousins Charlie Stevens and Francis Doyle. Of an afternoon the men and boys might knock off work for a game of baseball in a field. In a photo, the family has pulled the kitchen table and chairs out into the yard on a summer evening to sit and talk. My father is a teenager, sitting backward on a chair, leaning his folded arms on the chair back, as he listens. He is wearing a white undershirt. His face is open and tanned.

He told me how his mother, Elizabeth, came rushing up the stairs late one night in their little house, calling his name, calling his name. He was there, thank God, sleeping in his bed. Charlie and Francis had been out late, driving fast in a car full of boys. They sailed over a rise and hit a tree. Charlie and Francis were dead. The neighbors heard the crash and came running and spread the word. But who else was in the car? Who else was in the car? Elizabeth came running up the stairs, calling his name.

Ahead, my father steps over the tilled ground. He is measuring distance with his feet. He takes one stride, then drops the blade of the shovel he carries into the soil, twists it to open a small crevice in the earth. He has given me a pail of potato pieces to carry. Each piece has an eye. I have small steps; I cannot match his stride. I stumble up to each hole, fumble for the slippery potato, and lean forward to push it into the hole. It does not matter where the eye is, if it is pointing up or pointing down. It will find its way, my father says. He slides out the shovel's blade, and the earth closes over its new seed.

My father was a sickly kid, who suffered from asthma and allergies to barn dust. The doctor told him if he wanted to live, he had better get off the farm. He went to college and became a country veterinarian, and settled into a life of a different daily devotion. He liked cattle; he moved to the Thumb, where there was a lot of dairy farming, to make a life. In those days, in that place, his practice was a part of our family life. We answered the phone, we greeted customers in the clinic while my father got in a few mouthfuls of supper, we rode with him out to farm calls in his truck or the old family car stuffed with pharmaceuticals and equipment. We grew up, we said, on other people's farms.

As I grew I wanted to leave and I wanted to stay. I was taken by the pleasure of thinking, of turning ideas and words over in the mind. It seemed necessary to leave the life of the body to attend to the life of the mind. I went off to school, where lines were drawn. We were required to choose and narrow, choose again, in a branching set of decisions that led farther and farther away from a life that connected the land to anything else. If I was interested in international cultures, I was told, I would have to live in a city near an airport. I would have to pretend, I was told, that I was not married, that I was free to move from place to place as a company pleased. We worked long hours, caught airplanes, made presentations, aligned our work to a company mission, made money for an unknown someone. We set ideas against each other, to see which would win. I was among people living far away from their people. We were holed up in our jobs like solitary bees.

The country was a place where nothing ever happened. The summer heat pressed on the gravel and dust of the driveway, on the crops growing in the fields, on the small yellow and white butterflies encircling the chicory. My grandmother sat visiting on her porch swing, her housedress a faded print, her hands busy snapping beans. I caught a whiff of a new smell, the sharp smell of newly cut grass, under my arms. My grandmother saw me. Take a washcloth and soap and go wash, she said. Under the creaking windmill, an old pot caught drips from the pump, which my grandmother shared with the flowers growing there: zinnias and bachelor buttons. The bees buzzed the way time does, the most unsettling noise on the place. Around us the fields of growing things. The beagle Mac slept in his box of rags by the door and was otherwise free to go about his business. Farther back from the house were scraps of woods and creek. Nothing happened but everything grew.

I began to farm. I worked on a crew in Wisconsin, raising vegetables and flowers. I grew strong. I watched the moon and its transformations. The soil settled into the lines in our palms and the soles of our feet and could not be washed out. Some days I drove back into Chicago for meetings. I felt a layer of stillness around me; I had become unknowable to my city friends. One asked why I didn't bring her something from the farm. What would you like? I asked her, thinking of the beautiful vegetables and flowers we grew, tilling and planting and weeding and harvesting by hand. Bread? she said.

The next year I farmed a large old county work farm—450 tillable acres. I thought I might make a life there, but it turned out I was working in poor company, in a troubled place. We farmed wet ground in a drought year, and that saved us. I wanted to see the crops every morning, to know them, and through them feel reconnected to the cycles of life and harvest. We planted corn and beans and harvested hay, but the small field along the farm's entrance went unplanted, then filled with weeds. After the day's work, I would go out to my miserable garden plot and work there in the evening light. I stood and gazed at the fields on all sides of me, listened to a meadowlark sing on the power lines. There is something about long summer evenings that brings on lonely, that sets it ringing, like a slight breeze past wind chimes, the lowest pipe vibrating slow and tuneful. Those were my moments of standing on the earth, feeling warm soil under my bare feet, head swimming in vista and bird song. I had longed for the earth, and now I had it. But I needed my own kind as well.

This was back when I still thought it was possible to make a mark, to leave something behind. But the ground absorbs everything. All I have left now are memories of that single-mindedness, a few scraps of paper, a few photos. Hope took root and spread under the ground like a plume, headed nowhere in particular.

In the city, you can walk out your door and feel part of something, jostled and hurried. But in the country you are yourself, and you look out over a big space, a horizon as broad as an ocean's, long rows ahead of you. Sometimes after knocking off work we'd head for a swimming hole. I floated on my back and looked at the trees that fringed the water, felt how lives were bounded and unbounded. A life could be swallowed up this way, and why not. The killdeer call made a space around it.

My father died in the wee hours. I walked out of that newly quiet house in the morning to see an Amish farmer walking into the driveway. He'd come to town to visit a man in the hospital whose buggy had been hit by a car, and then he had walked up the long hill to see my father. He's gone, I told him. Come into the house. My mother would be glad to see you. I took him into the kitchen where my mother greeted him in her first act as a widow.

My father had told me how he caught a fly ball in Tiger Stadium as a boy. That was my moment of fame, he said, catching a fly ball in Tiger Stadium. His farm team had gotten to play. There was something about uniforms, how they'd never had uniforms and they scrambled to come up with something for their trip to Detroit. He was the kind of boy who would feel God himself smiling down on him as he fielded that ball, overcome with his own good luck. That little jewel of a memory he kept so close to himself that he never spoke of it except that once. Now all of his memories are scattered dust. Our flesh goes into the earth. But where do memories go? They are a kind of thought ash.

When you work with the ground, you can forget how to speak. You have worked all day, and now you are resting. Age is like this too. As you get older, you want to stop talking. You have come home at last, and your old people are gone. It is as if you were on a long sea voyage, and when you return no one remembers your old language. You remember the silence of your grandfather, whose silence was a field, a space around him. Nothing you see now is new; everything reminds you of something else, of someone else, someone you knew who is now gone. Wendell Berry says that you become like a tree standing over a grave. Some days you wish for someone to hear and see and witness all the memories you carry. Some days you understand that speaking of it only goes so far, only blunts the sharp edges. You are a vessel of memory, and there is nowhere to spill it except into the ground, which receives everything. And there is the earthworm again, making its way by mouthfuls, chewing and mixing: leaves and roots and minerals broken down and joined together.

Isn't this what you want for your feelings? For something to draw them out of you, draw them out through your skin, which has become porous.

You are a piece of ground, swallowing experience and all the wounds and joys that come with it. You are a receivership. Waiting in hope that some new gesture will find its bearings in you, and grow, and draw up its nutrients from what you have carried, and reach out its branches to the world.

■ ■
■ ■

To live among fields does something to a person. To live along a river, or on the Great Lakes, does something to a person. People from other parts of the country don't believe the size of the Great Lakes until they arrive, and then they exclaim: It is like the ocean. We know, we think. We told you.

More than once a friend from elsewhere told me my hometown was in the middle of nowhere—an idea I could not understand. It was a blind thing to say, when all around us the earth lay open and alive, dwarfing us. Even under snow, the curves of the world were voluptuous and riveting. It would be like saying, as you lie touching the body of your lover, that you are nowhere. You are at the center.

Look out over an expanse—the prairies, or the canyons, or the lakes, or the curve along M-81—and feel a low, slow stirring, like timpani. Felt, rather than heard, at the edges of perception, and then a swelling, an ache. Isn't this feeling a cousin to desire, the feeling that it is impossible to take it all in, that the senses are at last fully employed, stretching to contain an otherness, a reaching for what can never be yours. We never speak of it. I don't know if anyone else feels this way, but I think they do. It is the love of ground, which is like love everywhere: molecular and unbidden.

■ ■
■ ■

Where I live now was once a forest. The soil is poor and sandy, and lies over a layer of small stones. It can't hold onto anything—water and nutrients pass through it quickly—and yet the trees find purchase. The yard is filled with small green plants that require a close look. Moss: an assembly of individual pieces of jagged lace. I wait to see what comes up on its own. Yarrow. Oak and maple seedlings. A small forest orchid that no one seems able to name. In the wet part of late summer, mushrooms appear: red, tan, light brown. The air is alive with birds, with breathing.

Alison Swan

BEFORE THE GARDEN IS EXTINCT

I'D BEEN TO THE WOODS FOR MY DAILY HIKE. Back behind the wheel of the car, my body felt strong and capable—*I can climb hills in the sand, quickly. I know these unmapped trails as well as—no, better than—the back of either hand.* I was, as they say, *in the zone*: high on endorphins and good air.

Perhaps because I'd carried a bit of my woods habit of attentiveness back into the car with me, I noticed a brown fox trotting through the unmowed grass, April drab, of an abandoned golf course. She was so close to the road I could see she carried something small, gray, and songbird sized in her mouth. Thoughts flitted through my mind: Aren't foxes nocturnal? Is she a gray or a red? *You should stop. Work can wait awhile. Stop. Get out of the car. And go back and look for the fox.*

I talk to myself this way sometimes. It helps me settle in, focus, accomplish unquantifiable things.

This fox sighting was unremarkable, except that it happened right in the middle of the day. It would have been rash to let the moment pass, and I did pull the car off onto the grassy shoulder across from boat warehouses and condos, at least partially to prove to myself that I could, that I do indeed share some small bit of the talent for encountering wild nature that seems inexhaustible in some writers.

The sun beat down from the apex of its daily arc. Although it was midday, it was mid-spring and Monday, and so the road to the beach was empty: of cars, runners, bicyclists, lawn crews, of all the in-season bric-a-brac of resort towns.

I waded out into the deep grass. Lake Michigan reached me in sound waves, the surf so high it comprised the soundtrack a half-mile inland. I thought of the fox, hoped she had not moved on, and if she hadn't that I wouldn't startle her. I didn't have to walk far to reach the top of the sledding hill, which I crested in slow motion, going for a stalkerlike deliberation far removed from my usual habit of dashing. I imagine that this is the way successful hunters move. Two Canada geese floated on the pond at the base of the hill, and, as if they'd all three gathered at the water together on purpose, the fox nosed around in the weeds nearby. They seemed unaware of each other, the geese and the fox—and of me, but we have all played this game. No doubt they were keenly aware of one another—and of me—they just didn't let on.

At the very spot where I've launched my daughter on her sled, I lowered myself to a crouch very slowly, then wrapped my arms around my knees, also slowly. I didn't take my eyes from the fox, who did not so much as glance my way. Perhaps the northwest wind carried my scent away and the surf's roar absorbed my rustles.

The fox trotted directly up the hill toward me, still carrying the limp, gray creature. (Oh, for a photo of that to show you!) She was hunting, all purpose and intent. I willed myself to utterly still alertness. My unhatted hair flew about my head—like leaves, I hoped. Highly polished SUVs passed on the road. The odds were very good I knew the drivers. The glare off the windshields made it impossible to know. Without moving anything but my eyes and the corners of my lips, I glanced over quickly with the abbreviated smile that's my version of a neighborly nod.

The fox continued to climb the hill toward me. I noted her black-tipped tail and large ears, that she was more brown than red, and bore no black "boots," a gray fox then. She kept coming on. I kept still. When she was just yards from my lap, our eyes finally met. She didn't so much as flinch, and neither did I. Like flowing water encountering a boulder, she smoothly shifted direction. She turned into the wind, away from the road, trotted a few more yards, and began to poke through the gully of an old golf-cart path, along a crumpled orange snow fence that had long ago stopped serving any purpose. She'd managed to empty her mouth without my notice. Kits were probably heaped warmly in a nearby den. My own daughter was sitting in a classroom a couple of miles away. I wished she was here to see.

When the fox began wandering toward me again, I knew she'd determined that the darkish lump in the grass was not a threat, that I had succeeded in settling myself so carefully and quietly that she was carrying on the business of hunting. And so there we were: two mothers, one crouched and awed, the other trotting and intent, out in the wide open under a noonday sky, surrounded on all sides by the human-built world. That should have been enough for me, I see this now clearly, but in that moment I could not shake my desire for a picture. I desperately wanted a photograph.

A couple of times, the fox passed so close to me I could almost have reached out and touched her. I had never been that close to a fox. In fact, I'd never been that close to any wild mammal that was simply going about its business. (Neighborhood squirrels, we must admit, are not *that* wild.) I was struck by the intensity of her focus. She tracked odors on the ground the way I've watched dogs track odors, with starts and stops and starts, eyes slightly hooded. Maybe she wouldn't notice if I moved a little. I was pretty sure I could do so silently.

I decided to go for a picture. In one single motion I stood and began to lift the camera to my eyes without taking them from the fox—the better to watch the good mother immediately freeze, turn her remarkable eyes and ears toward me, then dash west into the tangled bank that bounded the other side of the overgrown fairway. In seconds, she had evaporated, and I was left standing there feeling impatient, graceless, and stupid, awkward in my human body. I suspect she'd known all along that I was a human, but that squatting humans do not move quickly, and maybe even that this squatting human was not any kind of threat.

Here is what I know for sure: moving through the habitat of wild creatures, on foot and quickly, with my ears and skin tuned in, and my eyes almost always averted, is what I do best, what I have always done best. I am not any kind of tracker, not one who shoots guns or one who shoots cameras. I like to be *with* and *among*. I do not like to be *above* or *upon*, and I certainly do not like to be *against*.

For the sake of the story and not because it felt like it was the right thing to do, I walked over to the patch of grass where I suspected she'd dropped her mouthful. I found a neat heap of vole corpses—there must have been a dozen, the work of the fox mother's morning. I did not touch them or step closer. While she had been patiently, deftly gathering fresh meat for her babies in that rewilding meadow, I'd been dashing through the nearby woods, imagining I could belong there for just a little while. Perhaps I can. Perhaps I do pass through without disrupting, too much. Perhaps it's okay, once in a while, to stop and watch. Gary Snyder has observed that, if we're of any use at all to animals, perhaps it's as entertainment. Maybe I'll play a role in the stories she tells when she gets back home. In any case, may other clumsy humans stay away long enough for her to notice the lump-turned-*Homo sapiens* that was me has exited the meadow, and may every one of those dead voles make it to the mouths of her babes.

A little bit of research reveals that the gray fox—and all foxes—are indeed nocturnal—or crepuscular (that wonderful word). The hunter with whom I'd passed the noon hour was likely out and about because of hungry kits. *Urocyon cinereoargenteus* ranges across the eastern half of the United States, across the southern states and up the West Coast. Gray foxes are less widespread but less shy than red foxes, and they like to build their dens in banks like the ones at the edge of the fairway we used as a sledding hill until it became the site of our town's newest residential construction project. They are the only American canids that will climb trees, especially leaning or thickly branched ones like those left for now in the rough of that old golf course.

I hope West Shore's foxes have found a way to live among the new houses that have laid claim to the sledding hill and its view of the tangled bank. And, yes, I hope I get to crouch near a hunting vixen again.

Stephanie Mills

NATURE IS PRIMARY, WONDER INBORN

WRITING IS ALWAYS DIFFICULT. At least for me it is. Writing or speaking about nature, especially in this era of extreme peril to the very elements of life—soils, waters, climate, and biodiversity—can be heart-rending. Yet hammering away at the many manifestations of the ecological reckoning bearing down upon us in order to shatter the natural-enough denial of them is not a kindness, but an incitement to the sin of despair. Rather, like Thoreau, I too would speak a word for nature. I would honor her prophets. I would hearten the reader for the challenges ahead with Rachel Carson's promise: "Those who contemplate the beauty of the earth will find reserves of strength that will endure as long as life lasts."

During the August and September weeks I struggled with this writing, daily walks around my neighborhood sustained my sanity. I now live in a very different kind of place than the Bay Area, a semirural county outside a small city in northwest Lower Michigan. Since I left San Francisco some thirty years ago, I have occupied the same piece of land. I helped build my house there. I've pulled up, cut down, and planted trees there. In good years my attempts at vegetable gardening in the beach sand that passes for soil at my place have yielded up to a pound of string beans. No sustainability coming from that quarter.

The bioregion where I live once was covered with the great North-woods, a forest dominated by sugar maples and beeches, interspersed with streaks of white and red pines as well as a score of other tree species. This forest was peopled by wolves, bears, cougars, flying squirrels, the late passenger pigeon, two dozen species of warblers—by an incredible host of beings. Although the terrain has been worked over by modern settlement, it remains a beautiful place to live, but not for sissies. There are four dramatically distinct seasons including a real winter. A recent year's total snowfall in our area, not to brag, was 220 inches.

Living there has been an extended education. I'm a slow learner, but in relationships with land, most of what's worth knowing can only be learned slowly. One thing I do know is that if I go outside and open my senses, I will meet up with a marvel or two.

On one of my mid-September walks I decided to filch some apples from an abandoned orchard nearby. The old fruit trees there are various, hardy and prolific, camouflaged by trees and shrubs that have grown up since the orchard was left to its own devices.

There is also an enormous ash tree in that tract of so-called vacant land. Its size isn't obvious from a distance, but up close you discover that its trunk is more than three feet in diameter at breast height. Before my apple heist, I made a pilgrimage to the ash tree, wading through the old-field vegetation of knee-deep dried grasses, bouncing bet, knapweed, and Canada goldenrod. There's a hedge of autumn olive, an exotic plant, around the ash tree's base. In disturbed landscapes autumn olive grows in dense thickets wherever birds can perch and excrete its seeds. I bashed my way through the alien shrubbery just to touch the great old ash tree. This ash might have been growing there a hundred years. That's a massive life experience, worthy of deep respect.

Meetings with ash trees are melancholy, though. Midwestern ashes have almost entirely succumbed to an invasive insect, the emerald ash borer, arrived here as an unintended consequence of world trade. Just as the Dutch elm beetle killed off the elms, and the blight the chestnuts, the emerald ash borer may administer the coup de grâce to the ashes, already stressed by deforestation and air pollution. Yet ash seedlings proliferate along the nearby roadside. Here and there are some ash saplings. With lucky genes, a few of them might resist the infestation. This mighty tree's will to live is in evidence all around.

Aldo Leopold, another prophet of nature, famously said, "One of the penalties of an ecological education is that one lives alone in a world of wounds." My encounter with the ash tree did not exactly contradict the gloom and doom. It gratified my sense of wonder, though, and was a sermon on steadfastness.

My ecological education has been at least as rewarding as it has been dismaying. The opportunity to get out and about with naturalists—scientists and laypeople who are living for something more than just a human agenda—has repeatedly renewed my hope for my own kind. Meeting people who are dedicated to saving species, witnessing their valor and their tenderness toward the fate of other creatures brings me tears of joy.

Although it's uncommon, human devotion to the survival of a rare plant, an endangered insect, or big wilderness bespeaks a deep understanding that in the community of life on Earth we are absolutely interdependent. The loss of any member of the community diminishes us all.

We human beings are in the continuum of life, subject to its rules, available to its splendors. Our membership in this community is not a romantic idea, but a fact of evolution. We are biological organisms. We exist because for five billion years life on this amazing planet has been developing, diverging, and colonizing niches—from the deep seafloor to the ice of the world's rapidly melting glaciers. No species lasts forever, but every creature embodies an inimitable saga of existence and adaptation. All life forms have moral standing and a necessary role in the order of nature. There is of course no life without the taking of life, but wanton destruction of other beings is a crime against life itself.

While climate destabilization rightly commands much attention, and human overpopulation as a driving force in the erosion of the biosphere deserves more attention, of all the calamities we face, perhaps the worst is the earth's sixth great extinction crisis, which humanity is precipitating. Because of what we are doing and how we are living, the rate of extinctions is now between 100 to 1000 times greater than prehuman levels, moving toward a rate that is 10,000 times greater. In this holocaust, the life and beauty of the earth are at stake.

Nearly sixty years ago, love for the living world drove Rachel Carson to sound the alarm about industrial civilization's chemical assaults on nature. Carson was a zoologist and peerless writer (educated, by the way, at a women's college, Chatham). Carson never married or bore a child of her own. Beginning in the Depression years, by the work of her pen, she supported her widowed mother, her sister, her nieces, and her grandnephew Roger. In 1962, after years of scrupulous research and masterful writing, her historic book *Silent Spring* was published. In it, Carson reminded the world that life is whole. She amply documented that pesticides and herbicides were killing or sickening all kinds of organisms, not just their intended targets. The decimation of bird populations caused by the then widespread DDT spraying against Dutch elm disease was particularly poignant. Carson's title invoked the terrible possibility that these chemicals could poison so many birds that their songs and calls would no longer herald the spring.

Silent Spring unleashed a storm. Foreshadowing the evils of today's global warming deniers, the pesticide manufacturers' and chemical companies' PR apparatus swung into action to slander the author and her claims. Rachel Carson's science was solid, though, and she braved the onslaught. Her powerful argument against the wanton destruction of other beings struck a chord. In 1972 the US banned DDT and a number of other persistent pesticides, making a gesture toward regulating the introduction of these chemicals into the environment. Rachel Carson emboldened countless people who shared her understanding of nature's integrity, thus launching the modern ecology movement, ever a David vs. Goliath match. Now climate change is disrupting the timing of bird migrations, and habitat destruction goes on apace; the musics of spring and even spring itself are imperiled.

How to persevere? Rachel Carson found her sources of courage and determination in deep communion with nature. This heroic woman spent her happiest hours at the edge of the sea and wrote three highly acclaimed books about marine and shore life before *Silent Spring*.

Carson would take her nephew Roger, even as a toddler, on her walks along the shore in Maine. The tide pools, the ghost crabs at the surf line, the periwinkles, whelks, and mussels all were there to entrance him. For Carson, fostering a child's love of nature was a paramount responsibility. Knowledge and concern would follow. She drew on these outdoors experiences with Roger in a lovely essay, "The Sense of Wonder."

"If I had influence with the good fairy who is supposed to preside over the christening of all children," she wrote, "I should ask that her gift to each child in the world be a sense of wonder so indestructible that it would last throughout life."

Years later, completing *Silent Spring*, then calmly facing the controversy that followed the book's publication, all the while suffering from the cancer that would cause her death in 1964 at age fifty-six, Carson's own sense of wonder sustained her. As long as she was physically able, she walked in the woods or by the shore, or gazed long at the night sky.

Aldo Leopold also was a scientist and a great writer who confessed himself unable to live without wild things. Trained as a forester in the early twentieth century, Leopold and others campaigned, with some success, for wilderness preservation, not just to protect unspoiled landscapes, but because there should be places where a person could know solitude, awe, and wonder in the presence of untrammeled nature. Although he would have been unlikely to couch it in those terms, Aldo Leopold's lifelong study of wild beings and wild places was a great work of love.

In his masterpiece, *A Sand County Almanac*, Leopold recorded his epiphanies. One of the most pivotal occurred in Arizona, where he first worked for the Forest Service. It was there, after shooting a wolf from the Blue River rim rock, that he learned how to think like a mountain.

"We reached the old wolf in time to watch a fierce green fire dying in her eyes," he wrote. "I realized then, and have known ever since, that there was something new to me in those eyes—something known only to her and the mountain. I was young then and full of trigger-itch. I thought that because fewer wolves meant more deer, that no wolves would mean a hunter's paradise. But after seeing the green fire die, I sensed that neither the wolf nor the mountain agreed with such a view." A humbled Leopold went on to describe what became of wolfless mountains. Burgeoning deer herds browsed every edible bush and seedling to death and defoliated every edible tree "to the height of a saddle horn." Predator control destabilized these ecosystems. "The world is green because carnivores eat herbivores," as the contemporary writer Julia Whitty puts it. To this day, in Michigan and throughout their range, efforts to protect and reinstate wolves to their wild habitats meet with fierce resistance. Wolf hunting still goes on.

As well as pioneering wilderness preservation, the science of ecology, and the field of game management, Aldo Leopold helped develop the land-healing practice of ecological restoration.

"A rare bird or flower," he wrote, "need remain no rarer than people willing to venture their skill in *building it a habitat.*"

Learning about the restoration work he did, first at the Arboretum at the University of Wisconsin–Madison, and then with his family at their retreat—a blown-out Depression-era "Sand County" farm near Baraboo, Wisconsin—brought me tears of joy. In 1992 I was able to roam around the Leopolds' place and see what nearly sixty years of intelligent attention and careful labor could accomplish in the way of land healing. There were pine forests, oak savannas, prairie patches, and wet meadows. Life's diversity had been welcomed back, and its pleasure was manifest.

In *The Book of Common Prayer* the Collect for Peace says the service of God is "perfect freedom." I titled my book about ecological restoration *In Service of the Wild* to evoke that. Restoration work is service to the wild, a way of doing something to combat extinction. Wherever I looked, I saw it liberating its practitioners from despair and sowing landscapes of hope.

A while back, at our natural foods co-op, I ran into my friend Richard, a gifted flautist and adept typesetter, whom I had not seen in a few years. When I asked him what was new, he fairly beamed. He told me that he had been working for the last few years on a Michigan monkey flower restoration along the eastern shore of a large inland lake. The Michigan monkey flower, a demure riparian plant with buttery yellow blossoms, is a state and federally listed endangered species. It likes lakeshores but so do people, hence the monkey flower's territory has been sorely diminished and degraded.

Most of what Richard and his partners were doing was weeding.

"You take the bad stuff away, and the good stuff comes back," he said.

Shortly after our encounter in the co-op, we met at the lakeshore, donned muck boots, and sloshed along the water's edge to visit the resurgent monkey flower, which was cohabiting with jewel weed, cardinal flower, turtlehead, liverworts, frogs, great blue herons, raccoons, possible spotted sandpipers (guessing at the tracks), and maybe even a mink. That field trip reminded me—and I often need reminding—that no matter how dismal the auguries, earth's myriad creatures are eager to live. They will hail the life force within us when we meet them halfway.

Over the next century or so we are bound to go through some hard times. We will either choose or suffer drastic changes in our way of life. We will perforce consume far less and produce locally more of what we do consume. And our responses to these exigencies must amount to more than just techniques for human survival. For as the late conservationist David Brower remarked, "You can survive in jail."

We hear about doing the right thing, and surely would, but our conception of rightness is often self-concerned and incomplete. We have tried to evade the laws of nature.

Aldo Leopold expanded ethics to include the living earth thus: "Examine each question in terms of what is ethically and esthetically right, as well as what is economically expedient. A thing is right when it tends to preserve the integrity, stability, and beauty of the biotic community. It is wrong when it tends otherwise."

If the future is to not resemble a cellblock, then in addition to learning how to meet human needs within straitened ecosystems, we must do right and dedicate ourselves to preserving the integrity, stability, and beauty of the living world.

Nature, humbly observed and rightly served, reveals the truths to steer by. If we can have the wisdom and the will to care for other forms of life, if we can have the vision to sustain wild beings and wild places, we will know joy and future generations may bless our memory. For as Henry David Thoreau declared, "In wildness is the preservation of the world." There could be no greater purpose than rescuing what we can of the earth's biodiversity.

Gather the resolve by connecting with nature, even in a vacant lot. Spend time with undomesticated creatures, go to places where human beings are few and wild things are many. Listen to the voices of the insects and the leaves. Watch the seasons change, sense life's great patterns. Join the wonder of it all.

Benjamin Busch

STANDING BENEATH THE GLACIER

I WAS BORN INTO WINTER. Nameless. December somewhere in the Borough of Manhattan, then delivered within days upstate for adoption. North. My new parents met me in a lawyer's office knowing only that I was small and had to be kept warm. They dressed me for the weather, covered me with blankets, worried about my exposed nose. By the time we arrived at their house down the street, I was wet with sweat. That is the story they told. There is no record of my ancestry, and I never asked. I've always just assumed I'm boreal, the lone survivor of a shipwreck, pulled from the ice floes, the last of my kind. I have hot blood. I was made for the cold.

My mother knitted mittens for me. She found yarn dyed for the early seventies, rainbow colors alternating through the threads. She hooked and braided it into the shape of my hands as if she could wrap my fingers in sunlight. Upstate New York had record blizzards, my soaked wool staining snowballs purple, red, and green. I tunneled into plowed mounds at the corners of streets, carved out chambers large enough to stand in, built battlements. I went hibernal for months of my childhood. Michigan was a mythological place then, somehow even farther north despite being largely on the same latitude as the hills of my youth. A peninsula of ice. I knew it only as a mitten on the map, a state even shaped like warm clothing.

My wife and I moved here with our baby girl in 2006, the year of its earliest recorded snowfall. We bought an old farmhouse in summer when the attic was hot with flies and the pastures were woolen with grass. It was a shell, hollow walled, the upstairs empty for decades, and by December we were forced to rent a house nearby until I could find a way to heat and insulate it. I built our way back into the bedrooms and hallways that year and the next. Inclemency was no longer a pleasure. It seemed to have matured with me, grown bitter, become an antagonist. I sealed it out, broke shovels throwing it aside, thought about frozen pipes. Cold season had become a landscape of chores. I didn't rush into it anymore. We dressed our thin baby until she looked swollen.

In our fourth year here the cold got deep. Plows scraped past, their wake left as white road. The hardened sky lingered over the view, pressed down, rubbed it smooth. Arctic wind struck our house on the hill, dunes forming on either side. Then the air billowed, clouds shaved into flakes, drifts spilling into the trenches I carved, my breath pulled east like a contrail. The land here rises from postglacial rebound, the mantel still filling its lungs after the weight of the ice age. Below me is the center of the Michigan Basin where a sea dried into fifty feet of salt and oil rigs still sip from a pool of rotten swamp. Nothing is final. Someday I won't be able to shovel anymore, but the snow won't know. Weather keeps no records of us.

The wind moves on, sky suddenly quiet, and snow falls lightly, packing itself around air. It catches on branches and stacks up, the other flakes passing, spreading evenly into the spaces below. As I shovel squares and toss them like pails from a boat, I think of how much of it was breath. I squint, forgetting I'm looking down at sky, forgetting that I stand beneath the glacier. It was right here, a tectonic plate of ice so large the oceans dropped 394 feet to feed it. It slid, grinding rock into paste, making clay and sand, rolling stones round. Our property is all aftermath, ghost ice returning every year. Winter in the north is a flood. Clouds fall and stay, sedimentary, everything covered for months. I wade through it as it drapes over the build of the land. I know, always, that if I lay down, I would succumb to it, drown in its cold. If winter could want, it would want us all frozen. Nival. Immaculate. I stand still, the weather in my head, freezing rain tapping my shoulders like moths bringing the spectrum from the atmospheric fringe, releasing rays at night, the ground glowing. It's this way on my birthday.

Our electrician had loaned me his tall stepladder. I used it to run wire to the outlets where he would later connect switches and lights. When I jacked up the house, I stood the ladder where the staircase had been. It soon lost itself in the regular rotation of tools and equipment employed for the restoration of our home. "MARSH" was clearly handwritten in black ink along its braces, but it had become mine. It replaced the plumber's ladder, left for the entirety of the preceding year, with "PHELPS" written on it. In all this borrowing, I learned why they were so clearly marked. A local couple leased our land to hunt, and I offered to build them a new elevated blind. It was to supplant an old shanty on stilts I planned to remove. As deer season approached, I took our truck and drove the "MARSH" ladder out across the fields to the edge of the swamp with lumber and bags of concrete. The site was half a mile from our house and overgrown with autumn olive and wild pear. Geese had already gathered and gone, all the leaves fallen. Our swamp was still dense with brush branch, but it looked soft now, a gray fabric that cloaked the mire like clumps of lint.

The trees were bare, like I imagined their roots to be if air and earth were reversed. I was beginning the work late, and cold had come, the soil trying to freeze as I dug. Sandy loam gave way to orange clay, hard as pottery. It had to be chiseled with a steel bar and scooped out with my fingers, my arm reaching down until my shoulder was pressed to the ground.

I measured the corners and set cylinder forms into them. I enjoyed mixing concrete. The water ran off the limestone powder like mercury until I pulled it together with a hoe. It warmed as stone formed. Twenty percent of the rock would remain water and continue to cure for a few hundred years, imprints of leaves preserved beneath the footings like fossils. The pyramids are limestone, cut and carved from formations made of seashells. Below me, like the salt, is Michigan's limestone bed, the hardened ocean trapped and interred. I decided not to scratch my initials, my work selfless as blocks of pharaoh's tomb.

I stood up the four-by-fours and braced them with temporary boards. It was hard to raise and steady a twelve-foot treated post alone, and I was left to lift braces to me from the ground with my feet when I ran out of hands. As I secured the last one and got through the complicated process of squaring all of the corners, a hard wind came from the west and knocked down two of them. I began again. The day darkened. Four posts stood as if, like the leafless trees, I had just finished building the blind underground and raised the posts to secure it to the sky.

The storms came, deer season began, and the posts rose out of the snow with no discernable purpose. Blank totem poles. The ladder stood next to them as a sign that more was to be done, but, given the circumstances, the construction would wait. The hunters used the old dilapidated stand beside it, shooting a six-point buck and a large doe without complaint. With work stalled until spring, I began to elaborate on the design of the blind until the drawings bordered on architectural wonder. Secret compartments for nothing in particular and a cross-gabled steel roof emerged. It was still just for hunting.

In December the electrician finally calls asking for his ladder. He wants to pick it up early in the morning of the next day on his way past, and I say that it will be waiting for him with my thanks. It's already dark outside. I'll have to haul it home from the swamp and melt it clean before he comes. On the floor by the door are our daughter's snow pants, quilted jacket, little hat, boots, and mittens all laid out. A child separated into pieces waiting to be zipped back together, held whole by buttons and Velcro. We make sure her slim body is warm. She is not like me. She was born in fall. I step over the warning signs, grab a work jacket, slide into rubber boots, and hurry out.

It's twelve degrees when I start walking across the field with my black Labrador, Jack. He bounds through the snow pushing his face into it as if he's a seal, and I run behind him, following his aberrant path. The land is a void, the air so cold it's dry, a near brush with outer space. I stop within a hundred yards and begin the trudge of a man walking against the current in a river. The chill gets into my lungs, and I slow to keep from cracking. I have not dressed for the weather. Jack turns back. The snow makes the sound of balled cotton being rubbed together. My steps are muffled, as if originating from somewhere farther away. The entire field seems to redistribute the impression of my tracks. It's like a lake laid over the land, matching its contours instead of gathering in the low points. More evidence that snow is something more than water, the tips of crystals part of a larger design.

I think of the war here, the desert, the snow a substance so completely different from dust, and the same. Nothing grows in snow, thrives from it. Nothing alive. It can stay together like the foam base of funeral flowers. I've built with it, bore through it, but never given in to it.

I finally arrive at the four posts. I smack icicles from the ladder and turn around. I'm exposed in the open land. As I forge slowly through the swells, I breathe hard, the air sharp in my chest. I hold a hand over my mouth and retrace my steps, the ladder on a shoulder like I'm carrying it into the ocean. Looking forward it seems like a long way, and my boots are filled with snow. I've passed over a rise in the land and into a drift close to three feet deep. The field spreads out to meet its edges, a blackened tree line all around, and I find myself stopped in its white center. I wonder what would happen if I collapsed and began to go numb.

The last freeze took the sea, stretched it porous and buoyant a mile high, the breath of mastodons trapped inside, the mantel weighed down enough to sink under an age of ice. We've burned too much, the last shelves rendering down, the grindings they pushed left in piles ten thousand years deep, heaped beneath us, these smooth hills unrecognized as the bone shoulders of glaciers. Farmers walk these Michigan mounds knowing they're burials, stop to kick seams around stones in the dirt. It's not enough. They have to bow to the ground, trace the edges like climbers searching for a grasp, stooped at first, then dropping to their old knees, hands slick with soil as they spin rocks cupped in bowls of roots. These are glacial erratics, round like skulls, found before they bend the plows, hauled from holes to line the fences, cannonballs carried off battlefields. Each one is cut out like bullets from wounds, lifted away from the land, elders staggering, cursing them as foes, as the pain in their joints, as animals, heavier than their children asleep, heavier than the dead they'd pulled from barns and beds, artifacts from the largest labor there is. They clutch them to their thighs. Snow still falls where the ice had been, a reminder in the thin coat of flakes that everything can be covered, our clouds of breath stored by the chill, our exertions locked in blocks of breeze for centuries and released again to blow cold over the places that will bury us too.

My wife knows that I'm out here, but she's pregnant and putting our first daughter to bed. She'll eventually call neighbors after I fail to return, and I'll be found hours later, dead in the middle of a niveous field, holding a ladder, on my birthday. They might wonder to themselves what I was trying to reach above the field, if I was trying to climb back into winter where I was born. Somewhere above the cryosphere. I would be sorry to tell them that it isn't even my ladder. They would know that winter got what it wanted.

Marcia Aldrich

EDGE

> In every man's heart there is a secret nerve that answers to the vibration of beauty.
>
> —CHRISTOPHER MORLEY

START WITH A DEAD DEER AT THE SIDE OF HAMILTON ROAD.
A major artery between Okemos and Dobie Roads, it is my route to work, to the supermarket, to the post office and bank, and the only means of access to Tacoma Hills, the subdivision in Meridian Township where I have lived for the last five years. The speed limit on Hamilton is twenty-five miles per hour, slowing to fifteen at the roundabout a quarter mile to the west. Nevertheless, a driver has struck the deer, and now it lies in the grass in front of a condominium complex. It is a white-tailed deer, *Odocoileus virginianus*, the smallest and most nervous member of the North American deer family.

How many deer have I seen dead at the side of a road in my lifetime? Hundreds for sure, maybe a thousand. The top of the deer's head points toward the pavement where it died, the neck stretched long in the grass and the single visible eye brown, glassy, and wide, as if a taxidermist had set it there, placed it in a patient form ready for portraiture or mounting. Among all animals, deer possess one of the most graceful figures, trim and defined, shapely and economical, finely tuned, vibrating with beauty. Fleet of foot, and short of life. I would like their portrait to be painted by Lucien Freud, bathed in bright light like his sleeping whippets, lying in an intimate mesh, without the shadow of death.

For days no one moved the dead deer. How many drivers passed by, saw the corpse, and kept going? A thousand? Two thousand? Thousands more drove by and noticed no carcass at the side of the road—so familiar and common as to be invisible, "an incident of roadside mortality," as the township's Deer Management Plan puts it. What about the residents in the condominiums—don't they mind looking out on a dead deer? Or are they skilled in not seeing it? They park their car in the allotted space and hurry inside, not noticing what lies in the grass about them.

To consider the dead deer, to dwell upon its prone body, is to risk being seen as sentimental. This infantile emotional overflow, this unexamined response, is well known to me. But I don't think my emotions are sentimental—that is, exaggerated and self-indulgent, shallow and uncomplicated. My neighbor feeds the deer to tempt them close, to ensure that she has pretty pictures outside her window. They're cute, she says, they're dear. *That* is sentimental. When I tell her that feeding wildlife can be detrimental, do more damage than good, she waves me off. At Christmastime reindeer lit with white lights are installed in her front yard.

Sighting, November 22. Before getting into bed, I open the sliding door a few inches to ventilate the room while we sleep. A loud rustle below our second-story bedroom. Snap on the outside floodlights. Hear more rustling and step out onto the balcony to see what it might be: two small deer frozen in the leaf-strewn ivy. Their faces turn toward me, and they don't move, not one little bit, as if a single light holds them in place and time.

None of the common attitudes toward deer I'm aware of entirely fits me. I'm not an animal rights activist who is set against hunting in every instance, not a biologist, not a certified naturalist, not a hunter who eats what he kills and believes he has a primal relationship with deer, not a painter, not a member of the township's herd management team. Perhaps I am a metaphysician, alive to the beauty of the deer—but that's only part of my feelings. Once we moved to our house set in the trees near the Red Cedar River, deer became implicated in my life, and I've become implicated in theirs. We share a home range; their lives and deaths intersect with mine. This much we share, but their lives are pitiably short and hard, and this brute brevity has burrowed inside to trouble me. Home range can be a tricky concept, and its extent depends greatly on the quality of forage, protective cover, water, and other factors. The range for the deer in my area may be as small as a one-quarter square mile.

When we bought the house five years ago, we had no idea what lived among these trees, near this river, what would pass through our property. At first my response to the wildlife veered toward the joyful, pure, and simple. I was made happy by the blue heron staking out a fishing spot every afternoon on the bank across the river. Waking on one of our first mornings in the new house, I saw three deer under the crabapple eating the hard little fruit that had fallen. I sighed with pleasure. My impulse was not to fly out into the yard clapping and screaming, as my neighbors did, bent on stopping the devouring of one's garden. My visitors moved from crabapple to hostas, tearing off one leaf and then another until mere ragged stalks remained. I felt no ownership of the yard. They'd lift a watchful head, chomping, green leaves the size of a peony sticking out of a soft mouth.

My first autumn in the house I tried to offer apples to the deer as if they were horses, a misguided experiment in presumption. I wasn't so stupid as to hold the apple in my hand and expect them to come to me. I threw the apples in their direction, but of course I merely frightened them. They didn't know it was a harmless and edible meal hurling through the air toward them. Next I tried leaving apples in spots they passed through. The squirrels got them before the deer.

Sighting, November 23. Early morning. Ice on the roof. Light in the backyard. Two deer, mother and medium-sized fawn, look up at the house, where I stand still in the family room behind the full-length windows. They're nervous, constantly alert for movement, sound, threat— I've never seen a deer that wasn't nervous, except the exhausted and the dead. They look back and forth between the river and the house. The mother moves first and in front while the fawn scours the ground. Not much left this late in fall—the deer have been through this yard more times than I can know. The fawn sniffs the dry hydrangeas, just reedy stalks and brown flower heads. The mother is too busy observing to eat. She can't relax enough to bend her neck to the grass; she must stand with ears pricked and eyes darting, the white ring under her neck clear to see. Eventually they skitter through into my neighbor's yard and are gone. Only then do I move from the window.

Our house lies in what the Michigan Department of Resources calls an urban/suburban area: residential developments and businesses mixed with undeveloped wetlands that can't be built upon, parks and natural areas, and open fields from the area's farming past. This suburban environment has created what deer biologists call *edge*, that is, crop fields juxtaposed with meadow and woods, natural preserves, and enriched residential yards. Deer need food, water, and cover primarily. My subdivision, surrounding neighborhoods, and intermixed open lands form a high-quality habitat where they flourish. No one knows how many deer this home range supports; no exact count has been undertaken. The main threat to the population is the high-density traffic that flows on arteries like Hamilton Road.

When I turn off Hamilton to enter Tacoma Hills, the houses are spread far apart on big lots, the trees become large and dense. We have no sidewalks, curbs, or streetlights, and neighborhood covenants prohibit fences in front yards. The houses circle a lagoon, back up to three natural areas, and cluster around a large commons between the two streets that intersect with Hamilton and are the only entrances to the subdivision. The Red Cedar River forms the southern boundary. I can walk out my back door, launch my kayak, and in minutes no longer see houses.

My house is placed in a wood of big oaks and maples, with more settled landscaping front and back. The deer browse here throughout the year, although in winter they may simply pass through on the way to better forage. In the warmer months they lie in the fallen leaves at the edges of the yard. Last spring a tiny fawn, separated from its mother, spent a whole afternoon in the tall ferns under the redbud tree. It slept so soundly that I worried it had been abandoned. I brought a bowl of water and set it five feet away, but the fawn never drank. After a long walk that evening, I found it had departed. Perhaps the fawn had been hidden under the redbud while its mother looked for food and was reclaimed.

Sighting, December 9, 4:46 p.m. 26 degrees, light snow on the ground, blue sky splattered with large patches of delicate pink tinged with orange. In thirty minutes the sky will go dark. The deer arrive at this turning time. A herd of twelve is running on the other side of the river, scattered out across the snow, bounding in what looks like wild abandon. I watch them from the kitchen sink as I snap the beans for dinner. Sometimes deer walk through the yard or along the banks of the river in single file, with a purpose, looking down for food, then freeze, listening for threats. No such caution tonight—they are like children who have been cooped up all day inside a classroom and have been released into the schoolyard for recess.

How apt it is for the word *deer* to be both singular and plural. Nouns with identical singular and plural forms are often the names of animals: moose, sheep, bison, salmon, pike, trout, swine, elk, and shrimp. We seldom think of them as unique, as singular, as individuals. Like the carcass at the roadside on Hamilton, deer are always off to the side, standing at the margins. Rushing by, drivers don't ask whether they know *that* deer or not. We see them out of the corner of our eye if we see them at all. Only the hunter sees the deer dead center in his sights. I want to move the deer to the center of my picture.

Do I know the deer? *Know* is too strong a word, for it implies a human intimacy and familiarity, an explicit relationship that I can't claim. Still, deer come through my yard regularly, and this Hamilton deer may well have visited a hundred times, stood below my window while I slept, munched my hostas while I watched. When its eyes were alive, our eyes may have met. If *know* doesn't precisely describe the relationship, what word does? We cohabit this range, are residents of the land and also temporary dwellers. I do not know whether I figure in the deer's memory or imagination or whether thinking in those terms is plausible. The deer establish patterns, I occupy a spot on their range map, and in that sense they know my house and the lay of the land around it. Do they recognize me? I doubt it, not in the sense humans understand the concept. But it is possible they recognize me in a form of sense memory. Primarily deer look at me to determine whether I am a threat. Do they learn over time that I am not, or is their reaction to me only and ever as a possible threat? Certain groups that stand at hedges, around the yards, in the fields and natural areas, I register as *familiar*—"That's the doe and two fawns that came through yesterday," I say to myself. Right now a group is browsing at my neighbor's two doors down; a doe pauses below the back balcony, munching a hedge she'd disdain if it weren't barren winter. Now a fawn, and another, joins her in the hedge destruction. They drift over to my yard to check out the bird feeder. This isn't the trio that before my eyes hungrily raided it the previous week. The doe is wary of the feeder, checks it with her tongue, sniffs something she doesn't like, and backs away. When one of the fawns tries to take a turn, she swats it away with her head. They move on to the backyard and find vegetation to consume where I see nothing.

There is one particular deer I catch sight of all over the subdivision. (I think of it as the same deer, though I may be collapsing several individuals into one.) A young deer, a buck, underdeveloped, a little ungainly, a smallish head without antlers or poise, and alone, always a solitary traveler. When I spot it alone across the river, browsing or lying down, I think, "That is the deer I know." At the same time, I am in doubt, thinking I am imposing a familiarity upon these encounters.

When I see the animal at the side of Hamilton Road, I worry that it is the deer I know.

Sighting, later. Full moon when we walk with the dogs after dinner. Omar the retriever senses deer before I do, and his ears go up. A moment after, two deer dash through on our right and disappear behind a house. Omar wants to chase them. When I am in bed later, the full moon hangs visible through the skylights. Its light beams into my face and wakes me. I feel shot through with cold light and called to the fields.

In Middle English *der*, in Old English *deor*, meant a wild animal of any kind, in contrast to cattle or other livestock that could be pastured on designated land. Deer aren't domestic, like a horse in a stable whose name is inscribed on the stall door, or cows in a barn. They do not saunter over to the fence to see if you have an apple. You cannot ride them for pleasure or compete in a steeplechase. You cannot derive milk from them for butter or cheese. You can't have a history with a deer in the usual sense. They're wild, and no pasture contains them. They belong to no one and come and go as they please.

December 11. Driving home on Mt. Hope, inappropriately named given all the animal deaths that occur on it, I knew long before I could see distinctly that a dead deer was lying on the grassy shoulder, a border lightly dusted with snow. The deer's head is facing the street, and blood has seeped from the front and back of its lithe body. Red dots of frozen blood in the snow. I can't reconstruct what happened here. If the deer was crossing from north to south, why wouldn't it be lying in the road; how could the impact throw the body to land in this position? I am probably the only person who wants to know how the deer assumed its posture. No one thinks about how it happened or why the deer assumes its final pose— not the way we are haunted by people in the last throes of life. We have to know that the heart attack came on suddenly as Uncle Harry was doing the laundry, and that's why he was found sprawled on the basement floor with a black sock in his hand. What is it in me that needs to know about this animal? And suddenly I understand—it is natural to grab a carcass by the hind legs to pull it away from traffic.

It will be days before anyone removes the deer from the shoulder. I will see it many times on my way to and from work—I'll be looking for it, knowing it is there, unattended. I feel alone and cold, aware that the deer turns me around on myself, standing apart from other people.

Home, I start to make dinner. Out the back windows are two deer lying down on the banks of the river. While chopping mushrooms and squash, I remember the survey the Meridian Township invited its residents to take in response to a plan to allow antlerless deer hunting on selected public, and perhaps private, lands. According to its website, the township had been receiving complaints from citizens saying, for example, "The deer are everywhere!" No statistics supported claims that the population had increased to an unhealthy, threatening number.[1] That, however, was the perception of the general populace. I knew it was pointless to fill out the survey, and that the township had already determined to allow managed hunts on parklands normally closed to hunting. Still, I answered the questions and voiced my concern about the lack of evidence in support of the conclusions reached. The survey asked for contact information, which I provided, so that I might be gotten back to. No one called, no one wrote.

Determining a good size for the deer population in a town like ours is not settled by figuring out how many deer the land can support. A decision also depends on what people feel about their interactions with deer. At one of the meetings of the environmental commission, an expert emphasized the need for democratic discussion to determine the township's stance on deer. Some residents—farmers, garden enthusiasts, and those who have experienced an automobile-deer collision—will prefer a low density, while others who have a higher tolerance for the problems deer cause will prefer a higher density. On the spectrum of possible values, I place myself on the high end of tolerance. Yet I am concerned with the quality of life and the health of the deer. If overpopulation can be demonstrated, along with the deterioration of health and habitat, I would favor a management plan.[2]

At a dinner party where the township's managed hunts were discussed, one of the women called deer "giant rats with antlers" and was pleased that their numbers would be thinned. She and her husband maintain a substan-

---

1. The township's draft Deer Management Plan reads: "It is difficult to obtain exact numbers of the deer herd population." In other words, the township couldn't say with any convincing authority whether the number had indeed increased. Local biologists were quoted as saying that damage to vegetation and incidents of deer-vehicle accidents were sufficient measures to justify the hunts. I could find no statistics that would indicate a recent surge in deer-vehicle collisions.

2. In all the materials deer are treated as a resource that government agencies have a right to manage. And manage they have—decreasing or increasing their number as the historical moment dictates.

tial garden and an orchard, and deer are the enemy. They occupy a place on the low end of deer tolerance. Her relish at their demise reminded me of a hunter neighbor who each year hangs his latest trophy from a jungle gym to drain the blood before dressing. He has a fenced backyard that would shield the carcass from his neighbors' view, but that would not display his achievement. Residents have asked him to move the deer, which disturbed their children, but he refuses.

At the dinner party I felt troubled in a way that has been familiar to me since childhood. Conversation about subjects I care deeply about at a dinner party will not allow me to express myself in a way that feels true or even okay. When I've been unguarded enough to say something real, the emotions blast out and spray everyone around me in the face, and it isn't pleasant for anyone. When it comes to my views about animals, I always feel at the margin. It was a group of educated companions who felt certain of their priority over animals—not troubled, not questioning, not pausing. No disturbed stirring arose that suggested the matter of harvesting deer was complicated. There was no place for feelings, or feelings of the sort I am burdened by. After my frustration with them and with myself built up sufficient pressure, I blurted out, "I prefer deer to human beings." I don't know if that is true, but I said it because I was enflamed, compelled to throw a hand grenade into the dinner chat. Afterward I felt embarrassed and exposed. I wanted to leap over a fence and disappear. You might expect that my daffy outburst offended my companions. It did not. They didn't take me seriously.

December 12. Dead deer still there at the side of Mt. Hope.

> *Sighting, late night. In the dark I let my dogs out into the side yard. On automatic pilot, sleepy, I do not think about the wildlife they might surprise. When I turn on the back lights, I see a shape at the bottom of the yard. The dogs don't immediately see or sense the solitary deer, much larger than usual. It moves slightly up from the river, and Omar sees it. He charges toward it but halfway to his goal stops. This deer stood his ground. When Omar comes back, he bounds up the porch steps and back into the house.*

December 13. Deer gone; removed.

> *Sighting, December 19, midmorning. Four deer, a doe and three semi-grown fawns, in the yard. In the daylight the deer often stay down by*

the river. The winter hunger is changing the behavior of this group—
they're awfully close. Between browsings, the mother licks the fawns,
cleaning head and neck, and then moving down the back. The fawns
lick her, too, and they touch heads and rub necks.

Midafternoon we drive on Dobie Road to our friends' house to drop off Christmas cookies. On the way home an hour later, I see a dead deer at the side of the road that wasn't there on the outbound trip. I wonder if I know this deer.

December 20, morning. I go out of my way to see if the deer is still on Dobie. I can't see it driving south. But when I turn around and return going north, I spot it. It has fallen a good way off the road and is shielded by brush and shrubs. "Still there," I say out loud. *Still there.* What is wrong with me?

December 20, noon. I take my camera and walk with the dogs across Sander Farm. We pass the deep-red barn on which figures painted in white announce the settling of the land in 1875. This barn and another a little farther north are remnants of the rural past, when the area was predominantly fields of crops. Stoplights have been installed along Dobie at several spots, but it's a terrible trap for deer—two narrow lanes, with a speed limit pegged to its semirural nature; if you swerve, you'll run into oncoming traffic or fly up on the sidewalk. But deer cross the road in numbers, coming and going from the Dobie Reserve, an undeveloped swath of land that the Red Cedar River runs through. My deer was on its way to the fence that borders the reserve, or had just surmounted it. Less than a hundred yards away is a stoplight, and fifty yards away a bus stop.

Last summer a small deer died in the commons. A member of the neighborhood association board of trustees called the Ingham County Roads Commission, which informed him that the ICRC only picks up carcasses from public roads. So a neighbor tilted the animal onto a tarp and dragged it out to the street. In two days it vanished. It was through this incident that I learned who removes deer from roads.

When I arrive home, I call the road commission about the deer on Dobie. The man I speak to says he'll fill out a work order to pick up the carcass since it is on a public road.

"What do you do with the deer once you pick it up?" I ask.

"Relocate it," he says, to a place where it can decompose naturally and won't bother anyone. If the deer is already too far gone to be moved, the road commission douses it with lime.

December 22. Something is building in me—I can't get deer out of my head or eyes. Wherever I look, I see deer. And I don't look away. I don't say I have something better to do. Out my study window in the side yard or at the bird feeder, in the back, down by the river, lying down, at night when I let the dogs out, there they are, in the morning under my window, walking in Sander Farm, dead on all the roads I drive to get to work, to go anywhere. I'm trying to sort it, as the British say. *Sort it* covers a multitude of meanings—figure out what's going on, what you feel, fix it—it being some form of trouble, confusion, malfunction. But in this case, I don't think anything is malfunctioning. All my senses and feelings seem in high alert, watchful, fully alive and engaged. Something inside me says, "Look, here they come, the deer, pay attention. This is a moment in time like no other, when what is ordinary becomes something else."

> *Sighting, December 28. Deer across the river, lying down. I get out my binoculars and count them: seven. Bright sun, blue skies, and biting cold. They're scattered, not far from each other. Hours go by in this resting position. At four thirty one deer gets up, and then another, and eventually all seven are on their feet. Not doing much. Cleaning, urinating, more cleaning, taking slow, leisurely steps down to the river, drinking. Calm. Then my husband lets our dogs out into the side yard before he feeds them. The dogs are on the other side of the river from the deer, a long way away. Each deer freezes and looks across the river at the dogs. At first none of them looks alarmed—they're just paying attention. And then, as if in response to something I can't detect, all seven lift their white tails and bound in a group out of the woods.*

With deer, we cannot know and we cannot be known in the usual sense—there's a freedom in that, freedom from the usual forms of feeling. The deer emerge out of the woods and take me away with them. I put down my task, look out, and suddenly the window becomes enormous and I feel shaken awake. Maybe the deer reintroduce me to parts of myself I thought I had lost or thwarted—a capacity for receiving a vibration of beauty that has rearranged the wiring of my brain.

> *Sighting, January 1. Off Dobie Road, on my way to a trailhead, a bit of undeveloped land. Getting out of my car, I glimpse in the corner of my eye a young buck on the other side of the railroad tracks that parallel the trail. I walk toward the opening of light made by the right-of-way.*

At first he doesn't sense my presence. When he picks me out of the land-scape, he rotates his head and focuses, like a camera adjusting a zoom lens. I expect him to disappear into the trees, for that's what deer do, flee, lifting tails high in white dismissal. But when this creature moves, he moves toward me. I try to hold my ground, but unwittingly I shift. And at that, the deer turns and leaps into the brush.

I keep after him, following his course. I spot him again, atop a mound of colorful cardboard boxes and other garbage, on the track behind him an abandoned railroad car, red and black with graffiti. His eyes hang on an invisible line running to me. We share a mo-ment. And then with a snort that hangs in the air, long, humid, and velvet-lined, he jumps for the woods and disappears.

If I could, I would follow him anywhere.

January 3. News reports say that residents of Meridian Township have responded positively to the managed hunts. Among respondents to the survey, 72.7 percent answered yes to this question: "Have you or a member of your family experienced or come close to a deer/vehicle accident in Meridian Township?" The question provides no time frame—in the last year, in the last ten years? What does "come close to" mean? It is impossible to ascertain from the results whether there has been a real increase in collisions, or a perceived one. A managed hunt was approved by 74.6 percent of respondents; 68.9 percent favored "encouragement of residents to hunt or allow hunting on large parcels of private property, defined as five acres or more." As of today, forty-one deer have been harvested, and the township board has approved an extension of the hunt through the end of February.

Holly Wren Spaulding

THE LANGUAGE OF TREES

EARLY AUTUMN, 2015. Artist Melanie Mowinski and I stand over black plastic tubs in her studio, sleeves up, swirling abaca pulp in water to make handmade paper, which we'll form into words for my short poems. Once shaped and dried, each word stands about eight inches tall, and will be legible from a distance of forty feet or more. This particular poem will appear along a public path in the Berkshires of Massachusetts.

> Look / Look / the / trees / are / making / beauty / we / can / breathe.

Melanie and I first met in her letterpress studio a couple of years ago, where I'd gone to learn how to hand-set type and print some of my poetry fragments as broadsides. I've given away most of those early printing experiments and I know that some of them have found their way onto bulletin boards and refrigerators, and even into picture frames. When introduced into the spaces we occupy every day, I imagine that these little poems will meet people who might not otherwise think to pick up a volume of poetry.

This possibility of a chance encounter with a reader is something I'm interested in, especially as our cultural relationship to books evolves, and even more so, as I notice the proliferation of text in our everyday environment. Billboards, signs and posters rarely inspire a second thought, or an association with beauty or art, but what if a poem appeared where once there was an ad for a phone?

As we operate Melanie's Vandercook Universal III proof press, we talk about our influences, and eventually discover a shared interest in trees, rooted mostly in our habit of walking in the woods. In different but related ways, our respective experiences in nature have impacted our internal environments such that we are not only making work in response to what we find and feel among trees, but the forest has become a place of refuge and spiritual renewal, where we can each connect with a more vivid sense of who we are, and how we relate to these other beings with whom we share our planet.

In one of her projects, a small, handmade book called *Into the Woods*, Melanie used text distilled from what had mattered most to her in Ralph Waldo Emerson's essay "Nature," creating a personal mantra that she recites as needed:

> In the woods
> we return to reason and faith.
> Nothing can befall me in life
> which nature cannot repair.
> Standing on bare ground
> all mean egotism vanishes.
> I become transparent.

Poetic texts have long served me in a similar way, especially during times of stress, uncertainty, or grief, so when I learned about how, since 2005, Melanie has also made handmade paper "empowerment words" using words like *honor*, *hope*, and *give*, which she wraps around the trunks of trees as a way of observing Earth Day and Arbor Day, I asked her to collaborate on something site specific, involving poetry in trees. People respond to her words with visible delight when they find them in parks and along city streets, and this resonance is a testament to how much a word or idea can mean to an individual, regardless of their relationship to art or poetry.

As a poet, I'm interested in what happens when we connect with language in such an immediate way as to feel it first, before our mind needs to understand what it means, or resists it based on reflex. As both a reader and writer, I find in poems a sense of "other knowing" every day. They give me pleasure, and healing, and a relief from the sharper edges and definitions of the more rational part of my brain. I also think of poems as antidotes to the more dominant forms of language that occupy our public spaces, whether advertising or directive signage, so I enjoy looking for ways not only to offer the alternative but, in a sense, to critique the paradigm in which corporations occupy the visual landscape—our shared commons—while quieter forms of expression become harder to perceive, even invisible.

Many years ago I read about the forest monks of Southeast Asia, who ordain trees by wrapping them in orange monk's robes, performing a ceremony, and subsequently persuading others of their protected status. Over time, these rituals have saved many of Thailand's trees from industrial logging. The images of "monk trees" moved me with their simple and dignified beauty, while the practice of ritually draping their trunks reflects imagination and a sense of hope. This poetic form of resistance inspires me to articulate my own belief that trees are sacred, that the whole of the natural world is sacred, and to draw others' attention in that direction.

We've called our poetry and trees project *Here, Stands*, because we're taking a stand against the many forces that continue to threaten our most beloved natural landscapes. We hope these poems will gently nudge viewers to notice the gifts of trees—spiritual and aesthetic, as well as practical—and maybe even consider the ways they could become more intimate with their natural environment or steward them. This kind of art invites reflection, emotional response, and even conversation—within ourselves and with each other—in a setting where the trees join and inform the dialogue.

October 2016. Melanie and I spend a full day installing five different poems along several miles of hiking, bird-watching, and ski trails at Notchview, a nature preserve within the Hoosac Range, not far from where we both live. One poem begins:

Slow / slower / still

You can't do this kind of work without hugging quite a few trees in the process, since wrapping paper words around each trunk and securing them with string requires both arms and sometimes both women, depending on the tree's girth. In the middle of one such embrace, Melanie remarks that as far as she is concerned, the experience of looking at and touching the trees *is the art*. The objects we've made are secondary to the process.

After six hours in the woods, sun filtering through evergreen needles and beech leaves, I feel gentler and more connected to this place, which is not my native bioregion, and so I'm still learning it. Still learning the names of the trees. This project fulfills more than an artistic vision for me. It is the necessary spiritual work of upholding, through action, some of the values that I hold most dear, including attention, slowness, and reverence for the natural world.

Several days later, after hanging more poems at the William Cullen Bryant Homestead, former home of the nineteenth-century poet and early proponent of the land conservation movement, we pass a woman and child on a cedar-lined trail as they encounter one of the first sets of words in a longer sequence. The girl of about eight or so is still learning how to read, so each word forms slowly as she says it out loud, and we listen from several yards away:

Linger / among trees

Fittingly, the girl wants to know what those words mean, and the pair discusses this as they amble deeper into the old-growth forest that Bryant had loved his whole life, and had influenced his own poetry so significantly.

I grew up on an off-the-grid homestead ten miles from any town, in an intentional community that comprised other families who'd left cities to move "back to the land" in the mid-1970s. Named Heartwood, after the hard, interior part of the tree, this social experiment was inspired by the idea that like-minded people could live durably on the land, largely independent of the cash economy, while making do with what we could grow, make, mend, or find in our environment. Everyone who lived there identified as some kind of artist or craftsperson or maker, and we all knew the land because we interacted with it every day, harvesting food, gathering firewood, making medicine, and creating what we needed from whatever was to hand.

As a child I learned many of the names of trees from my father, a carpenter and painter, who has interacted with wood every day of his adult life. He taught me to identify the grain, so that even without bark or leaves, I would know maple, walnut, cherry, oak, cedar, birch, and pine. My father also passed along the perspective that all living things have a right to exist, and are not here only to be consumed by humans. Ever since I can remember, a hand-painted sign has hung near the entrance to my parents' home on the Leelanau Peninsula: Earth is Heaven, Nature is God. If this is it—our one and only home—as I believe it is, then caring for our planet is not just a social responsibility but a moral and spiritual mandate. This fundamental regard for the natural world was reinforced by spending most of my childhood out of doors, usually in the woods, most often climbing trees and shimmying up and down saplings. Like all the other kids back then, I also gathered branches and plants to construct forts, always saying a quiet word of gratitude if I took something that was still alive—branch or leaf—to embellish my design. In my memory, I'm eight or nine years old, whispering, "Thank you, hemlock" and "Thank you, beech," and apologizing when I'd caused injury or damage to any of the plants around me. Eventually, with the exception of wildflowers, I decided to use only what I found on the ground.

I don't often talk about this time in my life because it's hard to explain what it's like to live in a more or less nineteenth-century way—our light came from oil lamps, our heat from the wood we cut and split and stacked, our food from an extensive organic garden—to those who know only about life with central air, televisions, and quick trips to the supermarket. But one of the clearest images of that time in my young life includes a giant willow where I spent many solitary afternoons, singing made-up songs and listening to the life of the swamp that surrounded me. If I wasn't already destined to become a poet, that corner of an overgrown meadow made me one.

The spirit of those early experiences and the language I absorbed as a result have made their way into my writing for years. *Catkin, thicket, deciduous, grove, anther, burl, bough.* Words help make my world known to me, and they also point to what I don't yet know but want to understand, like the combination of pressures and temperature that causes sweet sap to flow in sugar maples in early spring.

More than a science lesson, more than a metaphor, my family depended on this natural process, which gave shape to all the springs of my childhood. My brother Ethan and I would haul five-gallon buckets around the woods to collect the day's flow from the smaller metal buckets that hung from spigots on the hundred or so sugar maples used for that purpose, both of us struggling through the snow as we tried not to spill the precious liquid before we could pour it into the holding tank on the sledge, which our half-wild ponies, Ted and Molly, would pull back to the homestead, only occasionally ignoring my father's commands and taking us on a joy-ride instead.

Even the youngest among us learned early on how important it was for the days to warm up and the nights to cool, so that the sap would run and we could stock the root cellar with what we would need for the rest of the year.

Around 2000, I hosted a group of forest activists from the West Coast following a workshop on nonviolent direct action where they'd taught a group of anticorporate globalization activists how to use lockboxes made with PVC piping and chains, to conduct a hypothetical protest blockade. Their experience using these tactics to interdict logging operations in old-growth forests in California and Oregon resonated with a large contingent of us, who were organizing against the corporate privatization of Great Lakes groundwater, and hoped to create situations that would force the media, and therefore the public, to take notice of often invisible threats to our natural world.

As we drove north together after the workshop passing row after row of so-called plantation pines, John commented that these second-growth forests were conspicuously young and lacking in majesty, especially com-pared to the Douglas fir, giant redwoods, and sequoia he knew so well from his involvement in tree-sits. We talked about how the red pines' usefulness as timber and pulpwood failed to compensate for the fact that they make for poor habitat and possess none of the diversity, beauty, or resilience of a true forest. This one conversation helped me to begin to really notice the extent to which our landscape has been shaped by industrial values, often leaving me in despair at the ease with which we dismiss the more enduring values of beauty and sustainability.

Now, when I encounter wildness in its different forms, I make an extra effort to sense and see and hear the ways it is woven through with the signs and intelligences of forms of life, other than my own. When I'm walking in a natural area near my home, I make a point to touch the trees and en-courage my nine-year-old daughter to touch the trees, too. We smell their leaves and needles together. We sit beneath their canopies and listen to ᵗthe way the wind moves through branches and leaves. How the earth feels beneath a being that has lived its entire life in one place. These forms of interaction feel more urgent now. Not only do I want all of us, collectively, to act like trees and forests matter, but I want to save myself from a tendency to live indoors, and see the world in only human terms, and thus forget how rich and interesting the rest of our world really is.

Recently I came across a story about Melbourne, Australia, where each tree in that city has been issued an identification number and associated email address so that citizens can report problems like storm-damaged limbs and disease. Residents of Melbourne have bigger imaginations than that, however, and some of the city's trees are now receiving questions, confessions, and even love letters via email. *The Atlantic* reprinted several of these correspondences; here's one addressed to an elm, a species that thrives in many parks and gardens throughout Australia, but which was decimated by Dutch elm disease in the twentieth century throughout much of the Northern Hemisphere:

"My dearest Ulmus, As I was leaving St. Mary's College today I was struck, not by a branch, but by your radiant beauty. You must get these messages all the time. You're such an attractive tree."

An encounter with a giant redwood or a 3,640-year-old bristlecone pine can quickly illuminate the spiritual aspects of trees, but even a tender sapling will do. We are given groves, forests, and all else that flourishes in nature, so that we may finally realize that Creation holds far more within it than resources to be exploited. As the poet Jack Gilbert wrote, "We are given the trees so we can know what God looks like."

This month, as magnolias flaunt their petals, and cherries throw pink fiestas, something is emerging in me as well. As the natural world turns on, so do I. In part, this is what it feels like to be renewed in body and spirit by what's happening outdoors, which is the closest thing I have to a church. But it's also about the renewal brought by beauty itself. Natural beauty. All the little poems, the installations, the songs I sang as a child in that willow—these are my praise songs and devotions.

Trees cool our atmosphere, clean our air, filter our water, and hold our soil in place. Trees provide respite from the ugliness and clamor of urbanization. Can poems in trees provoke others to become more appreciative of any of these benefits and marvels? Can they inspire appreciation for the ways forests nourish our inner life or quiet the mind?

On Arbor Day last year, Melanie took *Here, Stands* to Nebraska and installed one of our poems along a path at Arbor Day Farm, not far from Kimmel Harding Nelson Center for the Arts, where she was an artist in residence for a month. Up close, the texture of the words betrays the white pulp we used to shape each letter, but at a distance they radiate, almost neonlike, against the darker palette of the woods. It's very hard to miss them if you're looking around, as we hope people will do.

Blue shadows / of trees / lay down / their cool / invitations

To read this poem, you have to walk along a meandering path, and it might take you a full minute to see and read all of the words, maybe even recognize that you're reading a poem. *Blue shadows.* Even two words can be a poem. You have to wonder about that, and maybe even say the words out loud to yourself or your companion. Without realizing it, *lay down* has made you think of doing so, perhaps on layers of leaves. Look up as you await the next word, and wonder what you're seeing and how it got there. This invitation to join the world in a particular way.

My words look a little bit like the new snow that will stick to tree bark after a storm. After a few seasons, this ephemeral poem will have disintegrated into the natural landscape.

A light breeze has just passed through the branches of the crabapple I observe each day from my writing desk. The slightest breath made a handful of petals release and drift to the ground, their brief season a symbol of the passage of time, but also the persistence of the sublime, even in a damaged landscape. These blossoms also remind me of the power of small things to enchant and sustain us, as this tree does, if I take time to notice it.

In recent years, a poem by Lorine Niedecker has served as a sort of personal credo and reminder of the fact that I believe a poet must stay awake to the physical world that surrounds her. In six short lines, Niedecker declares that our best work will happen if we stand among birch trees. It's a simple enough philosophy, but also radical, because in just seventeen words, she offers guidance, but also a challenge. One that I've tried to live by as much as possible. It takes effort. Very little in our culture world reinforces this ethos, and yet when I go to the woods, like Melanie and like Emerson, my work does benefit, and so does the rest of me.

Just this week, halfway into May, the larger oaks and maples around our home finally unfurled their leaves. Now, even the air seems tinted green. I have watched and waited for this, not wanting to miss any of the subtle shifts they make during this transition to true spring. I go outside and touch them. I write these lines:

Sycamore

Two hundred summers
so children will know
reasons for leaves

Works Cited

Gilbert, Jack. *Refusing Heaven.* New York: Knopf, 2007.
LaFrance, Adrienne. "When You Give a Tree an Email Address." *The Atlantic.* July 10, 2015. https://www.theatlantic.com/technology/archive/2015/07/when-you-give-a-tree-an-email-address/398210/. Accessed October 14, 2015.

Jerry Dennis

BENDING NAILS

FOR A FEW YEARS AFTER COLLEGE I HELPED BUILD CONDO-
miniums on the hills above Glen Arbor, Michigan. They were architectur-
ally complex structures, three stories high, stepping up the ridges like lines
of vertebrae, their top floors rising above the trees for that top-dollar view
of Lake Michigan. My mother had grown up playing on those hills and
had taken me there when I was a child, so I was saddened to see bulldoz-
ers shoving trees aside and cleaving roads through the hills. But jobs were
scarce then, in the early 1980s, and this was steady work.

In September, shortly after I began the job, my wife and I rented a cottage on the shore of Silver Lake, a small inland lake near Traverse City,
thirty miles from Glen Arbor. We would need to move in the spring, when
the owners returned from Florida, but it was a good place for the autumn
and winter and the rent was cheap. Our son was a toddler then, and although Gail planned to eventually resume her studies in graphic design,
for now she wanted to be a stay-at-home mom. Living on the lake seemed
an adventure at first—she loved taking Aaron for walks along the shore
while colored leaves fell around them—but by winter it would become te-
dious for her, trapped at home all day without a car.

Our aging Datsun sedan, which had run dependably in Kentucky,
could not adapt to Michigan's cold. On winter mornings I would rise before daylight and ignite a pyramid of charcoal in a garbage-can lid and
slide it onto the frozen gravel beneath the oil pan. With luck the engine
was warm enough to start by the time I was ready to leave for work. Then
I would spend a tense few minutes fluttering the accelerator and adjusting a hand choke I had installed, until the engine ran smoothly enough
to risk putting the transmission in gear. Often it would stall. One day in
January it stalled and refused to start again, and I was forced to abandon
it in the driveway, where it became buried beneath snow pushed up by
the county plow.

It would be late in February before we could save enough money to have the car towed to the garage and repaired. Until then, my employer, Paul Maurer, loaned me his Volkswagen Beetle, which he'd owned since college. It ran dependably and had a good eight-track stereo system, but like all Volkswagens of that era its windshield defroster was nearly useless. Also, its accelerator spring was broken. Instead of repairing the broken spring, Paul had secured the pedal with a length of cord, which the driver had to pull by hand to slow the engine. He showed me how to hold it like reins as I drove. To shift gears I would tug the cord to let up on the gas, engage the clutch with my left foot, slam the floor shifter to the gear I wanted, release the clutch, and accelerate again with my right foot. It took some practice. Eventually I became so adept at it that I felt like a novelty musician playing five or six instruments at the same time. Between gear changes I punched the track-finder on the stereo to change songs and scraped curls of frost from the inside of the windshield with a plastic spatula I had found in the glove compartment.

But all that was yet to come. In November, while the Datsun still ran, our crew worked overtime to get the condos framed and their roofs covered before the weather worsened. Already the days were cold enough to give those of us who were new to the job an idea of what lay ahead. At lunch breaks we sat on upturned five-gallon buckets, crowded around propane heaters, and told stories, one leading to another, some of them so engaging that at home, in the evenings, I would write them in my notebooks.

A plumber my age, who had grown up and lived most of his life in Northern Michigan but affected the speech and mannerisms of a good old boy from West Texas, had routines as polished as a stand-up comic's. He said: "This guy I drink with sometimes, he's good people, you can depend on him, but he drives a van so filthy you climb inside afraid a gitten rat-bit. Hell, there's stuff in there the dump won't take . . . Now Old Man Durgy, he was a mean sonofabitch. One day after a lifetime of bein' miserable and makin' other people miserable, he sat back in his rockin' chair on his front porch in Kingsley and put a shotgun in his mouth and blowed his head off. Later his daughter said, 'That dirty prick. He tattooed his brains all over the side of the house and I had to spend three days pickin' bone splinters out a the siding.' She actually said that. All a them Durgy kids is a little cockeyed, like the whole bunch is inbred. But she actually said that. I know 'cause my dad collects guns and she come to see him about a week after the suicide and asked if he wanted to buy the shotgun. 'Hell no I don't want a buy the shotgun,' my dad said, and she said, 'That dirty prick. I had to pick bone splinters out of the siding for three days . . .'"

It was unusual for anyone to tell a story without a Weese joining in to tell one of his own. The Weeses had been with Maurer since he formed the company seven or eight years earlier, and remained the backbone of the crew. The family patriarchs were the brothers Jack and Jerry, both in their sixties, who had been carpenters most of their adult lives except for a charmed interlude when they worked in the research and development division of a company in Traverse City that produced innovations for the aerospace industry. They would grow wistful remembering those days in their gloriously equipped workshop, carving helicopter rotors out of exotic woods and figuring out more efficient ways to manufacture fuel lines for Apollo spacecraft. Jack, the older brother, was the general foreman of Maurer's framing and finish crews, while Jerry was a loose-cannon loner who worked on whatever he felt like working on. Jack's twenty-six-year-old son, Kim, was foreman of my framing crew and was a Marine reservist who despised anyone who couldn't pull his own weight. Kim's younger brother, Shawn, worked with us periodically but was always making plans to move on to bigger things. Their cousin Larry was the quietest Weese on the job site and a skilled finish carpenter who would eventually run a crew of his own.

Of all the Weeses, I enjoyed listening most to Jerry, the lone wolf. He was an oversized, bearded, cigar-sucking grouch who never in his life cared what anyone thought of him. The first time we met, my first day on the job, when as The New Guy I was still nameless and faceless, he responded to my offer of a handshake by unzipping his trousers and urinating on the ground between us. He was an imposing man with a prodigious bladder—I had to step back to keep from getting splashed. At lunch, if he was in the mood, he would hold court, often telling stories about his and Jack's father, Cecil, a self-employed gardener and landscaper notorious in Traverse City for attending public hearings in order to agitate the city commissioners, whom he considered buffoons. Once, at a hearing called to discuss traffic problems, Cecil strode to the front of the room in his dirty overalls and elbow-torn flannel shirt, grabbed the microphone from the hands of a lesser being, and protested loudly his indignation at receiving a citation after a neighbor complained about his habit of urinating in his backyard, in plain view of her and her children. He bellowed, "The world is in a damned sorry state when a man can't piss from his own porch!"

Cecil once grew suspicious that another of his neighbors was stealing stovewood from his woodpile so he bored out the center of a chunk of maple, filled it with gunpowder, capped the hole, and placed it on top of the pile. Sure enough, a few nights later the neighbor's stove exploded, propelling shanks of cast iron in every direction, piercing the walls and demolishing all the furniture in the room. None of the family were in the room at the time or the shrapnel would surely have killed or maimed them, but to Cecil's way of thinking that would have been just punishment for their thieving ways. One night, during a thunderstorm, Cecil was sitting in his easy chair reading the newspaper when a bolt of lightning hit a transformer on a pole outside. A ball of blue flame the size of a cantaloupe shot out of a wall socket, danced across the room, and struck Cecil on the soles of his feet. The impact blew him out of his chair. He landed on the floor, his socks smoking, then leaped to his feet and ran laps around the living room, shouting, "I'm okay, goddammit! I'm okay, goddammit!"

I rarely spoke at those lunchtime sessions, preferring to listen, but I was not unnoticed. Once, on a day when I had filled my thermos with water instead of coffee, someone asked what I was drinking, and when I told him, he made a stricken face and said, "Water! I never drink nothing but coffee or beer!" Another day, somebody noticed that I had brought only apples and a candy bar for lunch. I explained that I'd overslept and hadn't had time to make sandwiches. Jerry Weese was dumbfounded. "You mean your wife doesn't make your lunch?" he asked.

I laughed. I thought he was kidding. When I realized he was serious, I said, "She's my wife, not my mother."

"Divorce her," he said. "And don't make the same mistake with the next one."

He must have gone home that evening and related the story to his own wife, because at lunch the next day he unwrapped his usual bologna-on-white-bread sandwich, bit into it, and turned a baffled look downward. When he tried to pull the sandwich away from his mouth, a neatly trimmed square of plastic-wrap emerged, coated with mayonnaise, and collapsed with a wet slap over his beard and neck, drenching him in condiment. At the bottom of his lunchbox he found a note informing him that from now on he could make his own damned lunches. He blamed me, somehow, and for days refused to speak to me.

Often the conversation circled around to opportunities for making more money, and especially ways to capitalize on the building boom in Houston, which, like the Trans-Alaska Pipeline, had acquired quasi-mythical status.

We younger guys debated whether it would be worth renting U-Haul trailers and moving our families to Texas, assuming we could put away enough money to make the trip and that our vehicles would get that far. We'd heard that contractors there were paying twelve dollars an hour, cash under the table, with time and a half for overtime. Good wages in those days.

The older carpenters knew all about building booms and promises of easy money and usually sat quietly through such talk. But they were attentive, and I could tell they liked the idea of working where it stayed warm all winter and they could live for next to nothing in trailers on rented lots and drink beer with their friends while their wives shopped the yard sales. Most of them had been working construction jobs all their adult lives and held out for the South as their best hope of reward. They limped when they walked and ached so much in their joints that after sitting through lunch they had to reach for a ladder or other support to help them get to their feet. Everyone pretended not to notice, and God help you if you offered a hand. They were proud, and quick to anger.

When I got to know them better, I would learn the codes they lived by—that it was disgraceful to complain, no matter how cold you were or how much pain you were in; that you always stayed on a job until it was finished and that it was never finished until it was done right; that you bought your own hand tools, the best you could afford, and kept them sharpened and clean. The veteran carpenters were as resourceful, practical, resilient, and uncomplaining as if they had lived all their lives on the frontier. They were fiercely atavistic and suspicious of authority and as stubborn as the oak stumps their grandfathers had rooted from the land, and they believed so inherently in the frontier ethos that it must have been infused in their blood. Of course the frontier had long ago been parceled into lots for ranch-style houses and duplexes, many of them built by these same carpenters, but they acted as if they could always pick up and move to the next valley north, where the forest had not yet been cut and the rivers not yet dammed, and where the game and fish were still abundant. They had become anachronisms, but they didn't know it or didn't care and went on resolutely trying to subdue the earth.

They knew the land was being taken from them by developers and out-of-towners and considered it part of the order of things. They watched the woods where they had grown up hunting deer as it was transformed into gated communities where they could not afford to live and into golf courses upon which they would never be invited to play, but a paycheck trumped hunting, and most of the time they were content with the trade-

off. There were many other places to hunt, on both private and public lands, especially in the national park. Sleeping Bear Dunes National
Lakeshore, with its sixty-five miles of Lake Michigan shoreline, two large
wooded islands, and hundreds of square miles of woods, swamps, dunes,
and abandoned farmlands, had been established since 1970 and was still
appropriating property from private owners, often against bitter opposi-
tion. On this subject, as in so many matters concerning the land and our
use of it, my coworkers were divided among themselves and within themselves. They alternately admired and begrudged the developer of the condominium resort, a top-of-his-class graduate of Harvard Business School
who had somehow managed to purchase hundreds of acres of prime shoreline property in the midsection of the national park, while other property
owners were forced to sell to the government. The men on the crew were
bitter knowing that the park was visited primarily by tourists and summer
people, and especially because it blocked further development, costing
them work. At the same time, they appreciated having places to go that
had changed little in their lifetimes, where the second- and third-growth
hardwoods, pines, and hemlocks were growing stately again after being
clear-cut eighty years earlier. And the hunting in the park was very good,
as was the fishing in its lakes and streams. The men wanted the place to stay
as it was; and they wanted the freedom to build on it at will.

I was already familiar with those contradictions, which I'd heard artic-
ulated angrily for years by my parents and grandparents and by my aunts,
uncles, and cousins who had been displaced from their homes to make
way for the park. I felt a blood sympathy but also had seen enough of the
world to know what was at stake. Like most of the crew, I had grown up in
this place and was nurtured by its woods and inland lakes and rivers and by
the immense freshwater sea that bordered it. I too had learned to fish and
hunt there and had absorbed the place and been absorbed by it long before
I'd heard anyone utter the word "condominium," so I felt I had the right to
question whether what we were doing on those hills overlooking the big
lake was right for the health of the land and beneficial to our own welfare.
But when I raised those questions on the job site, they were answered with
silence, as if they were irrelevant or naïve or, perhaps, an indulgence that
only a pampered college boy could afford. What mattered was the work,
the bone-and-muscle act of putting hand to hammer to nail to wood to
earth. Building something. Receiving a paycheck. If I had pressed the is-
sue, I think the others would have argued that the world was changing and
we were not the agents of that change, but that we'd simply been swept up

in it like everyone else. But that argument was never made. It didn't need to be.

Yet sometimes I would see glimpses of the kinds of understanding and appreciation for the natural world that can only come from deep engagement with it. In the spring some of the men would give up their lunch breaks to search for mushrooms in the woods around the building site, returning to show off gleefully the morels they'd found. Or they would bring bags of venison jerky to pass around while they told their hunting stories, and although we had already heard every story, we would chew the jerky and listen again as they told about walking before daylight to their blind in the apple orchard and the long cold wait as dawn broke and the buck that appeared silently out of the mist.

Many of the values taken for granted on the job were new to me. I had worked my way through college doing landscaping and mopping floors at night in department stores and laying track for a railroad, and in all those jobs slacking off was acceptable behavior, and cheating the boss was a favorite diversion. Here, though, slackers were never tolerated, and cheating the boss was unimaginable. We were more like a clan than a crew. Union carpenters had a saying: "First drop of rain to hit you is God's fault. Second drop is your fault." But we were nonunion and proud of it and worked fifty or sixty hours a week in all weather. Instead of collecting overtime, we banked the hours over forty and redeemed them weeks or months later for sick days and three-day weekends. In the mornings we always arrived well before eight o'clock, on our own time, to set up the tools and uncoil the power cords and shovel the night's snow off the subfloors. Those unpaid fifteen or twenty minutes a day were a way to demonstrate that we were serious about our work and deserved to be taken seriously ourselves. New employees who were not serious were bumped from crew to crew for a couple weeks and finally one day were gone. Often they came and went so quickly that we didn't bother learning their names. They were like replacements in combat. Somebody would say, "That new guy, all he wanted to do was screw the pooch. I knew he'd never hack it."

The men I worked with ranged in age from eighteen to seventy and in skill level from beginners to masters. Some were bright, some were dull. Some were broad-minded and inquisitive, others were small-minded and indifferent. A few were racists. One or two were practical jokers, a laugh a minute, but when they nailed a new guy's boots to the floor or filled his lunch box with fresh cement they showed themselves to be malicious. The most skilled of them performed work that was nearly flawless, their craftsmanship edging into artistry. By working steadily, with no wasted effort, they could accomplish twice as much in a day as anyone else. The older ones were reflective by nature or harbored private sorrows and worked quietly, but the guys in their teens and twenties were loud with bravado and would strut and flex their muscles, running up ladders with sheets of plywood and humping shoulderloads of two-by-fours across the deck, all the while shouting in lusty joy at being young, healthy, and alive.

I was young and healthy, too, and shouted along with the rest. Although I was not yet sure how to define manhood, I was learning what it was not: coasting into work ten minutes late with a hangover and a smirk; slamming a job together and saying it was good enough for who it was for; ignoring an unpleasant task because you hoped somebody else would do it; complaining about the weather, about the boss, about the difficulties of the job. I learned that being a man meant refusing to be a slacker or a whiner or someone who cared only for break-time and afterwork beer or payday. I recognized the ones who bragged about their endurance and pushed for every advantage yet were quick to fold under pressure, and learned to keep away from those who were weak in spirit or had eyes dulled by alcohol or drugs, or who pitied themselves and wanted only to be delivered off the hook. I was beginning to realize that the hook is precisely what we can never be delivered from. It's our responsibility, our test, our condition—it's what being an adult means. Women tend to learn this sooner than men, but men have always made more fuss about it. "Be a man," we would say, thumping our chests, while secretly wondering if we could ever be as strong as our wives and mothers.

The carpenters I came to admire most were exceptional in quiet capacities such as integrity, consistency, and attention to detail. Men like Jack, Jerry, Kim, Larry, Lars, and another guy my age, Ray Franks, who became my closest friend on the crew and remains a friend to this day, were invested in their work, maintained the same standards of excellence day after day, and performed their jobs with a seemingly effortless proficiency that left behind no evidence of the carpenter or his tools. They believed in the fundamental bargain of an honest day's work for a fair wage. They welcomed challenges and were deeply creative at solving problems. They had limited education but were intelligent, and they were so principled that I became ashamed of my own flawed character. Most could be extraordinarily hardy. I once saw one of the older men slip while using a chisel and drive the blade deep into the meat at the base of his thumb, splitting the flesh open like a peach. Without saying a word he folded his cotton handkerchief into a bandage and stanched the blood, then wrapped his hand and the bandage three or four times around with duct tape and went back to work. At the end of the day, on his way home, he would stop at the hospital for stitches, but he refused to go during working hours. Worker's compensation would pay for it, so it wasn't the medical fee or the lost wages that concerned him. He simply didn't want to fall behind on a task he'd been assigned.

For most of them, it was more than a job. If asked what they were doing for a living, they might shrug and say, "Still bending nails," but this modesty, so typical of working-class midwesterners, masked a conceit. Only those who knew the trade knew that swinging a hammer was the least of it, that it took years to learn the job and decades to master it, that the satisfactions ran deep and were rarely discussed. Though I never heard the words used, it was clear that most of my coworkers considered carpentry a career, even a calling. A few had ambitions to start their own companies and work for themselves, but most seemed content to remain on Maurer's payroll. As long as they received occasional raises, as long as the projects were interesting and the work was steady enough to keep them busy most of the year, they saw no reason to move on. Many considered it their life's work.

I had started too late to ever become a gifted carpenter, but I worked hard enough to rise through the lower ranks, from laborer to rough carpenter to apprentice finish carpenter. And although I had always known it was temporary, I liked the work. I had grown up dreamy and impractical, so it was a surprise to be thrown into such bountiful contact with the physical world and discover that I could change it to my will. I liked the smell of freshly sawn lumber and the heft and balance of well-made tools, the men shouting their pragmatic jargon, the screeching of the saws, the sharp satisfaction of driving steel nails into yielding wood. The nails closed gaps in the world. At the end of the day it was gratifying to stand back and survey what I had helped build from nothing. I would go home tired and satisfied, with sawdust in my hair, and lift my son above me and look into his eyes to gauge how much he had changed since morning. Every day overflowed with astonishments. I hadn't expected to find so much joy in ordinary moments.

I would stay with the company for five years, long enough to learn the fundamental skills and to equip myself with the tools I would need should I ever decide to build my own house. For a few weeks, at the end of those five years, I would be put in charge of a crew responsible for the final touch-up before new condo units were handed over to their owners. By then I was writing a book, my first, working on it evenings and weekends while my son played on the floor nearby, and though not many of the carpenters were readers, most were respectful of the task I had set for myself, if only because I described it as a second job to earn extra money. But a few interpreted it as a betrayal. Like most of the younger guys, I was supporting my family paycheck to paycheck in virtual poverty, with no health insurance or savings account, and I had no more advantages than anyone else on the crew, yet I would always be a "college boy" isolated from the others by what they perceived or imagined was a class difference. I reminded them of lost opportunities or narrowing options, and probably it made them feel trapped. They assumed that my university degree and my white-collar father with his house on a lake granted me choices that were denied to them, allowing me to walk away when I wanted to, while they had to stay behind. And they were right—I walked away, but not for the reasons they thought. They couldn't have known how much I learned from them. Even now, all these years later, I measure myself every day against the standards they taught me.

Sometimes the veterans would tell us about the winter months to come—how the boss gave us the option of not working when the temperature fell below ten degrees, but we would work anyway because nobody wanted to lose a day's pay; how we would spend an hour every morning shoveling snow off the deck and breaking the ice that cemented the piles of lumber together; how we would have to rub bag-balm on our hands to keep them from cracking and bleeding. We would hear stories about frostbite and loss of feeling in fingers and toes, about Jerry Weese's soggy cigar stub freezing to his beard, about Andy Willy touching his tongue to a piece of steel wind-bracing to see what would happen, and his brother John setting him free by pouring hot coffee over the steel. One often-told story was about a roofer who stepped on a patch of ice and slid down the condo's roof and would have fallen three stories to the ground if he hadn't slammed his roofing hatchet through the plywood at the last moment and hung with his legs kicking in the air until he got a foothold and pulled himself to safety—and how he went right back to work carrying bundles of shingles across the roof, without saying a word, as if nothing unusual had happened.

What they didn't tell us, but what we would learn on our own, was that it was all in a day's work, that cold and snow were an inconvenience not a hardship, that if you invested in a pair of Sorel boots and a stocking cap to wear under your hardhat and a coat with a hood and always had an extra pair of dry gloves in your pocket and kept moving, but not so fast that you worked up a sweat, you'd be fine, the buildings would get built, the winter would pass. And there was pride in it. By spring we would all be veterans.

When I look back now I appreciate most the moments of like-mindedness during which we were united by the work or by a story that made everyone laugh or by the all-is-right-with-the-world feeling at four thirty on a Friday, when the last nail was driven with a definitive slam and Jack would say, "Well, that about does it." One of those moments stands out above the others. It was during my first November, when a dozen of us were framing walls on the open deck of the third floor of a condo, when I was still trying to learn the codes the others lived by and how they saw the world and why it was so different from the way I saw it. From where we stood, above the treetops at the crest of the hill, we could see North Manitou Island and beyond it a broad expanse of Lake Michigan spread out to the horizon. Somewhere out there, beyond the curve of the earth, lay Green Bay and the shore of Wisconsin and two thousand miles of possibilities all the way to the Pacific. The wind off the lake was in our faces, harsh and bitter, carrying pellets of sleet and dragging winter toward us. Dark clouds trudged past overhead. A few leaves still rattled in the oak trees.

We heard noises in the distance, like the barking of dogs, and suddenly a string of Canada geese came over the hill from the lake and began passing over our heads. They were only twenty feet above us, so close we could have thrown our hardhats and struck them. Each bird was big against the sky, its belly the gray of the clouds, its craning black neck and white chin-strap standing out in contrast. They were near enough that we could hear the panting sound their wings made as they chuffed the air. They swiveled their necks and looked down at us, veering a little in surprise, and the tone of their honking changed from conversational to alarmed. Six, eight, ten, passed in a ragged skein. The lead birds disappeared beyond the trees, but others kept coming.

Canada geese were less common then and seemed almost a different species from the semitame birds you see now on golf courses and city parks. In those days they were emblematic of the northern wilderness. At night, when we heard geese calling, we hurried outside our houses to look for the V-shaped flocks passing high against the stars, listened to the lonely honking, and felt something primitive stir inside us.

So when the geese passed over our heads that afternoon we were as startled as they were. We stopped in our work. Saws whined to silence, hammers hung suspended. Everyone looked up to watch, even those who had never shown much interest in wild things. Twelve, fifteen, twenty—we lost count, the two branches of the skein diverging as they went over, each goose turning its head to watch us, then passing one after another out of sight.

I glanced at the men around me. All of them, young and old, veterans and greenhorns, the whole ragged crew in their worn Carhartt coats and orange hardhats, with their nail aprons bulging heavy with nails and their hammers and saws in their hands—all of them stood motionless, heads up-turned, watching. I was green, but not that green. I knew that every one of us was thinking the same thoughts: wings, flight, south—and here I stand anchored to the earth.

WATER

Jacob Wheeler

BILLY GOATS, BOYHOOD DREAMS, AND THE COMING APOCALYPSE

SOMETIME BEFORE SPRING, BEFORE SONGBIRDS RETURN TO the Midwest, my family of three and I will visit Chicago. We'll hop on the rickety old Red Line train and take it north to the Addison stop, where Sarah and I will introduce our nearly four-year-old daughter, Nina, to Wrigley Field. For us, this intimate ballpark tucked in a cozy neighborhood just blocks from Lake Michigan is baseball's sacred shrine.

I'll carry a stick of chalk in my right hand and a bag of peanuts in my left. I'll march up to one of Wrigley's red brick exterior walls and find four inches of space. There I'll write the following five names, separated by commas: Peter Brondyke, Anna Jean Wheeler, Norm Wheeler, Jacob Wheeler, Nina Louisa Wheeler. These are the branches of the family tree through which our love of baseball has been passed down, from 1900 until now. A love of two different teams, and cities along our Great Lakes shoreline.

A baseball is made by tightly winding a thread of yarn around itself a thousand times and wrapping the sphere in two pieces of leather that are stitched together. Through the cosmic dance of the universe, that same yarn also connects generations and binds a poor farmer (and son of Dutch immigrants who came to Michigan in the late 1800s) who survived the Great Depression to a bright-eyed and playful toddler of the present.

Not yet old enough to clutch a baseball in one hand, Nina nonetheless wore a kiddie Chicago Cubs cap and held a miniature "W" victory towel as she sat on my lap while we watched on television in the autumn of 2016 as our team made their historic march through the playoffs and ultimately won their first World Series championship since 1908—a statistically astonishing drought of 108 years.

It was after midnight, in the early hours of Wednesday, November 2, 2016, that the Cubs narrowly beat the Cleveland Indians, 8–7 in ten innings, to win the deciding Game 7 of the Fall Classic—one of the most nail-biting and dramatic finishes to a baseball season in American history. Prayers were answered, champagne sprayed, tears flowed, and Cubs nation in Chicago and in pockets throughout the Midwest, including up the west coast of Michigan, partied for days. My Leelanau County community, where steamships from Chicago once brought lumbermen and city dwellers on holiday, is one of those Windy City pockets. W's were spotted hanging from flagpoles, mailboxes, tent posts, and car windows, and we the faithful refused to blink or turn our heads, lest it all be revealed as some magical dream.

Newspapers published emotional narratives of men who sat and listened to Game 7 on portable radios at the gravesites of their fathers, or the chalk wall of names that spontaneously wrote itself outside Wrigley Field after the victory. One reporter found divine meaning in the well-timed rain delay just after the ninth inning; at that moment the Cubs were deflated after losing their three-run lead, but a retreat into the clubhouse allowed them to regroup, weep, bond as brothers, and score two runs in the top of the tenth that would ultimately wash away their curse.

The celebrations in the ensuing hours crested waves and traveled across oceans before surging back to Chicago in a November squall of Cubbie blue. The victory parade on Michigan Avenue that Friday drew five million attendees—reportedly one of the largest gatherings in human history. The next night in Manhattan, star players from the North Side team made a cameo appearance with actor Bill Murray and sang the Steve Goodman tune turned marketing jingle, "Go Cubs Go," on *Saturday Night Live.* (Goodman, a Chicago singer-songwriter and passionate Cubs fan, is best known for authoring the song "City of New Orleans," which he gifted to Arlo Guthrie and Willie Nelson. Before dying of leukemia in 1984 at age 36, Goodman wrote "Go Cubs Go" as an ode to his team.)

That blissful first week of November 2016, it seemed that our long-lost heroes and deceased ancestors were present, and our beloved game and our nation were innocent and righteous again.

Shoveling Coal, Picking Cherries

Here's how baseball traveled through my family.

Peter Brondyke, born in 1900, was the son of farming immigrants from the Netherlands who ended up in Oceana County, Michigan, in the state's west coast fruit belt. He and his wife, Hattie, had a farm outside New Era and were hardworking and loyal Christians who went to church every

Sunday. It's unclear how he fell in love with baseball; it accompanied his love for Hattie and his love for God. Perhaps the tradition and orthodoxy of his faith inspired Great-Grandpa Brondyke to spend the other six days of the week listening to Detroit Tigers games on the radio for three hours at a time—when he wasn't tilling the fields, that is. During the Great Depression the farm yielded few profits, so he took a side job shoveling coal to make ends meet. His daughter Anna Jean—my grandmother—would walk home from the country school and find him standing in the coal car, covered in soot; only his white eyes and pink lips protruded from the blackness.

Peter Brondyke frequently took his two daughters, and later his grandsons Norm—my father—and Jerry, to minor league ballgames in nearby Muskegon and Grand Rapids. Years later, in the early 1990s, when his body failed him, it was said that Brondyke's strong heart—strengthened from shoveling coal in the 1930s—kept him alive. My grandmother, my father, and I took him to one last ballgame at old Tiger Stadium before he lay in his casket holding the baseball my father had received from him as a boy.

Grandpa Brondyke was a Tigers fan, but radio signals, and Oceana County's Lake Michigan shoreline connection to Chicago, would eventually pivot our family's baseball allegiance. My father, Norm, a leadoff hitter and sure-handed high school second baseman for the Shelby Tigers, listened to WGN AM radio out of Chicago while picking cherries during the summers of his teenage years. All Cubs games were played during the afternoon in those days, and he listened to announcer Jack Brickhouse narrate the hitting exploits of Ernie Banks and Billy Williams and the pitching of Ferguson Jenkins, to the steady tap of cherries dropping into a bucket at the foot of the tree. Of course, the Cubs were lousy in those days, and so it was permissible to root for a feeble team in the opposite league such as the home-state Detroit Tigers. (In those days, there were no interleague games.)

When my younger sister, Julia, and I were old enough to understand baseball and its chess-match strategy—but still learning about its metaphysical importance to generations of Americans—Dad took us for the first time to Wrigley Field, which is considered the crown jewel of ballparks. It was April 27, 1989, my sister's ninth birthday. The Cubs' promising young pitcher Greg Maddux beat the Los Angeles Dodgers and the previous year's World Series hero, Orel Hershiser, 1–0 on a cold spring day with the wind swirling off Lake Michigan. I remember ascending from the bowels of the ballpark and seeing the outfield grass for the first time and falling immediately and hopelessly in love. Nearly every summer after that, through my teenage years, Dad and I would drive the five and a half hours to Chicago for a couple days of ballgames, dining at ethnic restaurants, and often a play at the Shakespeare Theater at Navy Pier—this was back in the days when rural Northern Michigan felt like a cultural backwater. Before Michael Moore brought the film festival to Traverse City. Before the wineries, the brewpubs, and the classy restaurants arrived.

We called these annual summer trips our baseball pilgrimages. We usually crashed in the extra room or on the couch of one of Dad's college buddies who'd left Michigan and landed on the north side, between Evanston and Milwaukee. (In the decades since then, I've observed an entire diaspora of Michigan natives end up in the Windy City.) The city on Lake Michigan seemed to offer more cultural opportunities for us than Detroit, which was fading into a depression following the rise and decline of the automobile empire.

The infection, the madness for baseball, grew on me. Dad taught me how to keep score, and I once wet my pants while following a close Cubs-Pirates game at Wrigley. Somehow I thought that if I left my seat, our team might miss an opportunity to tie the game. I stayed, pissed myself, and they lost anyway. I came late to other pursuits—girls, playing sports, partying—because baseball box scores and the grand summer game were all I needed. I watched Cubs broadcaster Harry Caray on WGN television, and to satisfy my Michigan roots, I listened to famed Tigers broadcaster Ernie Harwell on the radio. But love for the Chicago team always came first. The fact that they hadn't won a championship since before the First World War, and hadn't been to the dance since 1945, made their lore even more appealing.

Eventually, I gobbled up baseball books. In particular, W. P. Kinsella's *Shoeless Joe, The Thrill of the Grass,* and *The Iowa Baseball Confederacy.* One of Kinsella's short stories stuck with me for its fatalism. "The Last Pennant Before Armageddon," a work of fiction, is about a Cubs manager on the verge of his team winning the World Series, who lets the lead slip away in order to save the world. (He's having dreams of the apocalypse, and he listens on a radio in the dugout as American and Russian warships are about to face off.) For some, baseball offers a moral calling.

I marked the significant events of my teenage and young adult years by key wins and losses for the Cubs. A beloved grandmother dying overseas in 1989, the year they won the National League East division and were favored to advance to the World Series (but didn't). On the way back from a

1993 spring family road trip to the Grand Canyon, we were driving through Iowa cornfields (and, I think, about to visit the "Field of Dreams") and listening on the radio when new Cubs pitcher José Guzmán excruciatingly lost a no-hitter with two outs in the ninth inning. The year 2003 brought a difficult breakup with a girl and anger and rage within me following the US invasion of Iraq; the year also yielded an unlikely Cubs run through the playoffs and to the brink of the World Series. My team would have reached the promised land were it not for a comedy of errors that unfolded during an infamous eighth inning at Wrigley Field: a fan interfering with a foul ball, players visibly losing their shit, then making a succession of Little League–worthy errors. The pain of their collapse only strengthened the bond between the team and its fans.

I spent most of the Bush presidency living outside the country (Denmark, then Guatemala), and the wars, the reelection, and the inept response to Hurricane Katrina eroded any sense of patriotism I felt. Still, I would often fly through Chicago on my way back from Central America, crash with buddies in Logan Square, and then catch a Cubs game the next day. Despite the politics of the day, once I was inside Wrigley Field I could always stand and salute the flag when public address announcer Wayne Messmer sang "The Star-Spangled Banner" with the green grass and the ivy on the outfield walls as his pastoral backdrop. In this setting, I had an easier time honoring tradition.

Nevertheless, the "lovable losers" betrayed us in the end. They made a habit of trailing their opponent early, mounting a late rally and almost catching up, sprinkling their faithful with a dash of hope, then coming up short in the last moment. This happened over and over again, year after year. Being a Cubs fan was excruciating, as it had been for generations. Perhaps our devotion was fueled by the knowledge that we would never be completely rewarded for our toil.

When Nina was born in December 2014, I had almost tuned out altogether. The Cubs were awful, having finished in last place for the past five seasons in a row. I considered not introducing her to my team. Turning her into one more hapless, tragic fan seemed akin to child abuse.

Keeping the Billy Goat at Bay

Then a funny thing happened. In 2015 the Cubs started winning, and winning convincingly. They had a talented and inspirational young team, built largely by Theo Epstein, a brilliant and youthful executive from New

England who, eleven years earlier, had put together a Boston Red Sox team that exorcised its own storied "curse of the Bambino" and won a World Series. The Cubs would win ninety-seven games in 2015 and return to the National League Championship Series. By late summer I had capitulated and introduced Nina to the Cubs; some nights I rocked her to sleep by humming "Take Me Out to the Ball Game."

Then suddenly it was twelve months later, and amid the bewildering time vacuum of a second year of sleep-deprived nights and raising a restless toddler, suddenly the Cubs had vanquished the San Francisco Giants and Los Angeles Dodgers, they'd won their first pennant since 1945, and they were heading to the World Series to face the Cleveland Indians. The Cubs were hands down the best team in baseball, yet no one could quite believe they were headed for the Fall Classic. The dance. The promised land.

The narrative that bled from the sports pages of the *Chicago Tribune* and the *Sun-Times* was that these young stars—Theo Epstein's crew—were too infantile, too optimistic, too boyish, to worry about the great weight put on their team's shoulders. They'd gone 108 years without a championship. "Those were the mishaps of previous generations," the Cubs seemingly said in unison. "We live for today."

But history seemed to ride them the way a wet, heavy bundle of sticks rides an old donkey. When the 2016 World Series began, the Cubs didn't play like they had in the regular season when they won an astounding 103 games. They salvaged one of two games in Cleveland, then came home to Chicago and played badly to drop Games 3 and 4 in front of the home faithful, putting them on the verge of elimination. I distinctly remember watching Javier Baez, the Cubs' twenty-three-year-old middle infield wizard, boot several easy plays and strike out on a high fastball to end Game 3, and thinking, "The pressure is getting to him. These guys can't escape the arc of history, or the curse of the billy goat."

The legend goes that Greek immigrant and Chicagoan William Sianis put a hex on the team after they wouldn't let him bring his pet billy goat "Murphy" into Wrigley Field during the 1945 World Series. "They won't win any more," Sianis declared. And they didn't. Not even Joe Maddon, the Cubs' Zen-like manager, could turn the team's fortunes around. They found themselves trailing three games to one, with two of three potential remaining games looming in Cleveland. It looked like curtains for the Cubs.

But somehow the Cubs eked out a 3–2 win in Game 5 to send the series back to Ohio, then won a blowout 9–3 rout in Game 6, setting up the storied finale. (The Indians were suffering a drought of their own; they hadn't won the World Series since 1948.)

A Father-Son Victory

For a split second I thought about driving to Chicago for Game 7 and braving the teeming masses to get near Wrigley Field, where thousands would be packed into the streets watching the game on their iPhones. But when I read that bars in the neighborhood were charging over a hundred dollars for admittance—even though the game was to be played in Cleveland—I switched gears.

No, I'd watch the pivotal game together with my dad, older and hobbling, and a week shy of getting his right knee replaced. That meant meeting him at Art's Tavern, the traditional watering hole of my hometown of Glen Arbor, Michigan, where I'd seen a hundred sporting events on television, interviewed story subjects for my newspaper, the *Glen Arbor Sun*, even taken girls on first dates. Art's it was. We invited a small entourage of friends: Sudsy, the sports aficionado; Jim, my new colleague, himself a baseball worshipper; Tim, the tavern owner; and John, the union organizer from Cleveland (it seemed diplomatic to have one Indians fan in our presence.)

The Cubs leadoff hitter, Dexter Fowler, opened the game with a home run to send our spirits soaring, and by the fifth inning we had a 5–1 lead. The unimaginable—a World Series victory—seemed within reach. But then it all began to slip away, like so many games, so many seasons before. The Indians chipped away at the lead, and then in the eighth inning star relief pitcher Aroldis Chapman surrendered an excruciating, game-tying two-run homer to Rajai Davis. Cubs nation was absolutely deflated. The ghosts had entered the ballpark. Their billy goats wanted to graze.

With the score tied at 6, the ninth inning came and went quietly. Tension was building. But before extra innings commenced, the heavens over the Midwest opened and began to spit rain. What did this mean? What message were the baseball gods sending us? (The storm also knocked out cable TV for a group of travelers staying down the road at LeBear Resort. Bewildered and sopping wet, they knocked on the door of the tavern, the only light in town. This being November, and outside of the typical tourism season, Art's owner, Tim, had already closed the till and sent his staff home for the night. But understanding how much this game meant to us, he kept the doors unlocked, and the beer tap flowing, free of charge.)

Meanwhile, as it rained in Cleveland, the Cubs players secretly huddled together in the bowels of their clubhouse. They wept, they talked, and they concluded, "We can do this."

The Cubs scored two runs in the top of the tenth, the Indians scored one in the bottom half, a dribbling ground ball toward third baseman Kris Bryant turned into a routine out, and our cursed "lovable losers" had gone the distance. They had won the World Series.

In Chicago, the north-side neighborhoods erupted in pent-up joy. My friend Matt, who lives four blocks from Wrigley Field, attempted to walk out his door and approach the ballpark. He couldn't get very far before the wave of bodies pushed him back like a strong ocean current. Back at Art's, I didn't know how to act or what to say. The feeling was odd. I turned to my left, gave my dad an embrace, finished my pint of IPA, and watched the boyish celebration on the television screen as rain pattered the street outside. I drifted alone into my thoughts, deep into the baseball lineage.

Eventually, I returned home early that morning somewhere around two a.m., to my sleeping wife and sleeping daughter in the crib next door, and contemplated waking up the next day and trying to imagine a reality in which the Chicago Cubs were World Series champions. Euphoric revelry would ensue and carry us through the winter, I figured. Strangers who loved the Cubs would embrace each other on the streets from now until Christmas. And as icing on the cake, the following Tuesday a well-deserving woman from the Chicago suburbs would be elected president of the United States.

Before I closed my eyes, I thought for a split second about Kinsella's story "The Last Pennant Before Armageddon." Maybe this *was* it. Maybe we wouldn't wake in the morning. Maybe baseball wouldn't return to the land the following April. Maybe some strange geopolitical event would . . . never mind, I drifted off to sleep. And for the next six days—yes, exactly six days—I would share stories, text messages, happy tears, and cocktails with other Cub fans.

The Ghosts

Or maybe I didn't drive home from Art's after the game that night. Maybe I walked down to Lake Michigan and jumped into her holy, frigid waters, as I had told John from Cleveland I would if the Cubs won the World Series. Maybe I let the November wind dry me off, and maybe I hiked along the Sleeping Bear Point trail under a night sky that was suddenly, miraculously, full of stars. And maybe I looked southwest, across the Manitou Passage and the graveyards of forgotten schooners, and hundreds of miles away I could see Belmont Harbor in Chicago, dancing in Cubbie blue and red lights, and people bouncing up and down in revelry as if they knew the end was near. And maybe the Northern Lights formed the shape of a baseball diamond, buttressed by red brick walls and covered with green ivy. And maybe I heard Harry Caray's laughter rising from the lake bottom, but this time his voice described not balls and strikes but astronomical constellations in the sky while he sipped an Old Style beer. And in the dunes below me figures began to lope. No, not squirrels or deer seeking their next meal, but the familiar Cubs players of old. Ron Santo circling the bases on his legs ailing from the diabetes he kept secret from the baseball world; Ernie Banks, "Mr. Cub," joyfully proclaiming to a journalist, "Let's play two today" before snagging a line drive with his glove; Ryne Sandberg legging out a double in the gap; even Sammy Sosa, steroids and all, running out to right field and giving the Wrigley bleacher bums his customary two-tap fist-to-the-heart pump.

Oh, but what's this? I see a boat drifting toward the shoreline, a leaky canoe, tossing turbulently in the surf. In it, sitting calmly and clutching an acoustic guitar in his lap, is Steve Goodman, the Chicago singer-songwriter—come back to life after dying of leukemia thirty-two years ago. I strain to listen for his tune. The sound of the waves subsides and I hear it. No, it's not "Go Cubs Go," the marketing jingle that the franchise now plays like a broken record. It's Goodman's original anthem for the Cubbies. The one the team commissioned, then rejected for being too pessimistic. What he croons here on this drifting canoe is no victory ballad, but a thesis posed in the form of a question.

"It's late, and it's getting dark in here / And I know it's time to go / But before I leave the lineup / Boys, there's just one thing that I'd like to know / Do they still play the blues in Chicago / When baseball season rolls around? / When the snow melts away, do the Cubbies still play / In their ivy-covered burial ground?"

Six days later, the American people voted in a presidential election, and the electoral college selected Donald Trump to occupy the White House. To many of us, the apocalypse suddenly felt nigh. Had W. P. Kinsella predicted this? The Cubs winning the World Series, and the world imploding soon thereafter? I wanted to contact Kinsella and ask him, but I missed my chance. Kinsella didn't live to see how the story would play out. Ailing from a decades-long battle with diabetes, the Canadian writer took his own life with the help of a physician assistant six weeks before the Cubs won the World Series. Maybe he knew what was to come.

W. S. Penn

A HARVEST MOON

CLARA CALLS ME "BUMPA."

"Bumpa," she says, "when I told Ms. Hanson you were Indian, she said you weren't. She said Indian was insulting. You were Native American."

"Fine," I say, "except that there is no 'American' about it."

"What do you mean?"

"I mean that when Amerigo Vespucci fetched up on the shores of what is now our country, there were only Natives, indigenous people who had not yet learned the graft and glory of being Americans. True, there are theories that said indigenous people crossed a land bridge from Asia, a bridge that either never existed or exists no longer, kind of like Sarah Palin's Bridge to Nowhere. But then there are also theories by people without an understanding of metaphor that all of us came from a man called Adam and a woman called Eve, and that we had the good luck to be evicted from Paradise, which I've always imagined would be like living in Michigan, at two p.m. on a mild fall day."

"Yecch," Clara says. "That'd be boring."

"Not to mention always having to rake up fallen leaves."

"Which is why it's called fall, right?"

"That or it refers to 'fall back,' as we indigenous people turn our clocks back so we're on the same page with Geats and Celts."

Clara Bean frowns. "Bumpa!"

Got her. For the whiffiest of instants she considered the "fall back" business before she recognized that I was kidding.

Clara and I walk to the park, much as I did nightly with her mommy, telling stories of Stuart and Frankie. Stuart is a brown squirrel, Frankie black, and the first time I pointed again at a black squirrel and said, "Look, there's Frankie," she demanded to know how I knew that was Frankie, and I replied with authoritative calm, "He's black, isn't he?" and the logic of it convinced her. Just like her mother.

When she finally figured out that I might be not quite accurate—that brown and black were just squirrely metaphors—she had stopped caring, too involved with our stories of hunting and storing acorns, or dashing up and around trees like the red on a barber's pole.

Now I have to say, digressively, for those of you whose eyes are riveted to mobile devices and whose attentions don't exist outside of a squirrely twittering without the recognition of danger, there is no greater pleasure for a Bumpa (and by extension a Nana, Mommy, Daddy, Uncle, or Aunt) than to hold the perfectly formed tiny hand of his granddaughter and walk—anywhere. To the park, or Clara's favorite, the bookstore, is just an increase, though not of name but of being. Oh, and for the past eighteen months, she has loved Whole Foods because it gives out cheese and bread in small domes of tasting. She loves cheese.

"As for Ms. Hanson, 'Native American' is equally wrong as 'Indian.'"

"So she's wrong?"

"Not exactly," I say in a musing, here-comes-a-story voice. I do not want to undercut Ms. Hanson's authority. She is a wonderful teacher, underpaid, overworked, hardworking, and serious but cheerful. I couldn't do what she does, and her intentions are as good as any of the well-meaning people who believe that changing the words will change the experience, much of which is historical, already in the record books, so to speak. This old-age thing seems to cramp you all up and constipate you.

Lighten up, Bumpa. Or, as Clara's mommy once said to me on a dirt road into Glendalough in Ireland, "It's okay, Grumpity."

"So you'll come in and tell the class about being Native American?"

Aha. I'm a resource. Not unlike someone who plays the mandolin professionally. Except I am not a professional Indian. I know professional Indians, and I don't much enjoy them. Their Day Books are filled with snubs and verbal injuries that seem to injure the slight. I am as stuck with them as they are with me. I can't put it down and take up another set of attitudes or beliefs. But a resource, that's interesting.

"Sure," I say to Beaner, who snuggles up as we walk and gives me a sideways hug.

"Really?"

"For you, anything." And for the disbelieving, for Bean or for her mother or uncle I'd do anything legal, up to and including death, with which I have had more than my fair share of experience.

"What do you think I should talk about?" I ask her, expecting her to suggest, in her desire to have everyone enjoy my visit, "feathers and fandango."

But she doesn't. Instead, with all the seriousness only a seven-year-old can muster, she replies, "What you always talk about."

"Which is?" I say, thinking, "Always?" Do I always talk about one thing? You may imagine the anxiety with which I await Beaner's definition of always.

"Process," she said.

Whew. She's right. I do always preach process. There is no good story, but that it is well told, no good song that is not well sung, no human meaning without love. No joy without contentment, even momentary. No having experience, just experiencing and then remembering the experience in myriad ways as you tell and retell it to others or yourself, and if you don't want your fraternity brothers to pack up their Mickey's Big Mouth beer and leave you high and dry, then you'd better tell your travel experiences well.

Indeed, you may want to add some spice, at least some pepper and salt the way a good cook balances sweet with sour. Even if the spice you add is, well, not quite true. (Here you must pay attention to definitions of realism, as in believable, probable, possible: you may not sleep with a spacecraft alien on the poorer streets of Barcelona, but you may sleep on the sidewalk bunched together with traveling companions for warmth and protection, sleeping in poorer neighborhoods the police with teeny patent leather hats avoid.) If it keeps your reader/auditor engaged, it's worth the cost to fact.

Keep the details consistent, and worry less about "facts" and more about the truth of what the story says and about whom or what. If it is meant to aggrandize yourself in order to pick up girls (or boys), then it is by definition not a story, and you are engaged not with the process of telling a good story but with impressing others with a weak story, often involving money, drugs, or sex. Remember, too, that camera snapshots are, in fact, not factual because the human context of speech, movement, ambient noise, call and response is not present in that digitized fixity. Snapshots are boring, and no imaginative person wants to look at yours.

There are historical facts: blankets infested with smallpox were distributed to starving, freezing Indians; an estimated sixty million Africans perished in the triangular trade of slave ships; 6–7 million Jews, Romany, and other people Ayn Rand would discard in dustbins died in German and Polish extermination camps—but these facts are not stories. You cannot even get at the story. You cannot tell it well, because if you are a Human Being, your mind is incapable of imagining the actualities. Truths and historical facts are umbrellas for stories, large contexts for the stories that might be made out of the experiences, umbrellas under which teller and listener may temporarily keep dry.

The odd thing—at least odd when I think about it—is that you cannot tell a good story about any of those "truths" unless—*unless*—the story is about survival, not death, love, not hate, or, damn it all, forgiveness. A well-told story even about bad things—and come on, those are pretty bad things mentioned above—must have or offer, in whatever complicated understanding and alteration, hope. It must offer . . .

"Bumpa?" Her hand gives mine a squeeze as her engines begin to rev at the gates to the park and playground.

"Process from an Indian perspective, is that it?"

"Yup."

"How?"

Clara darts over to a fallen branch of maple leaves, all reds and golds, and hands it to me like an olive branch.

"Just talk to them like you talk to me."

"I can't."

"Why not?"

"Because they are not you." Beaner slips my hand and runs for the playground.

Kids are already there with their parents; others will inevitably show up. Though I greet the other parents, I take myself off to a triangular seat in the corner of the large sandbox to think about playing Indian for Clara Bean's class.

Hanging from a high branch of a tree and swinging from a worrisome height off the ground, Clara calls out, "Look, Bumpa!"

A mother named Mary comes over to bend with her scooped neck sweatshirt, playing trucks and graders with her youngest. Fortunately, another father with whom she is having an affair shows up with his boy. She unbends and leaves me watching her youngest, who seems unhappy and silently uses an old Barbie doll to beat a Tonka dump truck into submission.

I imagine myself in front of an overload of faces upturned like teacups for the fluid telling of what it means to be Native American. I'm nervous. After all, a few of these teacups are Clara's friends; others are the offspring of helicopters that hover protectively over them; and some—the digitized ones I want to recycle—will be rudely uninterested in anything I might say.

To be introduced—me without feathers or dark aviator glasses or hair grown long and tied with a turquoise studded band into the hair of a horse's ass—as Native American, when really all they wanted to see was some wrinkled old fart in beady leather, and then to launch into a lecture on process will cause even Beaner's best of friends to turn and look at her as if to ask, "What have you done to us?" the answer to which is "Don't blame me, blame Ms. Hanson." Not "Hanson," but "Ms. Hanson."

With that, I have it. Even Mary Bender of the Loud Affair worries at my excitement, as I gently pump my fist, once, like a restrained golfer sinking a ten-foot putt.

The day arrives. The room mother—a Person of No Color—who feeds on interest in things like Native Americans—asks me what I think of Michigan Indians getting a monopoly on wild rice. When I try to explain that my people don't do rice but pine nuts, she says, "Oh, so just what kind of people are you from?"

"Nu-mi-pu," I say. "The Wallowa Valley."

"Oh. You mean the Nez Perces."

"I guess."

Without effort on my part, I quickly get to know this person. She's a "Room Parent," a decent, generous, bombastic, pushy, know-it-all kind of loud mother who does good work by helping out Ms. Hanson. The last thing I want to do is enter battle with her, or in any way deflate her authority with the kids, who are beginning to mill and grin, fluff balls floating in the winds of our confusing blowhard contention.

"Explorers called them that. Francophone explorers ran across some who decorated their nostrils with bits of blue shell, Gothy piercings that got them thereafter called 'Pierced Noses.' The explorers even wrote it down, so it had to be true."

I could not help but add—I am a lot less than perfect—"Sort of like Nu-mi-pu meeting Catholics and calling them the 'Bent Knees.' Or 'Wafer Wolfers.'"

The woman knits her brow, trying to decide if I'm joking or if I've just told her something important about Native Americans.

Ms. Hanson claps her hands twice, and the kids go quiet, turning their attention to her. The Room Mother melts into the back beside two boys playing video games on handheld screens hidden below their desk. Beaner sits proud and upright, an epicenter of her friends, who all sit straight up with their hands clasp on the desk before them, expectant, looking from Bean to Ms. Hanson to me as the introduction promises them all more than I can deliver.

In the interest of diversity or the interest of getting them to start thinking about the fact that Indian people differ in custom and craft, I've brought a beaded headband, a Hopi pot, a Kachina, a marriage pot. What looks like a tree trunk with a face has the head of Coyote sticking out from the stomach: Bean's mother's hand-molded clay sculpture of Ilpswetsichs, "Swallowing Monster," from whom Coyote created the Western Peoples—the Big Bellies, the Flatheads, Umatilla, Cayuse, Blackfoot, and others. From the blood of the monster's heart came the "Pierced Noses," a people of courage and heart, the Nu-mi-pu, or Human Beings.

"Well, class?" Ms. Hanson asks when I've finished, a moment that is easily identified because our stories end, "And that's the way it happened" or "That's how the Nu-mi-pu came to be."

"That's a stupid story," says Ralph, whose name actually is Taylore or Vapide. "It's not even true."

How would he know? Even during my telling, he lifted his head only at Coyote's flint knife, his cutting, the blood from the monster's heart.

Bean flinches. She's ready to defend Bumpa against anyone. I lift my hand at my side, a subtle stop signal, give her a quarter frown and a barely visible shake of my head. "Wait," it says. "I can deal with this."

"Well, Vapide, last night Bean—I mean Clara—asked me why the moon hung so low and loud overhead, and had turned so yellow-orange. You know what I said?"

Vapide is doing his best to look all vapid, but in truth he's a touch curious. "Dunno."

Bean can't resist. She knows. Her parents have kept her from screens like congressmen keep away from the Zika virus. She gets the relationship between imagination and the relationships of respect. She raises her hand. "Clara?"

"Because the cheese is aging," she says happily.

"That's not true," Taylor says. "That can't be true."

"More like 'won't be.' You're right. It won't ever be for you."

Jessica Mesman

A CHANGING OF WORLDS

There is no death, only a changing of worlds.

—CHIEF SEATTLE

1. New World

At night I lie in bed and think of the cemetery gate on Monument Hill. It was a fairly steep climb up a gravel path and always left me winded, so I didn't often attempt it with our all-terrain stroller. At the summit is a clear view of the college grounds and a circular, enclosed graveyard where the founders' bodies lie.

I will likely never open that gate again. I wonder how long my arms will hold the recent memory of tugging at the rusted iron, the screeching of metal on the stone steps so loud it set my teeth on edge. I brace myself against the sound and pull.

I turn over in bed and rearrange the covers, hear the wind in the pines. The weather is already so cool in Northern Michigan, as cool as I remember my last winter in Virginia, and it's only September. I'm restless at night.

I close my eyes and reach for the gate. The grating of metal resounds in the earth and in my stomach. The kids cry out and cover their ears.

Inside the stone enclosure, the grass is lush and soft. The kids dance on the graves. The columbarium is their stage. They never want to leave, but I anticipate the long walk home. There are tears.

I'm romanticizing. I do that. It's how I've always managed; I tell myself stories, create tableaux.

For six years in rural Virginia, at home with small children, I lived in what seemed a world of my own creation. There were many hours to fill and few people to see. There were horses. There were two trees at the stable gates, the sentinels, who watched us sidelong as we came and went.

Were they maples? I wonder in the night. I realize I never thought to identify them, or even look at them very closely. They were like something out of Tolkien and seemed as if they might speak at any moment. *"Avoid their gaze!"* I'd warn, and we'd try to pass between them without a sound.

For six years I walked the Dairy Road, first with one child and then with two. We carried walking sticks made from fallen poplar branches in our yard. Unpacking boxes in Michigan, I pause and close my eyes and feel their rough wood in my hands, the gravel under our feet, a pebble stuck in the arch of my sandal. I smell the rank, wet scent of the old dairy and hear the nickering of horses.

We packed up six years in a week, six years taped and labeled or sold in the driveway. We sold so much we no longer needed—infant clothes, diaper covers, the sling, the play mat, the high chair, the blue plastic tree swing both children had outgrown.

We left for good reasons, the reasons anybody leaves any place: better jobs, more opportunities. I repeat the reasons as I rearrange the sheets, switch the pillow to the cool side.

But my thoughts keep returning to what we left behind: their babyhood, my young motherhood, the long hours of isolation, the endless retelling of tales, the cooing of the ladies in the bookstore and dining hall, the rainy winter days when I thought I'd die of boredom and loneliness but for their sweaty heads on my aching arm as they napped. I'm waking from dreams of who they might be, who I might be, into a world beyond my control.

In time, I will forget the feel and sound of the rusty gate. I may be a romantic, but I benefit, as Flannery O'Connor once said, from a lack of retention. For now, I keep the framed baby pictures in a box in the basement. I'm reading up on Michigan lore. I've learned the sandy soil has a name, *Kalkaska*. I told Alex about Paul Bunyan. Last weekend we went to Rainbow Bend National Forest, where the Little River Band of Ottawa Indians released baby sturgeon into the Manistee River.

Charlotte listened as the chief told of long-gone days of virgin forests and lakes, of a prehistoric fish that could grow to be eight feet tall and three hundred pounds and one hundred years old. He quoted Chief Seattle, though I'm not sure why, because I stopped listening after he said it: *"There is no death, only a changing of worlds."*

The drums beat as we walked with the children down to the riverbank, each holding a young sturgeon ready to be returned to the Great Lakes. Water sloshed dangerously over the sides of their tin pails.

"So I'll be 107 when this sturgeon dies," Charlotte said.

I paused just a moment before I answered, "Yes, you will."

I reached out to steady her on the slippery rocks, checked to see that

Dave was helping Alex. They knelt, tipped their buckets, and gave their fish back to the river.

2. My Soul Thirsts

My children's Michigan fact book says you can't go more than eight miles without hitting water in this state, but it must be less this far north. I imagine the land shifting and disappearing beneath my feet as it does at the shoreline, except I'm standing in my kitchen.

"You're basically living on a big dune," a woman says when I mention my back pain. I thought I'd pulled something lifting moving boxes, but she says transplants often complain of chronic pain. We go rigid trying to find our sea legs.

Today I imagine the strain in my back isn't from bracing myself against water but from shouldering a cross in the form of a giant clock, the old-fashioned kind that ticks loudly all night until it sounds a shattering alarm. I want to carry it into the woods and leave it, take it to the lake and sink it, float home weightless and free from an unhealthy obsession with time, from circling thoughts of finitude that have kept me awake since before my mother died young. They never leave, not even with my lips against the warm cheek of a toddler so full of life he can barely stand still for a kiss.

These are the thoughts that drive me to the page, and they used to drive me to the pews too, where I could escape for a moment into that ethereal world of hot wax and flickering light and melt into years of other people's faith in a place where death has no sting. But the churches up here don't seem any more set apart from the flow of time than their social halls do. They smell of musty carpet and HVAC systems and food.

A couple of weeks ago a parish priest thoroughly shocked and horrified me when he described stained glass and art—both lacking here—as distractions. My dear man, my inner Chesterton bristled, that's exactly why I'm here.

So instead of the pews, I find myself in the woods, searching for a place that is ancient and undisturbed. This, Northern Michigan has in abundance. I walk fast, headed nowhere, but trying to shake that devil time from my trail, looking for God shining in a break in the trees, on a bluff or a dune that gives way to a glassy lake like a portal to another world.

In Chicago for All Saints Day we visit St. Gregory's in Andersonville. I want to take a picture at the Pietà, a shrine to the Mother of Sorrows, but another woman approaches before me, and I back away to give her space.

She lights her candle and reaches for Jesus's cold, slack hand, the hand of a dead man cradled in his helpless mother's arms. She gives it a calm maternal squeeze, as if she's the one comforting him.

I take pictures of the shrine with my phone. It feels unseemly, but I need a souvenir to remind me that there are still places like this in the church, not just in my books about the church. I light my candle and let my sorrow flicker there with all the others, release it like a fish in the water.

Back in Michigan I proclaim defiantly to no one that instead of going to daily Mass on a steely November morning, I will be a nature-worshipping pagan. I'm sitting in my car by the bay, listening to NPR and the seagull crying on my parking meter, when I remember that the church downtown offers perpetual Eucharistic adoration.

There are several people there, kneeling in silence, and I feel awkward shouldering my way in with my heavy bag, full of extra clothes and Star Wars toys and a half-eaten banana. I sit and listen to my loud breath mingling with theirs. This is not St. Gregory's, where all that intricately carved wood will never not smell like incense and tears, where you kneel in the shadow of two towering sinewy archangels bowing before a gaunt crucified Christ.

This chapel is not beautiful. Really, it's almost offensive to me, with that mass-produced Divine Mercy tapestry with the laser beams shooting from the heart of Jesus, the slogan "I trust in you" in script across the bottom, and that white noise machine on the wooden table in the corner is just a little too mundane a reminder of my own bedroom. But to be an art-loving, art-making Catholic today is to struggle against the worst of the banal, the ugly, the artless every single Sunday and then some, to plug your ears and put out your eyes and feel blindly for the altar.

Because they say God is there. I say he's there. And the brass monstrance on that awful tapestry holds all of heaven, every soul who ever lived, every moment of experience, every beloved breath or soft patch of skin, hidden not in a bottle of dandelion wine but in a wafer of bread.

There is no more seductive promise to me than this Eucharist, the only real shot I've got at leaving my sworn enemy time behind, at least for fifteen minutes until I pick up my son from the preschool around the corner. So I can't quit this church, even if she stubbornly abandons or forgets all the other ways she offered escape from the relentless grind of the everyday that wears all things down to dust.

If I loved God better, I fear, I wouldn't need those transcendent chants, the dead language, the stained glass that obscures the present tense with stories from the swirl of history and the promised, longed-for future. But my starved (or is it overfed?) imagination needs help to conceive of a world and a love that is both like what we know and far greater, everlasting.

Without the Eucharist, I'd be left to my books, lost in the Northwoods, searching the cedar cathedral for a place where I can read God's language again.

3. Winter Is Coming

All of Northern Michigan seems to whisper a warning. The sun is slower to rise each day, and the mist clings to the lakes when I drive my children to school in the darkness. It's not yet Halloween, but our neighbors have been anticipating the first snowfall since we arrived here in August, when it was ninety-two degrees and sunny. They look stern and offer advice (much needed) on snow tires and vitamin D supplements.

I can't help but think of the residents of Winterfell in *Game of Thrones.* If the threat of such a long, hard winter wasn't terrifying to me, a homesick Southerner who has never owned a proper coat, I might find it funny.

When I open my checking account, the bank teller raises her eyebrows when I say we've come from Virginia. "Have much winter there?" she asks, knowing the answer. The lady at the shoe store tells me I need four pairs of boots, not one, "for the four types of winter days: wet, icy, snowy, and it's-May-and-if-I-wear-boots-another-day-I'll-cry." I suspect she's taking advantage of me, but later a real rugged Northwoods type confirms her advice.

"And don't get cheap boots either," he warns, "or you'll cry like a baby."

Our new doctor recommends a high-quality multivitamin and a ski pass. Skiing and snowshoeing and even ice-skating are all as foreign to me as a moonwalk, but I smile and nod and try not to look worried.

"You can't hide from winter here," she says. "You have to embrace it."

I sit by the bay on sunny days, straining to store up the sight of it for the coming months when earth and sky will—I've been promised—become an unbroken colorless plane. I think of the family in Ray Bradbury's *Dandelion Wine,* who collect golden summer weeds and press their liquor into glass bottles to line their basement shelves, so that in the dead of winter they can tiptoe down and commune "with a last touch of a calendar long departed." The words *dandelion wine*, repeated as a mantra, uncork a "sudden patch of sunlight in the dark."

The young Douglas, who comes of age in these stories, suffers from the dawning awareness that to be alive is to watch good things pass away. His perfect summer is marred by its inevitable ending, by the departure of his dear John Huff, by the thrilling but terrifying discovery of the body as a "clock gold-bright and guaranteed to run"—and thus to run out. This is a recurring theme in Bradbury, and the young Douglas, who wakes up to his mortality, isn't so far from the guy who is tormented by his own skeleton, the memento mori that supports his very being.

But this isn't just the stuff of fantasy or science fiction. Waiting for winter I've turned to books for distraction and consolation but find there instead a collective protest against the running of the clock.

Today the *Writer's Almanac* featured Shakespeare's Sonnet 73:

> That time of year you mayst in me behold
> When yellow leaves, or none, or few, do hang
> Upon those boughs which shake against the cold,
> Bare ruined choirs, where late the sweet birds sang.

Even in my kids' library, Leo Lionni's mouse Frederick collects the words of summer as a stay against winter's bleak and hungry nights, and J. M. Barrie's Mrs. Darling exclaims to the flower-bearing Wendy, "Oh, why can't you remain like this forever!"

Douglas decides in *Dandelion Wine* that the only way to keep things slow is to watch everything and do nothing, and he shouts angrily at dear John Huff when he sees him, on his last day in town, running in play, running out their last hours together.

First Douglas tries to convince John it's earlier than it is by winding his watch back, but John, the realist, can tell by the sun's fading that the day is ending. Douglas attempts to freeze him, literally, in a game of statues, and as he circles his motionless friend in the twilight, Bradbury circles his conjured memories on the page, uncorks the bottle, and finds "John Huff with grass stains on his knees . . . cuts on his fingers . . . with the quiet tennis shoes . . . the mouth that chewed . . . the eyes, not blind like statues' eyes, but filled with molten green gold."

" 'John, now,' commands Douglas, 'don't you move so much as an eyelash. I absolutely command you to stay here and not move at all for the next three hours!'

'I got to go,' he whispers."

John Huff knows that the watching of everything and the doing of nothing can lead only to madness and despair. Winter is coming. As the doctor said, "You can't hide. You must embrace."

And yet we can't help our mourning. We long for that perfection we sense is our destiny and the destiny of all we love and find beautiful—an endless summer, a golden flower that doesn't fade, a child that doesn't grow old, time unsullied by the pressure to remember the good things just as they are before they slip into the shadows, because goodness endures.

I am Douglas on my bench by the bay, memorizing the color of the October sky, and later, at my children's bedside, winding my watch and playing at statues. I smooth my daughter's hair and run my thumb over the patch of soft down on the bridge of my son's nose.

"Don't you move so much as an eyelash." Gather, press, store. Line pages with words and shelves with glittering bottles. Winter is coming. Dandelion wine.

4. A Winter Soul

The first time I saw snow, I was twenty-six years old. I'd moved to Pittsburgh for graduate school after a lifetime in southern Louisiana, where I'd never owned a coat, hat, scarf, or mittens. I remember I walked outside the coffee shop where I was studying and stood there, turning circles in wonder like some alien fallen to earth, looking every bit the yokel I was, overpowered by the beauty of the fat, white flakes, by the sudden hushed silence that seemed to descend upon the city, by the way it actually sparkled. I remember thinking, in complete earnestness, "*This is magic.*"

But Pittsburgh's winters were mild and short compared to the winters in South Bend, Indiana, where I moved after my wedding. After three years of bone-crushing cold and life under the "permacloud," which rolls in sometime around November and doesn't budge until May, I threatened my husband that I would never again live above the Mason-Dixon Line. He got a job in Virginia, and I swore we'd never leave. I said, many times, he'd have to dig my bony fingers out of the red clay. He did.

When I looked at the map to see where Traverse City, Michigan, was before he left for his job interview, I cried.

It is Up North (they capitalize that here). Way Up North: forty-fifth parallel north, three hundred inches of snow last winter north, subzero temperatures north, winter for nine months north.

I made the best of it last year. Really, I did. It pricked my pride to have so many people warn me about how awful the winters would be, and I adopted a mantra: "You won't break me." I'm a fast learner and a die-hard romantic. I would study northernness. I would write us into a winter story. We would not just survive; we would thrive. We would snowshoe.

I read Norse myths and Norwegian novels and memoirs and got a (temporary) tattoo of Thor. I told myself I had a winter soul, made for sitting by the fire and reading epic novels. (When we couldn't find a rental with a fireplace, I bought a fire pit and parked it outside the living room window so I could at least watch the sparks in the darkness.) I was determined to emerge from my first Northern Michigan winter victorious, sporting Viking horns and braids and a breastplate of bones and feathers.

I learned a lot. I learned to stop washing my face and hands with soap and water to prevent my skin from cracking and bleeding. I learned to wear makeup every day, not for beautification but as an extra protective layer. I learned to avoid cotton and denim and to invest in a down coat and the most expensive boots I could afford. I learned the terms *polar vortex* and *Alberta Clipper*. I learned, sort of, to drive in snow (I'm the one crawling along, holding up traffic into Traverse City—sorry). I learned several different ways to tie a scarf. I learned how to make a hot toddy and to drink fish oil with breakfast.

When we lit our spring equinox bonfire in snow up to our waists on March 21, I was a little discouraged.

On Easter Sunday, we hunted eggs in gloomy snow piles and walked in gale-force winds on Sleeping Bear Dunes. Admittedly, the temperature was starting to rise, and we were grateful to be outdoors at all, but the gloom was unrelenting. All I could think of was the dogwoods in full bloom back in Virginia, the daffodils long since up and withered. We drove the twenty minutes back to our gray ranch house in the gray Northwoods, and I crawled into bed and cried.

By the time I woke up to snow on my son's birthday in May, I was well beyond broken.

In hindsight, my naïveté seems cute. Now that I'm a hardened northerner, I know that winter isn't a time to thrive. It's a time to buy a light therapy box, take massive amounts of vitamin D, and get on antidepressants. In the worst months, January through April, anyone who can afford to leave for a while does. But most people just put their heads down, feed their fires, and press on. Or they ski. A lot. As my neighbor says, "There's no way out but through." And sometimes going through just isn't pretty. Sometimes you crawl to the finish.

Sometimes, winter breaks us. And maybe that's okay.

St. Paul reminds us again and again that without death there is no resurrection, no restoration. "Look around you, fools," he says, "it's the law of nature—that which you sow does not come to life unless it dies" (1 Cor 15:36). Suffering and death are necessary, not meaningless. A crusty old Anglican theologian named Richard Sibbes said that as "winter prepares the earth for the spring, so do afflictions sanctified prepare the soul for glory."

There is plenty of beautiful writing about winter as a fallow time—a season of rest and emptiness necessary for farmlands and humans to continue producing a healthy harvest. Caryll Houselander, my favorite Catholic eccentric, said in her Advent essays that many are too impatient with winter. "A seed contains all the life and loveliness of a flower," she writes, "but it contains it in a little hard black pip of a thing which even the glorious sun will not enliven unless it is buried under the earth. There must be a period of gestation before anything can flower." She urges us to trust that Christ grows in the fallow time, in our sorrow, and "in due season all the fret and strain and tension of it will give place to a splendor of peace."

This is all very nice and reassuring and exactly what might pop up in my Instagram feed as an inspirational meme on some February morning. But when February isn't even near the halfway mark of a northern winter, it doesn't quite get to the heart of things.

Fallow is too gentle a word for this kind of winter. This is not a season of quiet melancholy, a few weeks at a slower pace to be savored over a cup of tea. This is months trapped inside with small children. This is influenza and whooping cough. This is getting stuck halfway into the bank parking lot and blocking traffic. This is black ice and zero visibility. This is breaking bones in a fall. This is holes in the roof from the weight of the snow and the holes in the road that swallow your tires. This is what comes before the fallow time. This is a harrowing.

A harrow is a horrible-looking farm tool with wheels and spikes and teeth. It breaks up the earth, crushes, pulverizes, plunders. Sound too extreme? Then I've captured it perfectly.

New year, new mantra. As this winter gets underway in earnest, I say, "Go ahead and break me. Plunder me, take me down, so I can be made new." Maybe that is exactly what I need—not merely a rest but a reinvention.

If I can't be a Viking, Lord, make me the Darkling Thrush of Thomas Hardy's poem, who though "frail, gaunt, and small, in blast-beruffled plume" flings his soul upon the growing gloom and sings.

So little cause for carolings
Of such ecstatic sound
Was written on terrestrial things
Afar or nigh around,
That I could think there trembled through
His happy good-night air
Some blessed Hope, whereof he knew
And I was unaware.

If I survive another polar vortex, it will not be by my own schemes and strengths and romantic fantasies but by grace (and a nice long hiatus in New Orleans). My soul might be the only thing that can grow in this weather.

Jaimien Delp

PURELY WATER

I'M LEARNING ABOUT BREATH. Or more specifically, Ujjayi Pran-ayama, a way of breathing in and out through the nose while constricting the back of the throat—as if you were whispering—to release what is old or stale, and be filled again with what is new and fresh. Oxygen. This is during Hot Vinyasa, where I'm reminded, at least four times a week, that this is a *breathing* class. Even as the temperature spikes past 100, even as my legs stretch toward the ceiling, and my hands press into my mat, slick with sweat, and Lorde throbs over the dim evening light of the studio, I'm told, *"Return to your breath. Downward poses breathe out, upward poses, in. Be wholly and completely filled."*

Be wholly and completely filled. That means one thing to me, and one thing only, and it has little to do with oxygen. It's water that I lust after. It's waves and currents that I visualize, dipping below an incoming whitecap off the coast of Lake Michigan during the exhale, coming up wet into the sky on the inhale. It's Boardman and Au Sable currents that run through my chest during savasana, it's rivulets along the backs of my eyelids and lips, it's one unfathomably clear, turquoise curl and spray after another that I move with—as if I were purely water, too—to wash away the drudg-ery of everyday existence and come again into awe, into some sensual, watery place where love and liberation become interchangeable. Because really, isn't that what it means to be wholly and completely filled?

So then, yes, this becomes a love story; my love affair with lakes and rivers and oceans and occasionally, when I was misplaced on the globe (Manhattan, for example), even bathtubs, showers, a long, slow rain. Just enough to get by until I could return to Northern Michigan and blend my skin with flowing water once again.

I've often wondered where this impulse was born, how it grew so strong and absolute, when the birth of our interior landscapes began to take shape. Perhaps it's in the blood; in this case, passed down most directly from my father, a master lover of rivers large and small. Or possibly it began even before my memory of it, a story from my early childhood about jumping into a pool and, knees tucked to my chest, sitting still at the bottom. After a swift rescue, when asked what I was doing down there I replied, *"I was thinking."* Even then, well before I had experienced any true pain, I must have sensed that where there is water, there is clarity. Where there is water, my mind will release whatever is not needed, shed it like an old skin, a wave bound for elsewhere, and come into clear spaces. I can recall leaving a party and wading into a lake one night in a silk dress, heels cast to shore, and floating perfectly under a Michigan sky. I can recall shedding shoes and shirts and pants to be carried downstream in the Boardman on summer nights. I've jumped off boats in blue jeans, gone for long, hot July runs, and dived right into Lake Wahbekanetta afterward, sneakers and all, to feel that cool rush, fast. I've cried in water, kissed in water, crashed my fists into the current, used the deep pools to scrub off the touch of people or places I desperately wished extinguished, gone. I've exhausted my spirit in the deep haul of growing up and arrived at the shores near empty, little to offer those quiet pools, and every time, *every time,* I've been invited in, allowed to float effortlessly, as if some beautiful finned creature swam beneath me, its rainbow back pressed to mine, buoying me up.

For the better part of endless days and endless nights spent suspended in water, I never questioned the doctrine guiding our romance, which required so little of me as to require nothing at all. I simply appeared from wherever I'd been, slipped into whatever still or stirring surface presented itself, and for a brief while, inside the shelter of that body, I was free from thought, filled instead with something clear and light, water's gifts bestowed. Like a lover so wildly generous they ask nothing in return—only to hold the curve of a hip or smooth the edge of a recurring nightmare—so we were. At night I appeared, and in the morning I swept the dripping beads of whitecaps and currents from my shoulders and returned to my life.

When I learned, then,
that fracking purposes an average of *5 to 8 million gallons* of water
and toxic chemicals per fracture;

when I learned
about Marathon Petroleum and their mountains of pet coke
piled along the Detroit River;

    when I learned
about Canadian oil transport giant Enbridge
spilling *800,000 gallons* of diluted bitumen
into the Kalamazoo River;

    when I learned
that the twin pipelines weaving along the wild,
public bottomlands of the Mackinac Straits
were built in the early 50s
and suffer dents, rust, missing
supports, and corrosion
even as *20 million plus*
gallons of oil
continue
pumping daily;

    when I learned
a leading freshwater research scientist
classifies Line 5's location as
"the worst
possible place
for an oil spill";

    when I learned
that such a spill
could surrender
up to 700 miles
of Great
Lakes coastline
to devastation;

    when I learned
that the Great Lakes
have
quite
literally
been colonized
to transport crude oil
for Canada,

the Great Lakes XL,
live for you
now;

   when I learned
that the DEQ had
recognized Nestlé's request
to increase withdrawal rates
from the Muskegon River
by the
hundreds
of gallons
per minute,

   to bottle and sell
away
from our shores,
to cap
and ship
off
such beauty, such
basic
human
rights . . .

   When I learned and learned and learned,
the truth is, for a long time, I didn't really *learn* very much at all. I couldn't
quantify or visualize the magnitude of such numbers, let alone their impact, so they floated, dim abstractions that they were, directly outside
my field of vision. The facts were like the wingtips of predatory nocturnal
birds, working overtime to evade the one thing that could expose and van-
quish them—light—doing their bidding, instead, at the edge of a horizon
so dark as to disappear from me almost entirely. I couldn't fathom such
impersonal and terrible terms in regards to the landscape I knew so intimately, that appeared, to me, for all practical purposes, unchanged. Bitumen? What the hell was bitumen, exactly? And it was rain and snowmelt
that dictated the water levels as I knew them, that ebbed and flowed, but
always, I thought, returned to relatively the same place. And didn't that

pure and unimaginable shade of blue always appear again when the ice melted, no matter how bleak the day, the night, the year . . .

Perhaps, in this sense, much of the assault on Michigan's water is not so different from any other assault that doesn't leave immediate and violently visible public wounds; nothing a quick smile or witty deflection or act of beauty can't distract from, and for a relatively long time, if the assaulted remains lost for words, or afraid, or perhaps she wishes to unknow that part of her landscape, of the uninvited there, as well . . . *So you want to see what's happening deep below the surface . . . Around that bend . . . Here, first let me wet your lips, you seem so troubled, my love, so thirsty . . . yes, like that . . . shh, don't say anything, let me . . .* And so you let her—of course you let her—close your eyes with fingertips so smooth and fluid you fall asleep wondering how it is they hold such wild currents inside of them, whatever it was you glimpsed to make you wonder what was beneath her thoughts—a slight shift in her body, her gaze—now no more than a single petal dropped to the river of memory, and so far downstream as to be gone from you.

And therein lies part of the problem. It's so easy to redirect a viewer's gaze from even the most painful injustice held veiled and way off to the left, with a clear and pretty picture directly to the right. And she's full of pretty pictures in every direction: the view from Pyramid Point in late August, that spot where seven creeks run together in the hills beyond a bend in the Boardman, the slow, endless arc of Platt Bay. She has any number of coasts and shores where you can run and breathe unbridled, where you might give all of yourself to open, exquisite beauty, protected in the knowledge that nothing of you can be lost here, only returned, and made more whole in her presence. It's unfathomable, when her waves are running through you and the sun is dipping down and every part of her is catching the light, to imagine that somewhere, people with no purity of intention want to touch her, and that somewhere, someone already has.

It's a technique the aggressor is skilled in, though their motivations are quite different . . . Their deflections aren't born of fear, or sorrow, or the ache of denial. Rather, the aggressor's deflections are born of a desire to deceive. Take this scene, for example: Imagine a rectangular screen. From the left, an arm is reaching in, extending in its hand the offering of a single drop of water. The drop is white, *pure*, dipping softly as it floats, like a note in a lullaby, just above the cradle of the palm. White arrows direct the eye from the droplet over to the right, where now two hands rise up from the bottom of the screen, cradling the Northland, "the Mitten," the unmistakable topography of Michigan. The droplet, it seems, has found its way home, though we sense, from this image, that such a homecoming was inevitable; this droplet could never have been lost, never have been harmed, not with such gentle, guiding hands surrounding it. The soothing outline of our coasts, the curve of her thumb, every secret peninsula and inland creek and sacred well—it's all there, it's all whole and clear and *there for you always,* its purity implicit in the way the hands seem to honor it, something holy dropped down from the sky. The lines of the image are softened, as if a slight rain has just washed through and carried all controversy away with it. Words surround the image—careful words, self-assured and easy words, like "preserve and protect" or "good water stewards" or "we take great care to operate in a responsible way." It's a place you might like to stay, an easy riverside café you might think to linger in for one more glass of wine. After all, there's nothing else you have to do, all of the work is taken care of and the air feels so fresh, suddenly, the river so especially pretty . . .

Born to any number of different orientations to the world, perhaps I might have taken one look at Nestlé Waters' marketing and believed it all. Perhaps with an alternate definition for success, or a different education (say, one that failed to stress the importance of studying one's sources for legitimacy), I might have rested my mind in the cradle of those hands, too, and never thought of any of it ever again. But the truth is, the image you've just studied so closely, perhaps thought about framing above your bathtub or over the entryway at the lake house, is the antithesis of truth. Those arrows? They're pointing in the wrong direction. That droplet? It isn't going home, it's being pumped *away* from home, to a factory where it will be treated, bottled, and then sold from one corporation to another. The truth is, those dark birds on that looming horizon have names, and they're Nestlé and Enbridge and Marathon; they're Corporate Gain and Government Interest and Fossil Fuel Culture; they're High Profit and Clever Manipulator and You're So Fucked If You Actually Buy This . . . And their wingtips, of course, aren't coasting on the currents of "sustainability" or "preservation and protection" or "community engagement," let alone wind or light or grace . . . Rather, they're coasting on *money*: billions and billions of dollars' worth of negotiations toward a highly profitable, industrial nightmare.

Here is an image that's true: Somewhere inside of me is a single feather, gifted to me at birth by a bird that feeds only on light. This feather moves not according to the breeze, but to water, to the currents and waves I run to. Sometimes in dreams I wear it like a headdress, this feather so white it glows against the dripping gold of my braids, and I wake up believing that I've discovered a word to save us all. Then the dream catches up with the day, the daily news, where the word becomes ten thousand other words, half of them distorted by PR reps and lobbyists and clouds of manufactured smoke, and not enough in the world are truly listening to distinguish between them, not enough know what to do with so many sounds . . .

So I go looking for the word again, under river stones and at the peaks of whitecaps and on still evening surfaces . . . Like those summer nights, just after dusk, when I take my paddleboard down to the lake. I slip under first—I want her dripping all around me—and then I shove off. Sometimes, with the sky vast and turning around us, I lie down and stretch my arms so my fingers dip to the tips of the waves, and I think of a poem by Stephen Dunn, about walking the marshlands with his daughters. "The world beyond Brigantine awaited their beauty," he writes, "and beauty is what others want to own." I listen to the clear, soft stir of my own breath against the clear, soft stir of hers, and I think how different our doctrine now, the deep debt I owe for being able to appear before her as I do. Now, I come to the water as a woman, changed—the way, if we're lucky, we grow back into the spirit of our childhood selves, that we then learn to dress and protect in the wake of a difficult world. I think of the cracks she has filled, the rage and fear soothed, the sorrows softened, that I might dive whole into love. I think . . . what I wouldn't do to save her . . . I think . . . what is that word, please, it exists, I have known it, I have felt it. . . . I think . . . please, currents, tell it to my fingers, tell it to my lips, and I will write it—*I will breathe it*—here, now.

Kathleen McGookey

AUGUST AT GUN LAKE

The coming storm stirs up waves that break over my little wishes—less bickering, a cleaner floor.

Main Street Bridge has been out six months.

Let's not talk about the sunrise, how it reflected roses and gold on both water and sky, how it started slow, then vanished inside its own light.

My daughter loves the number 44.

Each day, part of the house-falling-into-the-lake appears in the orange dumpster. Today, one wall, windowless, propped up, remains.

"Your average cloud weighs 1.1 million pounds," my son says.

Here, inside the sunrise, I will build us a glass boat to drift on apricot currents of light. I will pack blankets and a thermos of sweet milk. Here, inside the day's flush, we begin and begin, our plans suspended like dewdrops: plant a sunflower seed, write a note in purple marker, help a box turtle cross the road. You might lean against me and stroke my hair. If the weather changes, we'll pull on yellow slickers and hats and say the gray clouds feel soft as fur. When the sun rises over a farm, we'll look down on goldfinches flickering through the cornfield. When the sun rises over Gun Lake, calm as a cat's clear eye, our other, watery selves will wave up at us.

Let spiders nest in my daughter's paper lanterns, hung from the porch for her slumber party. Let fireflies and moths light the extravagant dark, thick with biting insects doing their work. Let those with broken wings find someone determined, armed with scissors and tweezers and glue. When the storm sweeps across the lake, all wind and hard rain, let rain and lake boil in a frenzy of spray. Let yellow jackets bury their dull buzzing underground. Let the toddler dressed as an owlet escape her flimsy cage, because a real owl perches on the zookeeper's arm, right out of a book. And because we leave the bookstore at midnight, let the yellow animal eyes of traffic lights blink us all the way home. The next morning, if a fledgling robin flies straight into our window, let it die quickly, its spotted chest pearly as twilight on the grass. Now we can get as close as we want.

Night opens like a culvert we must pass through to reach memory, that flat and silver lily-covered lake. Someone rows his black boat from shore to shore. Each time an oar breaks the surface, the smell of dead things rises up. Far above, an egret carries the key to my secret wishes. In the kitchen, rows and rows of ripe peaches, burnished like embers, flare into rot.

Image placeholder

That couple with their heads full of clouds is sailing on stirred-up August water, more green than any shade of blue. She reclines on the seat, a rolled-up towel under her neck. When the boat tilts, she grabs the edge. He's careful, usually, but wind's capricious—rippling or dying, flapping the rainbow-striped sail. She closes her eyes. She doesn't mention the child's spider bite, new shoes, new notebooks, new blank forms, the lemon cake she'd like to make. Instead, she imagines clear bubbles in the sailboat's wake, swirling before they dissolve. The water smacks its small mouths against the hull. They might hold hands, briefly, here inside the wind's rush and lull, give and take, until he pulls the mainline in. What happens next is out of their control. Sometimes an eagle flies overhead. Sometimes, a gull.

Anne-Marie Oomen

TWELVE WAVES

1. Childhood at Lake Michigan. My father threw me up and over his shoulder, and I laughed as I tumbled in the waves. Later, he told me waves come by the dozen, not sevens like others said. But then he said, "Don't try to count." He laughs. "You won't know where to start, or which is which." Still I watch, paying close attention for the big three somewhere in the middle.

2. This one: Blue beyond blue—even when it's gray or steel or any of the blue-induced shades of fierce. Blue that is not blue but the cold wonder that could crush ships or even your spirit, not break it as in some insipid cliché but crush it with depth, beauty, wildness so stunning it stills the heart, the finest way to die—if there is a fine way. I learn waves are ideas, not numbers. Counting them keeps time with water, an essence of sorts.

3. As I grow, big water becomes the miracle of coolness and play. The surface a dance floor of glitter and glamour to swallow you whole. Beach, swash, shallows, depths. Dive in. A world of mystery. You open your eyes: a golden and blurred place. I come up for air wishing I could live down there, scared out of my mind. Dad is always there: "I'll save you." Water in my eyes, cleansing outside and in.

4. Nothing could save him. When my father died in that white hospital bed, all afternoon fluid in his lungs, a reduction of the body's internal waves to something salivic and mucosal. I kept asking the nurses to suction it out; they looked at me sadly. Once or twice, they tried. That wet wheeze always came back. They knew but would not say; then the moment I understood.

5. That wave knocked me over, nearly drowned me.

6. That wave knocked me over, nearly drowned me.

7. That wave knocked me over, nearly drowned me. Then, storm rising over water, shouldering itself, stalling on the horizon, roiling inside. I thought it would never move. This was grief, a water large and shuddering, surface slashed with white keening. I could not see the other side.

8. Wave of time. One day, I see a woman walking on water. She looks like a slim bird dragging one narrow wing. I learn: on a paddleboard, a woman may mourn like a lake, like big water, breaking gravity by not going under but gliding over, dipping in.

9. At first, I fall so often my face is never dry. One rainwater day, a shallow balance. Finally, toes gripping board, I feel the vibration of underwater currents, old stories, a loneliness that will not hurt you if you simply stand in it, let it flow through and around you. Out there, woman becomes gnomon. Water, a liquid something. Soul. You lift and dip one narrow wing. You can find your way.

10. One of those things that just happens. I'm out on the board, trying to hear my life, just beginning to sing. I don't know if the woman I found would have died. Hypothermia is unpredictable, especially for swimmers, especially in the waters of Lake Michigan where the temps can jump and drop those few critical degrees depending on the subtle currents that curve around bluffs, spits of dune. She stopped swimming; she called. I turned the board with the long stroke, shallow and wide as I had been taught, and came alongside her. She reached for the board, slipped, then clung. I leaned away, balancing her weight with my own, then knelt, lay the paddle crosswise, and we began to work her body onto the board. I thought for a moment I would lose her. But she had enough left to pull her own body out of the chop. Her skin like cold nectarine. The air above her smelled blue and empty. She could not speak, shivered so hard I could feel it through the board. I stayed on my knees, as we do when we pray for miracles, paddling over her head, an awkward but necessary stroke. As we came in, others took her in and warmed her. I looked at the water, lifted it to my face, kissed its cold power, that it would let me rescue one of its own—who was me.

11. This is the wave of evening, one that quiets. Out there on the board, as the temperature dropped, the moment when I felt him. His spirit, east wind, flying over waves, intensely curious, beyond these waves into the waves beyond beyond. I tried to match and rode the waves so hard I was almost beyond seeing the shore. The blue there was deep and fast and pure. Where, where, where was he? The wave told me; he was fine. I stopped, pulled back to earth.

12. Oh lake, oh father, oh woman on the water. Take this water I am made of and depend on; keep it pure and blue, this healing liquid, held in a body of being. Lifeblood that comes in the shape of waves.

W
IN
D

Fleda Brown

MIRRORED TRANSOMS

OUR NEIGHBOR HAS BEEN RENOVATING HER CONDO FOR almost a year. Just cosmetic changes, she said, but the place has been gutted, the hundred-year-old chair rails and trim are gone. Now there are all sorts of soft-gray built-ins, floors stained fashionably dark, wallpaper, and so on. I know because we live next door and I poke my head in from time to time to fret over what the workmen are doing.

It took me weeks to see what's been done to the high transom windows (our ceilings are eleven feet high) over the doors and the front entryway. I kept thinking there were lights on in there, but one day I just stood and looked. I got a flashlight and shined it on the windows. The light bounced back at me. She'd had them covered with mirrors! What I'd been seeing was the lit hallway.

If I stood on a ladder, I'd be seeing myself.

I can't help looking up every day as I pass, harboring a vague sense of being shut out. A general sense of a soft glimmer at the junction of what I can and can't know. I wish I had words for this feeling.

Not exactly glimmer. More like a thought that travels past the boundary, past the gravitational field, and thins outward until some distant source sends it back to you. More like the way you see a creek running under grasses when the sun hits it. Oh, there it is! Like when I head out for a walk behind our historic buildings, along the warren of trails up on the hill. I'm exploring, in a sense, another world: this summer a peace sign woven of vines hung from one of the trees. Who put it there? Who took it down? The flat old water tank in the woods is decorated with amazingly skillful graffiti, overlaid so thick on the old graffiti, the whole is a blast of cartoon-fat signatures and designs from the secret world of teenagers, of gentle insurrectionists.

The path is soggy these days, leaves making the slopes, especially the rocks, slippery. Where the trail dips down into the cedars, the broken-down organic matter is black as tar and clings to my shoes. It is secret and dark in here. Now I am "in here." Wherever else my thoughts have gone, when I reach this stretch, I am entirely here. Alien and muddy, at the lowest spot.

There is something crucial about this: wandering to the low point, as if I have to feed on it. There are no words there, but that's probably the point. I have to stare into that, and later, the words are never right, but I have to try. There was my cancer, then the words for it, then words for me (*fear*, *sorrow*), and then the wordlessness beneath the words.

The same feeling from high up instead of low, when Jerry and I were standing on the Cliffs of Moher—cocooned up there, same as cocooned down there, for a few minutes, a strange and looser attachment to the mundane earth. The whipping wind—and my mind then turns to our condo, on the third floor. When the wind blows—as it does particularly hard off Grand Traverse Bay a few blocks away—the sound is eerie, other-worldly. Our huge building used to be the Northern Michigan State Asylum. I can imagine the mental patients living here long ago, hearing the sound of wild, uncontrollable spirits, trying to eat, dress, bathe, with the spirits raging in their ears.

Everything I write eventually bumps into that mirror. When I can't see any farther, there goes my mind, taking on the problem. When I was a child, at our lake there was Old Dave, who lived in a little house not a quarter mile up what's now called Woody Knoll Road. We walked all the way to the top picking wild blackberries for Old Dave, we said, wanting an altruistic reason for the picking. When our buckets were full, we walked back down and timidly knocked on his door. Very scary, a bearded old man in a ragged flannel shirt in the middle of summer. Inside his house it was dark, with magazine pages stuck on the walls from the Joe Louis/Max Schmeling fight. He'd thank us for the berries and tell us about the fight, which he remembered in detail from the radio.

Now I can tell you that Joe Louis was the most important black athlete of his age, a focal point for black pride in the 1930s. Schmeling represented Nazi Germany. Against the backdrop of the Great Depression, the fights stood for the struggle between democracy and fascism. I can tell you that in the first fight, Louis was knocked out. Old Dave's magazine pages were probably of the rematch. The poet Maya Angelou, who listened to the fight over the radio in her uncle's country store in rural Arkansas, said that when Louis was on the ropes, "My race groaned. It was our people falling. It was another lynching, yet another black man hanging on a tree. . . . It would all be true, the accusations that we were lower types of human beings. Only a little higher than the apes."

And then he won. Bands, dancing in the streets. How did Old Dave feel? Where was he then? Not in his little house, but at the top of the hill in the old Airstream trailer that's turned on its side now, the one I used to explore and take away a cup, an old coffee pot, as souvenirs. Like Old Dave, I collect artifacts and press into them as far as I can.

Now I can tell you that his family moved him down the hill so that they could bring him food in the winter. He was a little crazy. He was a hermit. We children called him a hermit, loving that word. What did we know of a hermit? What does any of us know? Only that he—or she—exists at the bottom, or in a cave at the top. We don't know how to understand someone who won't conform. So we bring him berries. Sometimes we think he's a sort of god, because he seems to need nothing but himself. His mind furnished pictures enough to make him content, so it seemed.

The stone foundation off his house is still there, on Woody Knoll Road, in the front yard of a newer house and planted with flowers. I've thought of him often. Some neighbors at the lake know his history, his family. I have not asked very many questions because each answer seems to flatten the story, deflate my imagination. The work of the imagination is to press on, beyond the barrier of facts. Not to ignore facts, not to discredit them, but to see through them into the space where the separations into here and there, then and now, are no longer the point.

The management company for our condo association has sent our neighbor a letter, chastising her for what she's done to the historic space, although there's not much that can be changed now. The mirrors are clever, though, and I commend her for that solution for privacy. Jerry and I argue a bit about this. He is an eighteenth-century scholar and lover of all things historical. He doesn't like it when people mess with history. He's studied and written about the history of the novel, starting with Cervantes's *Don Quixote* in 1605 and springing to a wide and popular genre in the eighteenth century. The modern novel is intimate, private. You can burrow into its secret life. The novel—as is true for visual art, for all art—began as gesture, as mimic of "real" life, as close to a mirror image as possible. A play, onstage, on the stage of the mind. After photography, after the splitting of the atom, after the big wars, when art began to turn inward, the direction of seeing reversed itself. Instead of mirroring the objective world, it was our own minds we thought we saw in the mirror—the textural excitement of Van Gogh, the balletic distortions of Matisse, the multiple angles of Picasso.

Our section of the building, we've been told, housed the seriously crazy patients. The whole huge complex was designed to allow patients to work, meet, socialize, in as attractive and supportive an environment as possible. Yet our section was a locked ward. I sometimes sit in our bedroom, which is also my study, and try to imagine what it was like to be a patient here, hearing the wind howl, the mind turned back on itself so that all it knows is the story it makes up, full of demons and spirits.

Spirits, being weightless, float upward. Demons are heavy, downward urging. The concrete floors on the lower level of our half-mile-long building sit over joining tunnels, tunnels higher than your head, rounded at the bottom, arched at the top, just like the Romans built them. Before the renovation, kids used to sneak in and wander through, smoking, drinking, listening to their echoes. A forbidden zone. Tunnels used to connect all the buildings. Nurses, doctors, and workers could walk through them, and there were steam and water pipes, electrical conduits, bracketed to the walls. Some were shafts to pull fresh air throughout the hospital and out the spires on top. An ecosystem, a cosmos, literally a bricks-and-mortar version of Dante's universe.

Or of *Paradise Lost*, maybe. The height and depth and breadth of Milton's cosmos was the height and depth and breadth of his mind, of the minds of the prophets, added together, so dense they curved space to make a safe enclosure.

Across the huge lawn from us is Willow Cottage Assisted Living, one of the other renovated buildings on this 480-acre campus, where my ninety-seven-year-old father lives. The residents there are pretty much safely contained within own ecosystems. Sweetly, for the most part. If they were hostile, they'd live somewhere else. Their minds have grown less limber, less able to maneuver in the outer world. So the front door opens with a code, the stairway doors with a different one. But even for us, who are still agile in that way, the stories we tell ourselves about what's true can easily admit no external world. That's what crazy means, isn't it?

For the patients in the locked ward, there is only the present. For those who live as external a life as possible, the sober fact of death can be held in a locked closet for a long while. Until a diagnosis, for example. Yet with or without our permission, the moment of death brings the interior and exterior to the threshold together.

My father has said for years he wants to die. But really, his talk about it is his way of warding it off. He's afraid. No point in trying to examine why. I know how it is, since my cancer. Isn't it sane, after all, to dread seeing our great good fortune of being born human, intelligent, and capable come to an end? Others at Willow Cottage sleep their way slowly toward their end. Others forget who they are, so fear doesn't know where to lodge.

Mother officially died from choking on a piece of Halloween candy. She'd been having mini-strokes all along, so probably she had a stroke as she was chewing. By the time I got to the hospital from halfway across the country, she was lying there unable to speak. But when her three daughters gathered around her and bent down to kiss her, tears ran out of her eyes. The MRI soon after showed no brain activity. I thought many times about her fear of the enclosure of the MRI and imagined that she was still alert enough to feel that fear. I wondered what she felt when we were gathered in her room, waiting for death. She seemed unaware, but the nurse came in and shouted in her ear, "I'm going to aspirate your throat, Mrs. Brown, so you can breathe better." The nurse turned to us and said, "They can sometimes hear, you know." I keep that image with me, the trouble in my mind about what my mother knew and didn't know, when she fully crossed the threshold and what I might have done or said at that moment that could have held her gently in the passage.

Not that I ever knew my mother, not really. I've tried to see into her, and my heart hurts. She remained innocent. She was battered by a life she didn't know how to get out of or fix. She was kind and gentle. And cheerful by nature. When she threw herself across the bed in tears, she would recover like a child, with little residue of sadness. Or is that what I'd like to think? I had to ignore her suffering so I could grow up myself. That's what it felt like. It felt as if, had I been inside her mind, I would have died of sorrow.

Do unto others. I wanted to be good, and kind. I was offered that conduit between heaven and earth that Sunday School provided. I lifted mine eyes unto the hills and tried desperately to see beyond. To live beyond. I sat in a tiny chair in a semicircle with the others and sang "What a Friend We Have in Jesus" to the flat notes of the piano. This was the group worship session with words read out of the booklet. Then our individual classes, where we trekked through the Bible stories, week by week. If we weren't sure what to make of them, the moral was printed at the bottom of the page. What was soaking into us during those years, those of us who were faithful?

We prayed. Sat in a circle and bowed our heads in submission to Something Greater Than Ourselves. Something separate that we needed to reach. That's what I thought; that's what we thought. As if the thing greater were not located inside ourselves. As if there were anything separate from anything. Everything felt separate. My small athletic body, restless; my nose, with its own separate awareness of the musty smell of the wooden floors, the old classroom; my fingers playing with the pages that held each week's scripture, plus a prayer; my ears, tuning in and out. I was only marginally a believer by nature. I had inherited my father's atheism in my rational brain, but there was also my mother's irrational belief in something else, something called "out there." Called "Greater" by the Sunday School booklet. By the minister.

What was my Sunday School teacher thinking? How did her belief work? When her mind bumped against the unknowable, did it move on out into space, or did it stop at the border and turn back, turn the page and read to us what was written there. Look, these words stand for what I don't know. But the words know. They are words, and they must know something.

There was Bessie, who taught the adult women's class, had taught it for years. One morning she got up, went to church, taught her class, came home, ate dinner, took a nap, and died. I have thought about this as a good life, a good death. And then I think, I don't know. Is this life any better than the drunk's, the criminal's? What if the criminal sees the truth and can't get to it, keeps trying, by all the twisted routes he knows? Through whose eyes is there a judgment? Is there a point of reference out there that doesn't shift, that is the same now and forever? And what about the person whose last moments are filled with pain and anguish that aids the leaving in some crucial way? We can't know.

Who can fathom death? I ask this in all earnestness, as I've come up against it myself. But then, who can fathom birth? Ovum, sperm, an explosion of cells, each marked to build its portion of the structure. Then here comes the spark of life, out of nowhere, and the human mind that learns to say, "This is life." Learns to mirror itself.

Our great water, Grand Traverse Bay, is often glassy-smooth this season, late into the winter with no snow. When it finally comes, and it will, I'm sure, the surface will cloud over with ice. Below the ice will be walleye, pike, and perch, and the fishermen will set up their huts, cut holes through, bring their kerosene heaters and beer, and sit there for hours, leisurely fathoming what might swim up to their bait. Imagining. Their minds will be a mirror of their desire.

And I will be imagining them in their ice houses and writing what I think goes on there. What is their cryptic male conversation? Are they retelling fish tales? I have one for them.

My grandson, Zach, was fishing from the pontoon boat, way up the Chain of Lakes. He was ten, I think. The water was very clear. He saw northern pike down there, hovering, as they do, huge submarines. Then the jerk on his line and, oh lord, the fish to contend with, the terror of its rising with its prehistoric teeth, out of the other world, bent on destruction or return. Zach, his face gone white, pulled against the fearful thing, pulled until at last the line snapped. Shaky with relief, he looked down at the water reeds swaying, the fish gone already, the tale beginning to form in the absence of flesh.

Absence is a grand palette. When we moved in here, the huge, wide halls had nothing on the walls. Now we have art. This year it's multicolored abstract paintings, with pieces of brightly colored wood planks and branches attached. A pleasure to see every time I walk down the hall. But ever since I figured out the mirrored transoms, my eyes turn to them instead. They're more fascinating than the paintings, the sculpture in the elevator foyer, the boots outside other people's condos. They can't look back at me because they're too high. I can't see myself. The light is a soft shimmer, almost like a window, but you can tell it isn't quite. And there's a slight telltale reflection of the wood trim at the sides. Not absence; not presence. It's enticing in a spooky way. Not a metaphor for anything, really, but still, I feel a bit floaty when I look up. Nothing is what it seems, and maybe I'm not either.

Toi Derricotte

RUTH STONE'S FUNERAL

Ruth Stone received the National Book Award at the
age of 87 for her collection of poetry *In the Next Galaxy.*
She died November 19, 2011, at her home in Ripton, Vermont.
She was 96.

HER DAUGHTER MARCIA MADE THE COFFIN. When I arrived it
was still on the kitchen floor with curlicues of soft shaven wood around it.
There was sawdust everywhere; the kitchen table was, shall we say, buried
in it. And the antique tools, rust-stiffened on the table and floor, without
a toolbox, the paint-layered hammer; and yet the pine box was beautiful,
smooth and sand white. I had no idea that an ordinary woman could make
a coffin in the middle of her well-used kitchen—its plainness, the veins and
streaks of caramel running through it in long flat ribbons. It was the simplicity of it that made it beautiful, the straightness and exactness, the un-
adornedness, the smoothness of the grain, the four sides equal and fitting,
their edges like rough sandpaper, the bottom so flat against the kitchen
floor. Everything equal, every part in its place, a four-cornered thing. It
was a surprising reminder of the woman it would contain. It underlined
what we loved most, her directness, her plainspokenness, her lack of pre-
tense and makeup. Marcia said she certainly wouldn't have wanted to be
riding in the back of a hearse. She would have written a hilarious poem
about herself, dead, powdered with stiff hair.

I met Ruth in 1988. Our beloved friend, Sharon Olds, had invited her to
NYU to do a reading. I seem to remember Ruth and me walking down
a gleaming street in the rain—perhaps I was delivering her to the reading—me helping her out of a cab. She was so light when I took her hand,

in her seventies and girlish—both of us giddy, as if she were Cinderella, as if I were her prince. Who knows why you instantly fall in love? For me it happens once every eleven years.

Was it her high-voltage laugh? Her brass-red hair, thinning—that streak I never questioned as anything but real even up into her nineties—a handful of which she would grab and pin up, wildly, to whatever place on her head her hand went to? Her presence so intense you might think she was aquiver, a tuning fork; the skin of her face like onionskin, translucent, pearly? Was it her irreverence for the big boys? Among the giant men, she could so easily, with so few words, cut down to size, and laugh, which was a worse cut than anger. For sure it was the depth and quickness with which she saw through appearances, and how in a phrase she could make us see.

After readings sometimes so unsure of herself that she would almost beg to be affirmed. "Was I any good?" she'd say, distressed. "I don't think they liked me." No matter how convincing you were, there was always another way for her to turn her questions. I loved her, for she was like me, with her self-doubt; but she was not like me, with her assuredness and purpose. Once I wrote a poem about the violence in my childhood, in my infancy, as if out of a dream. When I read it to her she sat still, as if she had been wounded; finally, she looked up with a kind of despondency. "You almost died, didn't you?" she said. I hadn't known until that moment the degree of my suffering.

■ ■
■ ■

So, Marcia, Nora—one of her granddaughters—and I (whom they had told to "Please come, you are the only one but family, she loved you so much!") made the holes for the rope handles and threaded them through, Nora tying the square knots left hand over right so that they would hold against the hundred-pound weight of the coffin, and the hundred or so pounds of Ruthie (my nickname to diminish and bring closer my beloved, a familiarity for, in a way, a god). The three of us checked by lifting the rough handles to make sure, and then carried it through the ordinary furniture of the living room, bumping against the legs and arms of things, turning it on its side to get it through the back door (would we have to tip Ruthie over on her side to get her through the back door?) and to the outer room, Vermont winter cold as a freezer. We laid it on the floor head to toe with Ruthie, who lay on a platform bundled in clean sheets.

And when I saw her body wrapped so tight, even around the head, with only a small oval of face visible, and a little wisp of a silver curl resting lightly on her forehead, she looked like a baby in a bunting, swaddled so tight—as they do so that the child feels held and safe—layers wrapped roundly and neatly (no raggedy display). And, around it all, a thick woven rug like an Indian blanket, perhaps of a coarse hemp, also fitting, and opened like a shirt at the collar, ready for the last fold to fit everything inside, to hide it as you might put a cloth over rising bread to keep the heat in.

She looked like a mummy, regal, the many layers of wrap so much larger than her body. We had fit a foam pad, like one of those you put on top of a bed to make it soft, neatly and exactly in the bottom of the coffin, which had a pattern in it of circles and wavy lines that now looked as if it was hand embossed.

Robert Lowell wrote a poem about collecting his mother's body in Italy and sailing back to the US with it in the hold of the ship in a "black and gold casket like Napoleon's." He said, "The corpse was wrapped like pannetone in Italian tinfoil"—an image that I thought diminished his mother and showed his ambivalence. No, not Ruth. She, in this most humble of dressings, seemed larger than life, cared for by intimates (for they must have washed her, though I never asked) who regarded her precious, who had not yet distinguished the dead Ruth from the living.

She was wrapped and laid in a cold outer room, born to her new life on a hard platform, her face visible for those who for, whatever reason—the body is always beautiful to those who are madly in love!—wanted to say good-bye. She did not want to die in a hospital among doctors; she did not want to be handled by strangers, pickpocketed for a lie—that only experts can clean us; take death away, and leave a black spot.

Her daughters made the funeral up like a poem, for Ruth refused to talk of her death, ever. She truly believed, and said, that she wasn't going to die until the end of the world. On the last night, as she struggled to breathe, Marcia climbed into bed with her—where she had enthroned herself since her blindness, where she listened twenty-four hours a day to British novels, books about science, and fairy tales (she wouldn't listen to poetry, which she feared would harm her voice)—and held her. When Ruth couldn't breathe, she said, as a midwife says to the woman in labor, "Relax, in another thirty seconds the air will come freely"—and it did. Ruth looked at her daughter and said, in full control of her senses, "I don't want to die." Is it better to die when we are ready? When we ask for it? When pain has beaten us down so low that we want anything but to be here?

She was a great teacher because she made an opening to impossible things, and we, not blindly, but for love, followed. We knew that what she said sounded crazy only—even if it was the craziest thing—because it was crazy to put yourself in the danger of saying what you truly thought.

This morning, the day after the funeral, her seven-year-old great-grandson, Henry, quoted a poem—it was in the middle of an ordinary conversation over his oatmeal when we were talking about my visit ending, and he said Gigi (what he called her) said everything ends, but then it never ends. I thought he was just saying something that he had made up, but Marcia asked him to repeat what he said, and he said the lines, exactly the way they were at the end of her poem, "All things come to an end. / No, they go on forever."

A monarch, in humble sheets that smelled like fresh laundry hung in the sun, even though it was November, a little shrunken woman, at the end, bereft of many of her powers, blind, barely able to stand on her feet, hating even to sit up, and, for many months, while I had thought, hoped, she was scribbling poems, she had stopped writing, Marcia confessed. As if the blindness had also brought a silence. Still, the incessant tapes; perhaps, Marcia speculated, to stop her ears to what she didn't want to know.

As always in the past when I have visited her, I have to drive the roads up and down the mountains. I am afraid of heights. Here in Vermont, that's the only way you get anywhere. The navigator directs to dirt roads. "Turn down Pencil Lane," the lady commands, and when I turn thinking this must be a shortcut to the highway, she says, "Drive twenty-one miles." No one is here beside me except an ill will to drive the two-ton car over the edge. The only way I stop myself is by this tension, going forward and, at the same time, holding on to the one who keeps saying no, holding on by the seat of my pants. I said out loud, "Ruthie, every time I visit you I have to face my fears." Is love, great love, always like this? Do we always come to the place where we might drive off the cliff?

Yesterday the local man with a backhoe opened a six-foot pit behind the house she loved so much in Goshen, Vermont, the seven acres she bought when she won the Bess Hokin Prize, using the four thousand dollars, against her husband's will, to be out there in the hubbub of the storm, in the quiet of nothing; in the house in the woods where she lived so freely, without heat or running water until she was seventy-five, where her grandchildren, as one said, didn't have to bathe for weeks, in the same underpants, living in the wide and generous warmth of a grandmother who brought in great baskets of raspberries from outside the kitchen door, and who, Nora said, made the biggest thing over any little thing they did or made—of their poems. "Send it to the *New Yorker*," she'd yell over her shoulder. Don't we always love the adventurers the most?

In that place she made for herself, she said she took poems from out of the air, from out of the universe, as if she could lift her hand as they passed and snatched them. She said, "Get them when you can, what you don't get is gone." Perhaps the way you honor your mother is to remember what she gave to you, to honor yourself.

As they lifted her coffin out of the back of Robert's truck, I held myself in; and her sons-in-law, grandsons, and uncle (brother to her dead husband, who was also ninety-six, who also refused to think or speak about his death) carried her. We placed the coffin over the bleak carved-out hole, the bottom of which held several inches of water (we explained to five-year-old Chloe, anxious and complaining, that we had put plastic inside so that Ruth wouldn't get wet), on two plain pine boards that held the weight securely. They had carried her a bit precariously, since, of course, she hadn't been tied down, so there was a possibility that, should the coffin tip or, God forbid, fall, there would have been, if not a terrible display, at least some uncomfortable shifting! The way was slick with Vermont mud (it was sunny and in the sixties after a week of snow), but all was carried out with dignity, while an alarm clock CD player that Phoebe carried in her hand sang the now scratchy voices of the great chanteuses Ella Fitzgerald and Edith Piaf. "September Song" was her favorite, which her daughters said she sang more beautifully than any of the recordings. We stood around the grave and a few read letters about their love, while most read a favorite poem or two and, one by one, shoveled two shovelfuls of earth on top of her. Her brother-in-law went first, announcing that he had learned how to do it from his mother-in-law, who, when she was ninety-six years old, had buried her own daughter, his wife.

Now thinking back, I was shocked when I had looked at her face, and, yes, as much as I hate to admit it, a feeling of revulsion came over me, as if my spirit succumbed to something I hated. Yet I wouldn't move, I was glued by my desire to stay, to see whatever had to be seen through. And it wasn't her; in fact, she was gone—even though there was a bit of that quizzical smile that seemed to be pressed into the flesh from the inside. It was she, but not.

That is the only time I almost cracked, after they lifted up the casket by its cord handles, pulled out the boards, and began to lower it by the blue-and-white ropes—gently, if a bit unevenly—as Chloe noticed (it's all right, we put a pillow under her head, we assured her)—and let the weight sink. The water must have been coming in; perhaps the body was, even as we stood there shoveling one by one, already kin to the earth and water. She had said in a poem that we would be carried out on the river, that we would become part of what was larger, and she is—whatever is left, whatever Ruth Stone was and is, is being carried out.

▪▪
▪▪

Funny I should say that because her granddaughter Bianca remembered her days in the country with Ruth, remembered how sometimes at night she was frightened by the darkness and hated it when Ruth would leave her. She said when Ruth went into the bathroom, she would wait by the door; sometimes it seemed to take forever. She told Ruth she was afraid of ghosts, and Ruth told her she wished there were ghosts. I'm sure she was thinking of her dear and shockingly dead husband, who hung himself on a closet door, and whom Ruth wrote love poems to, poems of longing and puzzlement and rage for the next sixty years. From the day he died when she was in her thirties, to the day she died, at ninety-six, she never stopped wishing for him, even remembering so exactly the bones of his elegant feet.

▪▪
▪▪

I was unhappy with what I felt during those days. I didn't cry like most of the others. In therapy I had been talking about abandoning myself, how, in order to survive a violent parent, I had to abandon my deepest self and concentrate, as much as possible, on where the next blow might come from. So there I was standing not six feet from the hole, with hardly a tear. My face, even my heart, not dry, but not pouring out sorrow either, as if I was temperate, as if I was a woman in control, as if I had to be.

▪▪
▪▪

Once I was on vacation with my partner and his daughters, whom I had just met. One of them, imperturbable, was so careful to pay her way that, no matter how hard I tried, I couldn't find a way to treat her. I decided the only way was to unbalance her. So I walked up from behind, grabbed her hand, and said in the meanest voice possible—a voice not even mine— "You better take this, bitch, I'm sick of all this fuckin' around"—and as I said it, I stuffed a twenty-dollar bill in her hand. This girl who was forever in charge of herself shriveled for a few seconds, her hand dropping loose, then clutching the money as I had told her to.

Of course, in just a few minutes, figuring out the joke of it, she gave me the money back. But why had I done something I never would have done to anyone else? And when I told the story last night to Marcia as we sat around after the funeral talking about the loves in our life, she explained, without even a thought—knowing the depth of my own distrust and feelings of unworthiness—"You trusted her." Yes, that was it. I did something completely outside of my fearful boundaries, I acted on an impulse for fun, I surprised myself.

How many times did Ruth tell me I was her daughter, how much she loved me; how many times did her daughters tell me, and when I asked Marcia could I stay for two nights instead of one (I was afraid to drive back to the airport over those unknown and high dirt roads), she said, "You can stay forever; you're blood kin." How many times did Ruthie tell me, almost scream at me, holding her ear with her hand still indicating how deeply she had listened to my poem, "Toi, you are a great poet." She said this to me many times every year, every time we talked or saw each other. She said it to me the first time she read my work over thirty-five years ago, and she said it to me the last time we spoke. How does a woman change what she allows herself to believe? Do I say Ruthie was just being kind? Yet she was so insistent, so determined I hear. She wanted to go deep in me, deep down to the water, to the elemental self before the self that got twisted and dropped the wrong way.

As I was standing over her grave, for a split second I saw myself through her body, saw myself in the pine box wrapped tight in linens, blankets, me sinking down in the darkness, me disappearing, and I felt an instant of what it is to be gone, to not be even in the memory of others—as if memory were a cloth like a magician's and that cloth disappeared.

Her great-grandson Henry, probably as smart a kid as I've ever met, said to me this morning, "Yesterday was like a birthday for you." "Why?" I asked. "Because you got two presents." He had grated nutmeg with a grater for half an hour and put it in a medicine bottle his mom had washed out and dried with a paper towel, filled it all the way to a third with fresh-grated intensely eggnog-smelling nutmeg. It was in the air, on his hands. I told him I'd put it under my Christmas tree, and he snatched it back and gift wrapped it in Xerox paper, put a masking tape seal on top and printed in those hard printed letters of an eight-year-old his signature, "HENRY." "Yes," he said, "you got two gifts." (This morning at seven a.m., he was grating more nutmeg. Who knows for whom?) "And the second one?" I asked. His aunt Phoebe, Ruth's second daughter, had given me one of her novels and signed it. "Yes," I said, "it was like my birthday," and, even as he continued grating, we looked each other in the eye.

Yesterday he had said to his mother, "I think people at the funeral wanted me to be sad, but how can you look sad when you don't feel it?" And I thought of my confusion at the gravesite. Could it have been that a part of me was happy, is happy, no matter what, even at the gravesite, and is there a part of me that I can't bear to see? Not my grief, but my dancing ecstasy, that I loved her so much, that I am alive.

I am grateful to Henry, who acknowledged his happiness in the middle of the funeral day. Would Ruth want the world to come to an end? I suppose that is what ghosts are for, to harbor such ill wishes on our brief time. And since there are no such things as ghosts, then we are free to experience it all, whenever we sit in the middle of ourselves, the flare of the spirit that flares when we least expect it.

There is a secret. Her beloved dog died on the same day she died. Ruth had called her the palace guard dog, for she was so small and yet regal; she looked like a short-haired red-brown fox—now stiff as a board, but in a comfortable position, relaxed, on her side, her legs crossed in front, her round eyes wide as if still watching. When Marcia had said she wanted to bury her mother in a pine box in her backyard in Goshen, someone had said, how could you bury her with the dogs (for Ruthie had buried her dogs behind her house). It may be hard to understand—for a great poet to be buried without the many who loved her in attendance, without the great poets who were her friends, without the ceremony. And indeed there will be a ceremony. But this WAS the honor that she deeply courted by her life. So we put the little dog at her feet to keep her feet warm—she fit perfectly—and covered her up so that she was completely hidden. She'd like the joke—that Ruthie was actually buried with the dogs.

Michael Steinberg

FROM MANHATTAN TO LEELANAU

HOW PLACE SHAPES OUR SENSE OF SELF

Someone once said that if the Leelanau Peninsula has a polar opposite, it's probably Manhattan.

—KATHLEEN STOCKING, *LETTERS FROM THE LEELANAU*

It's just after dawn on New Year's Day. My wife, Carole, and I are at our Leelanau County cottage in Michigan's Northwoods. Carole is in the loft working on a painting, and I'm standing at the bay window nursing a cup of coffee, gazing out across Lake Michigan. A few embers still glow in the fireplace, and the smell of smoke intensifies when I stack more logs on the grating. Outside, a pale sun rises through foggy mist above the bay, and a new snow begins to coat the evergreens. It's an idyllic winter scene, to be sure; yet, my imagination, like the fire, suddenly flares. And the scene that's forming takes place back in the early sixties, when I was living in Greenwich Village.

An early October morning, and the air has just turned nippy. I leave my West Village walk-up and stroll through Washington Square Park, past white-uniformed nannies wheeling baby strollers, and scruffy teenagers making their morning connection with seedy-looking drug dealers. I pause to watch the old men in pea jackets and wool caps playing chess, and I see a group of NYU students gesturing with their hands and talking loudly as they head for their morning classes.

Picking up a *Times* at the Sixth Avenue newsstand, I inhale the musty aroma from the subway grating and watch the spiraling steam rise, while my feet are warmed by the burst of compressed air that's been pushed up in the departing train's wake. I walk by the tiny asphalt park across the avenue and pause to watch the neighborhood kids playing hooky basketball on the fenced-in asphalt court known as "the Cage."

As I head up Bleecker, I wave at the Italian storekeeper stacking the morning's shipment of produce on the outdoor stalls. My last stop's at David's Potbelly, where I linger over a hot cup of coffee and kibbutz with the usual coterie of neighborhood writers and painters about the Yankees' season-ending loss to the Red Sox.

At ten o'clock, I leave the Potbelly and head over to the New School to attend my weekly fiction-writing workshop.

Part recollection, part invention, that scene has been nagging away at me since we arrived up north a few days ago. Perhaps I'm more sentimental than usual because I'm disappointed that Carole and I won't be going to Manhattan for the holidays. It's one of the few times that's happened since we moved to Michigan some four decades ago. We're here at the cottage because I'm trying to meet a January 15 deadline for a memoir about growing up in New York—a book that, even five years ago, I could never have imagined myself capable of writing.

Since we couldn't go to New York for the holidays, we decided to bring Manhattan to the Northwoods. On the day we drove up, Carole packed two carousel trays containing slides we'd taken during our last few holidays in the city. And I made certain to bring along a handful of CDs and some books about New York in the fifties and sixties.

Ever since we bought the cottage, I'd been reading books by writers who either grew up in New York or came to Manhattan from somewhere else. Many of them write about hobnobbing with the Beats—Ginsberg and Kerouac, in particular—that raffish, exotic group of avant-garde writers that captivated and in some ways inhibited me when I was growing up.

Back then, the New School, downtown, and Columbia, uptown, were the "in" places for would-be intellectuals and aspiring artistes; while the Greenwich Village clubs, like the Gate and the Vanguard, were the late-night spots where you'd go to hear the likes of Monk, Coltrane, and Miles Davis. And some of the local taverns were well-known watering holes for cult artists and writers. Allegedly, the Beats frequented Chumley's on Bedford Street. And they also held court at the White Horse Tavern on Hudson and Eleventh, where legend had it that Dylan Thomas took his last drink—his sixteenth of the night—before checking out for good.

What would it be like, I wondered at the time, to be part of that world?

In preparation for the next morning's writing, I was leafing through Dan Wakefield's *New York in the Fifties* at the same time as Carole and I were listening to Mel Tormé's "Songs of New York." Which, of course, tripped off a rush of memories.

I recalled with a mixture of sadness and pleasure those Christmas break reunions with old college friends at Grand Central and Penn stations. Carole, meanwhile, reminisced about taking the New York Central up the Hudson to Scarsdale to visit her sister and niece. And she waxed nostalgic about meeting *her* college friends for lunch at the Tavern on the Green.

Midway through that evening's slide show, I was brought up short when two successive images clicked on. One was of a photo we'd taken in 1996 on Fifth Avenue, in front of the Doubleday Book Store, and the next slide showed the facade of the Scribner's pavilion, a few doors down. Both reminded me of a recent feature column in the *Times*, a piece that mourned the loss of the old New York bookstores—Brentano's, Doubleday, Scribner's, Books and Company, Shakespeare and Company, and the Abbey and Pomander bookshops.

Maybe, just maybe, transporting all this memorabilia wasn't such a good idea after all. Because the more we reminisced, the more we longed to be back in Manhattan. But which city would it be: the New York that exists right now, or the New York I've conjured up in countless daydreams over the four-plus decades since we've moved to Michigan?

I grew up in Rockaway Beach (Queens) in the late 1940s and all through the fifties. Like Leelanau County, Rockaway is a long, narrow peninsula, and it's surrounded by the Atlantic Ocean and Jamaica Bay. In the summer, from Edgemere, to the north of us, and Riis Park, at the southern tip, the beaches and boardwalks were as crowded as those at Coney Island or Jones Beach.

Because we were set apart from the clamor of the city, our little peninsula had the feel of a small town. Three blocks from my house, 129th

Street was the neighborhood shopping street. Between Cronston and Newport avenues stood my grandfather's drugstore, Sam Cahmi's deli, the Peter Reeves supermarket, Cushman's bakery, Irv's candy store, Tishman the tailor's shop, the Tydol gas station, and Johnny's shoe repair place. At night we hung out at Irv's, smoking cigarettes and fabricating stories about our sexual successes with the girls in our junior high classes; we schmoozed with neighbors while standing on line at the bakery; and we caught up with the local gossip while sipping egg creams at the drugstore's soda fountain. The only real skirmishes arose when the Irish Catholic kids from St. Francis de Sales would taunt us Jewish kids for being "Christ killers."

As a teenager I had visions of becoming a writer; and so I was drawn to the mystique of Manhattan as an exotic literary Mecca. But that dream began to fade when I started reading about the Beat writers and going to late-night jazz clubs. The Beats were cocky, even arrogant iconoclasts; they were heavy drinkers and smokers, and, according to some critics, Kerouac and Ginsberg were deep into hard drugs—tendencies and activities that were the polar opposite of my own. Because back then, I was self-conscious and unsure of myself, always wondering what it would take to be accepted by the popular high school cliques—whether it was the jocks or the preppies.

The myth back then was that the well-recognized writers, painters, and jazz players lived their lives on the edge. And since I wasn't a risk taker or a self-proclaimed outsider, I'd already decided that I had no business thinking of myself as an artist of any kind.

An English major in college, I found myself becoming increasingly envious of and intimidated by the writers whose works we were reading in our Modern American Literature class—most especially Hemingway, Fitzgerald, and Faulkner. Like the Beats, they all lived extreme, even self-destructive, lives. But it was also clear that they possessed the gifts and talents I lacked. And it didn't help matters much to know that I was regularly getting form-letter rejections for what I knew even back then were generic poems and derivative, unoriginal short stories.

By the time I was a junior, I'd pretty much given up on my dream of becoming a writer. While my writing was regularly getting turned down, though, most of my literature professors were praising my critical/analytical papers. Small consolation to the likes of me.

When I graduated, I applied to a handful of grad schools. I was hoping to stay in New York, but Columbia, my first choice, turned me down. And so when Michigan State offered me a teaching assistantship, Carole and I (newly married) reluctantly moved to East Lansing. My plan was to get my PhD in English and head right back to New York.

But that's not how things eventually turned out.

Home for the last forty-plus years has been East Lansing. Surrounded by lush, flat farmland, East Lansing is a lively but generic midwestern college town. Grand River Avenue, its main thoroughfare, comprises mainly hole-in-the-wall student bars, sweatshirt emporiums, and the kinds of fast food stores you're likely to find in most college towns. The new high-rise apartments behind the main drag seem sadly misplaced in this chintzy milieu.

Two miles to the west is the city of Lansing, the state capital and East Lansing's larger, blue-collar neighbor. And during General Motors' heyday, it was Oldsmobile's home base. To a couple of former New Yorkers, Lansing/East Lansing was no more or less stimulating than Columbus, Ohio, or Des Moines, Iowa.

From the start, life in Michigan was not an easy passage. My difficulties, I'm sure, were rooted in disposition as well as geography. During graduate school, I struggled to attune myself to the far less urgent pace of midwestern life. It perplexed me that on weekends my neighbors were content to play with their kids, wash their cars, watch TV, and take care of their lawns. I whined about not being able to get the *New York Times* each day, or about having to drive for an hour each way to Southfield and back just to get a good bagel. I made a big fuss about not being able to get an egg cream in Michigan; and I never quite got the hang of driving directions. In New York, the streets have numbers and names. And we say things like "swing a left on Fourteenth," or "hang a right on Ocean Parkway." Here, they tell you to go north or south and then they give you nebulous markers, like a church or a school. You need a compass to figure out how to navigate even a small town like East Lansing.

Trivial concerns, maybe; but to a congenital New Yorker everything's an inconvenience. Part of our ethic (and, I hope, our charm) is to complain.

A tougher accommodation, though, was adjusting to the inbred politeness and reserve of midwestern friends. It's taken me years, in fact, to understand even simple telephone etiquette. When a friend says, "I have to let you go now," it's a polite euphemism for "You've been talkin' my ear off for an hour and I wanna get back to my life, okay?" Which is what most New Yorkers would have said. And since I moved here, I've been advised more than once that I'm a whiny, opinionated easterner. It's funny, because when I was growing up I was the least assertive member of my family.

It's interesting, is it not, the ways in which geographical locations influence one's sense of self.

Like a lot of other writer wannabes, by the time I finished my graduate course work, I reluctantly chose the preferred default career—that of literary critic. And for my doctoral dissertation, I wanted to work on F. Scott Fitzgerald's fiction—largely, I believe, because I could identify with his main characters' unsuccessful dreams.

In my dissertation I tracked the theme of dream and disillusion, which, to my mind, runs throughout Fitzgerald's works. But what fascinated me even more, I found, was Fitzgerald's nonfiction, especially those essays and letters that described his often failed attempts at writing—a struggle I was intimately familiar with.

Halfway through the dissertation, I began to re-experience that same sense of guilt and regret—and frustration—the same demons that used to surface intermittently in college. It became clear to me then that instead of analyzing a given writer's work I desperately wished I was capable of creating my own.

For a few months—and with great apprehension—I went back to my writing. By that time, though, I'd become so critical of my stories and poems that I judged and dismissed them before they were even rough drafts. And because I lacked confidence in my writing, I was too embarrassed to show my work to anyone, much less submit it for publication. Over time then, this became yet another self-fulfilling prophecy—one that would continue to derail my writing for many years to come.

When I got my doctorate—in the mid-seventies—I could see that positions in the arts and humanities were very scarce. A college job in New York was simply out of the question; and I didn't want to move to Iowa or Kansas to teach five sections of remedial writing at a junior college. So I compromised; I accepted an offer to stay on as a freshman composition instructor at Michigan State—all the while thinking, once again, that within five years something back east was bound to open up.

I recall when the realization that I wouldn't be going back to New York, or even back east, sunk in. I'd been living in Michigan for almost two decades, and I was kvetching, as usual, to a colleague about how much I yearned to be back in New York.

"Everyone on the faculty here," she said, "I mean EVERYONE, has wished they were somewhere else—Yale, Columbia, University of Chicago, Berkeley. Get over it. It comes with the territory."

Since we've lived in the Midwest, we've intermittently longed for the city's romance and allure—the stimulation of the theater and museums—as well as for its dissonant ambience, the subway and the tumult and animation of an urban neighborhood. And there were times in those early years when I especially yearned for the aggressive give-and-take of those commando coffee klatches I used to participate in back in the Village.

But things have changed over the decades. In some ways, the part of Michigan where we live has become more like New York than people here are willing to admit.

All of a sudden there were *too many* shops that sold imitation New York bagels, and a glut of stores masquerading as New York delis. And can somebody tell me why it costs twice as much for an abridged edition of the *New York Times?*

I shouldn't kvetch so much, though. Over time, I've become grateful for several things about Michigan. For one, Carole and I can own a home and live comfortably on moderate fixed incomes, something we could never have managed in Manhattan. Plus, over the years I've assembled an enclave of ex-New Yorkers whom I meet with regularly for coffee. And there is of course the alluring landscape of Leelanau County.

Leelanau County is to Michigan what Cape Cod is to Massachusetts, what the Finger Lakes region is to Upstate New York. It's a prized locale of woodlands, rolling hills, wineries, and cherry orchards—surrounded on three sides by the blue expanse of Lake Michigan.

From the first time I saw northern lower Michigan, from Traverse City to Mackinac Island, I was drawn to its ambience, mostly to the presence of Lake Michigan to the west and Lakes Huron and Superior to the east—all of which reminded me of my days growing up on the Atlantic Ocean.

Another enticement had to do with the peninsula's mythology and lore. Kathy Stocking, whose book *Letters from the Leelanau* is a paean to the area, describes the Leelanau as a "Michigan Eden with [its] trilliums and northern lights. " And depending on whose version of the myth you believe, the word "Leelanau" is the Indian name for "land of delight" or "beautiful lost Indian daughter."

Stocking also says that the Leelanau will be the site of the second coming of Christ, "with the next Messiah to be born . . . at the forty-fifth parallel—right about where the roadside picnic table is, north of Suttons Bay." Stocking writes that "these myths and legends and fantasies about the Leelanau Peninsula are, as much as anything, a testament to the way the delicate beauty of the place touches people's imaginations."

Whether one believes these stories or not, the peninsula does indeed have an undeniable aura and spirit about it. Because when I'm "up north," as the natives call it, my imagination and sense of wonder are ignited in ways that rarely occur when I'm back in East Lansing. The catalyst can be anything from sitting on my deck listening to the roar of the lake, to watching a midnight sky lit up by the northern lights, to coming upon a sudden blaze of sumac in the woods on a nippy fall day, to walking the rocky beach at dawn, watching the slow infusion of pinkish-orange light creeping across the lake's horizon.

After twenty-five years of living in a landlocked college town, we wanted a more exotic setting, a place without the usual interruptions and distractions of home—a retreat where Carole could paint and I could maybe jump-start my writing. So, just before I turned fifty, we decided to have the cottage built.

Despite the fact that the guy who delivers my firewood, the local furnace man, and the kids that clean the chimney in October continue to refer to us as "fudgies from downstate," having the cottage built has turned out to be first a sanity-saving move, and later a life-altering decision.

Like the Rockaways of my childhood, the Leelanau Peninsula is a loosely integrated network of small communities: Empire, Leland, Suttons Bay, Lake Leelanau, Peshawbestown, and Northport, the village where my cottage is located.

Situated right at the tip of Michigan's little finger, Northport often reminds me of 129th Street in Rockaway Beach, and even of certain small neighborhoods in the Greenwich Village of my college days. From the Rose Street Marina at the easternmost intersection of Nagonaba and Bay streets, I can survey the entire downtown. There's Tom's Market and, across the street, Dog Ears, Pamela Grath's used bookstore. Her husband David's art gallery is right next door—they share a bathroom. At either place, at any given time, you can count on running into a neighbor or acquaintance.

Northport Building Supply, the hardware store across from North Country Gardens, is still a family-owned business. If you need a ten-cent widget or gadget, they'll find it for you. Haserot Park, right next to the marina, has a public beach and a band shell for summer evening concerts. And some of the roads on the edge of town—Craker, Garthe, and Gill's Pier—are named after families that settled here in the middle of the nineteenth century.

There's also the pizza parlor/Dairy Queen, where the local high school kids hang out. Edee Joppich's art gallery is around the corner from Barb's Bakery, which is on Mill Street. Barb opens and closes the shop according to a schedule only she can divine. On most summer mornings, though, you can sit and linger over coffee and one of Barb's sweet rolls and catch up on the local gossip. In the summer, you can even get the Sunday *New York Times,* that is, if you get to Tom's before nine a.m.

In the early nineties, shortly after our Northport cottage was built, I underwent two successive cornea transplants, each of which gave me a significant block of time away from teaching. During my hiatus, I began to feel a nagging, insistent urgency—sometimes even a visceral feeling that was, in effect, warning me that despite my lifelong failures as a writer—even if I failed again—I'd spend the rest of my life regretting the fact that I didn't at least give it one more try.

While I was AWOL from teaching, I spent several weeks each month at the cottage. Most of it was time given over to writing. And to my surprise, I found myself composing short sketches—mini-personal essays, really. I could see that most of these narratives lacked conscious shape or structure. But as I reread them, I noticed that the ones in which the writing seemed most alive and compelling were those short pieces about—what else?—growing up in New York City in the late fifties.

For a long time, it had been clear to me that I had neither the sensibility nor the craft to be a fiction writer or poet. But for the first time that realization didn't diminish my desire to become a writer. Because during this period, I discovered that the forms that seemed to animate me and suit my sensibilities were the personal essay and literary memoir—genres I'd been teaching in my comp classes for decades. And the more I wrote and studied these forms, the more curious I became.

It's true, I couldn't write the kind of literary fiction or poetry I'd most admired. But writing personal essays/memoirs seemed to bring out my best writing self. And given my sometimes analytical, sometimes expressive nature, they seemed far more suited to my temperament.

■ ■
■ ■

As I became more energized and confident about my writing, I continued to worry that I daydreamed too much over what it would be like to live in New York again. So, in my midfifties, I set up a meeting with Ken Klegon, our financial advisor, to discuss the possibilities of early retirement and moving back to New York.

When I asked him about the prospects of getting out at age 57, Ken told me point-blank that before we could even think about that, we had to cut back on our annual trips back to New York. My initial resistance was predictable. Ever since we'd moved to Michigan, those New York trips were a tonic, even a lifeline—my way of reconnecting with my old roots.

But Klegon also said something to the effect of "Mike, you're always complaining about not having enough time to write. Instead of going to New York, why not get your ass up to your cottage and work on your book?"

I whined and kvetched, of course. But it caught my attention. I thought about those post–eye surgery excursions, the days, sometimes weeks, I'd spent at the cottage—writing. Why had I allowed myself to get away from that routine?

The truth is that it did take a while for us—for me, really—to wean myself away from those annual New York excursions (escapes?). But eventually, go up north we did—more frequently, and for as much time as we could.

Five years later, I was able to take early retirement, and when I left the university I was revising and finishing up an essay collection made up, for the most part, of reworked versions of my post–eye surgery sketches. And at the same time, I was roughing out a memoir. Neither book, I'm sure, would have been completed had I not taken my financial advisor's advice to heart.

Just as Klegon had predicted, coming up to the cottage to write did indeed help temper my feelings of displacement. And yet, I still daydreamed about my old life in Greenwich Village. But in more reasonable moments, I began to recognize that the New York I dream about and the Leelanau County I romanticize are as much states of mind as they are physical settings.

Other writers, I know, have experienced a similar disparity. In her anthology *Leaving New York,* Kathleen Norris writes that Willa Cather "experienced her best writing years in Greenwich Village from 1912 to 1927, when the most celebrated of her Nebraska novels were published."

"To do fictional justice to Nebraska," Norris says, "apparently, [Cather] found it necessary to remain in New York." And ex–New Yorker Leslie Brody says in her memoir, *Red Star Sister,* "I had to leave New York in order to preserve its poetry."

And isn't this similar to the arc of my own writing? Perhaps writing about New York had, over time, become a substitute for living in New York. And this has caused me to speculate further: I've lived in New York, in Michigan, and in an imaginary New York. Let's say I did move back to Rockaway or the Village. Would I then become nostalgic for my Michigan retreat—or for my even more mundane life in East Lansing?

I'm thinking here of something one of my East Lansing coffee klatch cronies once told me. "New York," he said, "is that old girlfriend you hope won't show up one day and, God forbid, start hitting on you. Because just like you, she'll be sixty-five, and not the young girl you remember."

He's right of course, because recently I saw two more articles in the *Times*, one proclaiming that WQEW, the last New York station for jazz and pop standards, has become a Disney-oriented children's station; and the other noting that the Brasserie, one of my old always-open haunts, is being remodeled for the first time since it was built in 1959. The new one will feature rows of computer monitors and will no longer serve cappuccino and desserts after midnight.

I know I'm sounding pretty retro here. But when I'm thinking clearly, I'm aware, as my coffee klatch crony had observed, that locales invariably do change. Especially a constantly evolving city like New York. Part of Manhattan's charm is that it's always reinventing, redefining itself. And I'm not unaware that people too can change. Myself included.

For decades the New York of memory and imagination has represented excitement and wonder, the opportunity to be caught up in the whirlwind of a more stimulating, sometimes even enchanting existence. At the same time, my equally self-invented Leelanau landscape offers a grounded, meditative state of being. At different moments, in different moods and phases, I'm alternately drawn to one or the other. Sometimes simultaneously to both.

At some level then, I realize that this ongoing struggle is about learning to accept the life I have, not the one I fancy. And just as I've started to come to terms with that, a writer friend has begun to chide me about it.

"Haven't you ever had a fantasy about living in a more glamorous place?" I asked him.

"Sure. I'd love to have a pied-à-terre in Paris that I could go to whenever I wanted a taste of that life."

"What's stopping you, then?"

"Well, if I did," he said, "then it wouldn't be a fantasy anymore, would it?"

As I stand in front of the bay window, I watch a tanker glide across the lake's horizon. Then I turn away and see Carole's art displayed on the walls. I pause to gaze at David Grath's Leelanau landscape, "Manitou Dreams." There's an inscription that reads, "To Carole and Mike, living in paradise."

I look at the bookcase to my left, the section of the bottom shelf that's reserved for my writing. That's when I spot the blinking cursor that beckons me back to my morning's work. In that long moment, it occurs to me that my midlife memories of Greenwich Village are not unlike my early dreams of becoming a writer. And now, some thirty-plus years later, I am a writer, but I've done all of my best writing here, in Michigan, not in New York.

So as I walk the few steps to the computer, in my imagination I'm crossing Sixth Avenue again, after my writing class has ended. The afternoon sky is turning dark. The nannies in the park and the old guys playing chess have long since departed. But the basketball games at the Cage are still going full bore. I swing over to Bleecker and stop at the Italian market to pick up a loaf, before heading back to the Potbelly for my late-afternoon ritual—a mug of hot cider and some hard-nosed, down-home New York City kibitzing.

Robert Root

CROSSING THE CUESTA

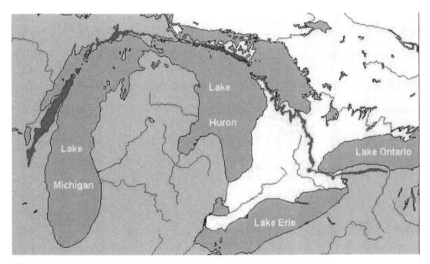

The Arc of the Escarpment

I IDENTIFY MYSELF AS A GREAT LAKES BOY. I grew up in Lockport, New York, with Lake Ontario half an hour's drive north, Lake Erie three quarters of an hour southwest. For most of my adult life I've lived in Michigan and Wisconsin, spending time along the shores of Lakes Michigan, Huron, and Superior. When I resided elsewhere, I never felt quite at home, always sensing the absence of a Great Lake.

However, Great Lakes alone weren't all that encompassed the trajectory of my life. It was also enclosed by the Niagara Escarpment, a geological formation roughly a thousand miles long, traceable all the way from central New York to southeastern Wisconsin. It parallels Lake Ontario, runs between Lakes Erie and Ontario after forming Niagara Falls—it's what the Niagara River falls over—then arcs up the east side of Lake Huron, crosses the northern edge of the Straits of Mackinac, and stretches down the western side of Lake Michigan, ringing the places where I've spent most of my life. A mere coincidence, I would think, if I hadn't been born in a town created by blasting through Niagara Escarpment strata to build locks on the Erie Canal and hadn't moved late in life to a town twenty miles from its western end. Awareness of that synchronicity fostered within me a growing affinity with the escarpment until I felt compelled to come to know it—to walk it, climb it, spend time in its company, understand its complexity. I needed to connect more strongly to this landscape, in effect to locate myself in its span of time.

That compulsion brought me again to the Upper Peninsula, now newly familiar with its geologic history. Over four hundred million years ago, during what geologists term the Silurian Period of the Paleozoic Era, shallow equatorial seas sprawled across a vast area of what would become North America, their depositions building ever thicker and varied strata. In the middle of the Silurian Period, distinguished as the Niagaran stage, resistant layers of limestone and dolostone were formed. Where Silurian strata are exposed today, subsequent depositions from later periods have been removed by centuries upon centuries of weathering and by the scouring of Ice Age glaciers. That weathering and scouring created the distinctive bluffs of the Niagara Escarpment, so prominent at Niagara Falls and, in Michigan, along the western shore of the Garden Peninsula. Middle Bluff, 150 feet high, lining Snail Shell Harbor in Fayette Historic State Park and arching out into Big Bay de Noc, is one of the Upper Peninsula's prime exhibits of the Niagara Escarpment. That cliff face is precisely what you hope to see when you go looking for an escarpment. But though geologists trace the Niagara Escarpment formation all across the UP, the bluffs of the Garden Peninsula—Middle Bluff, Burnt Bluff, Garden Bluff—are the only scarps, the only cliff faces, the only bluffs—that anyone can find.

An escarpment is not a fence or a wall; it's a place where terrain has been sheared away vertically from an extensive landform known as a cuesta. Escarpments form from the persistent wearing away of the edges of a cuesta over vast periods of time. Once, Middle Bluff and, farther south, Burnt Bluff were higher, and their cliff faces—their scarps—extended farther out into the bay, until they were worn back by the forces of erosion and glaciation. Behind them the same stratigraphic layers of deposition exposed on their faces go on and on, for the most part unexposed and unnoticed. Every escarpment fronts a cuesta; we have to cross the cuesta to reach the top of the escarpment, and when we leave that escarpment, we leave across the cuesta.

The Niagara Escarpment is essentially the rim of the lower Great Lakes; it always faces outward, away from them, and the cuesta always slopes toward them. The arc of the escarpment forms the northern boundary of the Michigan Basin, the depression occupied by Lake Michigan, the Straits of Mackinac, Lake Huron, and the whole of the Lower Peninsula. Evidence of the Niagara cuesta can be found across the southern portion of the UP, from the Garden Peninsula in the west to Drummond Island in the east, roughly two hundred miles of a relatively narrow geological corridor, a dozen to two dozen miles wide. Once the cuesta dips below the northern shoreline of Lakes Michigan and Huron, its Silurian strata plummets deep below the lakes and below the Lower Peninsula landscape, buried under successive depositions of later Devonian and Carboniferous strata. The farther you go into the center of the Lower Peninsula, the deeper the Silurian strata is buried and the younger the strata is nearer the surface.

If, however, you go north from the Straits, you are going further back in time. Across the Silurian layers you encounter Ordovician layers; along the northern shoreline of the Upper Peninsula you are on Cambrian layers; heading west along that shoreline you cross Precambrian bedrock, the rock of the Keweenaw Peninsula, the Canadian Shield, and the geological core of the North American continent. In other words, when my wife and I were driving from the center of the Lower Peninsula, where we lived and taught, through the Upper Peninsula to the tip of the Keweenaw Peninsula, we were crossing a landscape undergirded by strata ranging from 300 million to 635 million years old.

When you look at terrain in geological terms, your sense of where you are changes.

Maps of the Niagara Escarpment always show it arcing across the bottom of the Upper Peninsula, but anyone expecting to see a scarp that compares with Middle Bluff or Niagara Falls will be disappointed. There is none. The line on the map traces the limits of the geologic formation, and the terrain south of it to the shoreline of the lakes is the Niagara cuesta. The cuesta is not as conspicuous as the escarpment, though far more pervasive, and as we cross it I ponder how I might come to feel as though I've seen it. To do that will involve finding a location where enough glacial till and outwash have been washed or scoured away to expose the strata on which they were deposited thousands of years ago. It may also mean finding places where the cuesta has been cracked open and excavated.

If a large hole is dug in the ground and if what once filled it is carted away, it often happens that rain and snow melt and groundwater and newly exposed underground springs flow and settle into its lowest levels. The rock walls and floors of a dolostone quarry seldom provide a natural outlet; a puddle eventually becomes a pond that eventually becomes a lake. In some communities what might have been a civic danger becomes a recreational gathering place. Manistique has such a site, Quarry Lake, in Manistique Central Park.

Quarry Lake is the center of the park, with sport facilities scattered near it and a half-mile-long footpath running around its kidney-shaped circumference. A small sandy beach fills a narrow section at the north end, the waters here noticeably shallower than the rest of the lake. The waters deepen where the lake broadens and the quarry was most thoroughly excavated.

From a wooden lookout deck we look down the east side of the lake. Stone walls occasionally rise as much as ten feet above the water, but most often they are considerably lower. The surface of the walls is rough and uneven and worn, sometimes crumbling and broken up. Evergreens line the top of the wall intermittently, and small shrubs are often rooted in the talus close to the water's edge. Near the overlook, where the wall is the lowest, the stone is well weathered. Beyond the shallows beneath the bright green water rough tiers drop off quickly. In places the lake is fifty feet deep.

Remembering Middle Bluff at Fayette Historic State Park, that high wall of stone exposed to view by glaciers and lake waves, I imagine the quarry walls here once exposed to a similar extent, in depth rather than in height, by commercial excavation. If not for the waters that fill Quarry Lake, the quarry walls we gaze at would be the industrial equivalent of a scarp, a man-made display of a portion of the Niagaran strata. Now the rim of layered stone I see above the water serves only as a retaining wall for the lake rather than as an indication of how deeply the quarry penetrated the cuesta.

Whenever I stand before an escarpment or look down from the lip of one, I can't help being aware of the forces that created it—the incremental buildup of strata over vast periods of time, the play among forces of deposition and consolidation and erosion, the landscape's power to shape itself. Whenever I stand on the floor of a quarry or look down from its edges, I'm always aware of what I can't see, what's no longer there—I always notice the scars and debris and rusted detritus that commemorate the industrial energy that emptied the space in as short a time as it could. At Quarry Lake I realize I've come for the quarry but should only have come for the lake.

In past travels in the UP, I avoided Palms Book State Park, about a half-hour's drive inland from Manistique, where the main attraction is the chance to raft across Kitch-iti-kipi, the Big Spring. I hadn't been aware then that the big spring flows out of the Niagara cuesta; now it feels necessary to visit it, to gaze into it, and perhaps learn what part it plays in shaping its environment.

It's a busy place. We walk a short, winding trail through cedar forest to the dock where the raft is moored and join a short line waiting for it to return across the pond. In the green water close to the dock, submerged tree trunks jut toward the center of the spring, lime coated and pointed. Kitch-iti-kipi is two hundred feet wide and forty feet deep, the largest freshwater spring in Michigan, gushing over ten thousand gallons of water a minute, and the slow progress of the raft across the pond and back allows plenty of time for passengers to look around, to gaze into the deeps, to scout the shoreline.

When our turn comes to file onto the raft, I find a spot near the long rectangular opening that offers a view beneath the vessel at the depths of the spring. A sign above the opening explains that the water comes from rainfall and snowmelt seeping into the ground through glacial till along a layer of interbedded dolomite and shale beneath a layer of the Burnt Bluff Group, one of the Niagaran strata that run through the southern UP. The water dissolves soluble elements of the bedrock and becomes more and more pressurized until it squirts through cracks in the rock above it into the pool. There it creates, as the sign terms it, "a dancing layer of sand." It's an apt phrase.

Concentrating on the depths, I see abundant trout swimming lazily beneath the raft. Below them parts of the spring bottom bubble and roil, circles of gray sediment churning in the waters rising from the Niagaran dolomite through continuously flowing vents. Though forty feet below, in the clear water the circles of moving sediment seem somehow near. As we return to the dock, I see the encrusted tree trunks again and realize that, below the trunks, I can see the dolostone walls of the pond. It's an all-too-brief internal view of the cuesta, excavated and inundated by degrees over immense intervals of time.

We shuffle off the raft and off the dock, past an equal number of people waiting to board and crank themselves across Big Spring. I cast my thoughts back to Quarry Lake in Manistique Central Park and remember the flooded floors of other quarries, nonrecreational pools created by rainwater and snowmelt. Something there is that doesn't love a man-made hole in the ground. Such lakes and pools remind us of industrial impacts, both historical and contemporary, shaping the landscape. Looking into them we can't help thinking of what isn't there, of what's been removed and made it possible for something else to fill its space.

At Kitch-iti-kipi, in contrast, I can't help thinking about the natural processes that formed the spring, processes millennia old and still in operation. To comprehend them, I have to understand the strata under my feet, the strata below which the water flows and through which it spouts upward to roil the floor of the spring. Water and rock engaged and interactive, reminding me that the cuesta is something more than simply the strata behind the scarp. It's an enduring, active presence.

Aware that the cuesta slopes beneath Great Lakes waters and disappears below successive strata at the center of the Michigan Basin, we head for a place where we can see the meeting of cuesta and lake, the shoreline at Seul Choix Point. We stroll past the historic lighthouse, its tower a white brick column rising over seventy-eight feet high, topped with a metal catwalk below the lantern room. Taking a path through the trees beyond the lighthouse and museum, we emerge onto a broad flat rock beach. Shrubs and grasses are abundant in crevasses and either lake water or crunchy white shells often fill deeper indentations. We weave our way toward the water across eroded strata, broken chunks of flat rock lying in the small pools, dark mosses spilling over cracks and fractures. Glacial erratics rise above the waves offshore. Gray waves match the grayness of the clouds and the grayness of the rocks. Where the waters darken farther out I have a sense of the distance below the lake that the Niagara cuesta soon slopes.

Where the rock surface is most uneven and the depressions most pronounced, I squat down to consider what has been exposed by the elements. Some of the rocks that have broken from the cuesta are rounded and smooth, well weathered by Lake Michigan waves. Other rocks are almost neatly formed, flat on the top and the bottom, mostly straight on the sides, as if chiseled off the strata nearby. They resemble on a small scale the larger slabs visible in the talus below cliffs and bluffs elsewhere along the escarpment, wherever the scarp face is prominent. In places I can see the exposed edge of the rock and the tight layers of strata that built up over time to form the cuesta. The edge of the rock seems as neatly cleaved as the walls of a quarry or a cliff face. The distinction is a matter of scale.

Sue and I circle the point, sometimes pausing to watch the waves roll in, the offshore erratics resist them, and the clouds drift slowly above the lake. It seems a timeless scene, and we are slow to move on. In places we trudge over huge mounds of white zebra mussel shells, so thick and dense that they bury the rocks, adding another layer of strata to the coastline. The shells almost seem to have replaced the outwash deposits of receding glaciers that the lake had long ago carried away. They obscure the cuesta centuries of wave action have exposed.

We return to the parking lot and notice an SUV with surfboards propped up against it and some men busy gearing up in wetsuits. We stop to ask them how the surfing is on Lake Michigan and learn that, though the near coastline is only ten feet deep, a little farther offshore it becomes forty feet deep, guaranteeing good waves when the wind blows north up the lake in summer. I immediately imagine the gradual incline of the cuesta offshore giving way to a steep slope plunging down below the waves and envision surfers riding waves from the deeps inland to ever shallower waters. It occurs to me that, in their knowledge of the water acquired on its surface, the surfers have also gained an innate, largely unconscious knowledge of the cuesta below the lake.

While Sue stays behind in Cedarville to catch up on her own work, I drive to DeTour, take the ferry across the DeTour Passage to Drummond Island, then make my way across the island. Maxton Plains, its western end jutting out into Potagannissing Bay and its northern edge running along the North Channel of Lake Huron, is an Ecological Reference Area. Its more than four thousand acres are managed in part by the Michigan Department of Natural Resources and in part by the Nature Conservancy. It preserves a broad, flat terrain dominated by horizontal plates of bedrock atop Niagara Escarpment strata.

Scraped and scoured repeatedly by glaciers up until ten thousand years ago, the surface at Maxton Plains has never built up a soil layer more than ten inches thick. The plants and flowers that find purchase in cracks and joints in its limestone pavement are a mix of prairie, tundra, and Great Lakes vegetation. Trees amenable to long winters and fierce winds—aspen, fir, spruce—border the alvar. In *The Drummond Girls,* her memoir of annual reunions on the island, Mardi Jo Link describes the area as "an ancient place, a flat circle of silver and gold a half mile across and surrounded by florescent evergreens." She was struck by the metallic sheen given off by the moisture on the flat rock. On the morning I arrive where she first beheld the place, at a Nature Conservancy crossroads kiosk, I seem to be entirely alone at what does seem like an ancient place.

Determined to see the western coastline, I drive slowly across the open space. The wildlife on Maxton Plains seem not much concerned about tourists—pairs of deer and pairs of sandhill cranes drift across the road and through the grasses, and a solitary rabbit observes my passing like a calm pedestrian. I lessen my speed whenever I see them. Winding my way through thick forest to a place where I can park, I walk out to a marshy shoreline. Half a dozen Canada geese wander lazily through it. Beyond a rocky beach, the shallows, like the grasslands across Maxton Plains, are dotted with boulders, glacial erratics protruding above the water, dropped during the last glacier's recession into Canada. Gazing at the shoreline, ignoring the tree line in the distance, and recalling the alvar plain behind me, I can almost imagine that the ice sheet didn't leave here so long ago. Fully immersed in the contemporary moment while simultaneously absorbed by a sense of being somewhere ancient, I bask in a transitory feeling of experiencing timelessness.

Crossing the preserve again, I occasionally pull to the side of the road and leave the car. I step lightly across rocky surfaces, making my way out into open spaces where the flatness and growth on the limestone slabs of alvar are most evident. Once, between thickets of trees on either side, I find the road's surface to be entirely a bare patch of alvar. It is easy to see why people refer to alvar as a "limestone pavement." The joints in the pavement look as if their origin were industrial rather than natural. If not for the grasslands and trees around it, the space could easily pass for a small urban parking lot. I'm reminded of the joints and fractures that make the levels and layers of dolomite in a quarry so convenient as building stones, nature modeling manufacture. The illusion doesn't last long. I soon come upon rough patches where wind and weather have made the surface less even and gravel has blown into the indentations. Here lichens have gained a foothold and hang on tenaciously to make the meager most of their environment.

It's been claimed that Maxton Plains is the best place to experience alvar in the Great Lakes, though there are other significant sites on the Bruce Peninsula. Elsewhere it's found along the shoreline of Estonia, in Sweden (where the term comes from), and in a few places in the British Isles. It is often flooded in spring and drought ridden in summer, and its plant communities include rare species with strictly limited range. At times it seems as stark and challenging as an escarpment cliff face.

On my slow, solitary crossing of Maxton Plains, I stop every so often to gaze across a wide stretch of grassland interrupted by formidable glacial boulders, some as large as my car. Throughout the grasslands bare patches of stone appear, as if in all these centuries grasses and shrubs have never been able to secure a footing there. Wherever there is soil, it's a thin layer. In the distance the alvar and the grasslands are fenced in by rows of mixed conifers, spruce and fir and red pine. When I detect movement in the grasses, I discover more pairs of sandhill cranes and stand for a time to watch them, as if I hadn't seen any others all morning. I'm the only stranger in the landscape, and they ignore me as if they haven't noticed me at all. In clear sky and cool breeze I don't bother to tell them how far across the cuesta I've come to be here, to see what they and their kind have gazed upon for countless generations.

Waiting in a line of vehicles for the ferry to arrive and disembark island-bound passengers, I step to the side of the road to gaze off at the Drummond Island shoreline. In the clear water I can see a rocky shelf below quiet waves and feel a touch of clarity myself. Crossing the cuesta has given me a new perspective on both the Niagara Escarpment and the Upper Peninsula.

In the UP what has absorbed me has been not the scarp—the cliff face—of the Escarpment but the cuesta behind the scarp—or, so often here, instead of the scarp. Rather than looking down from or up at the heights, I've been paying attention to what lies below the surface and the ways the surface changes when it slopes away from any potential scarp. Yes, quarries gouge out their holes in the cuesta, but the nature of the cuesta's composition lets water have its way with it, find its own way of burrowing beneath it, rising up through it, smoothing it, undermining it, changing it in slower increments over immense amounts of time. The vulnerability of karst, the imperturbability of alvar, the roiling of springs, the persistence of waves, the ways in which constant change still maintains a presence that calls no attention to itself—all these reward awareness and concentration and willingness to be in the moment. The cuesta is a lesson in the balance between continuity and change; the lesson is a reward for crossing the cuesta.

Keith Taylor

AT SPRINGHILL FARM

FOR MANY YEARS I WORKED AT SHAMAN DRUM BOOKSHOP,
a small independent store half a block north of the central campus of the
University of Michigan. We described our market niche as "academic and
scholarly books in the humanities." Many of our customers were professors and graduate students, but the store was also supported by a large
segment of Ann Arbor's overeducated population. We prided ourselves on
the obscurity of the titles we carried and were startled, even a bit disgrun-
tled, when we found that a book we stocked had made it onto someone's
bestseller list.

In addition to the usual methods of acquiring books for our shop,
we were always looking for ways to find a few more titles for a little less
money. Several times a year we purchased review copies sent to the academic journals that had their homes in small offices and basements scattered around the university. Usually those books were so obscure that the
editors had decided no one would ever choose to review them. We were
able to get them for pennies on the dollar. Periodically we'd go through
the boxes of these review copies and pick out books to add to our inven-
tory, to sell as used books, or to sell as drastically reduced books on our
bargain tables, the ones that stayed outside all year long through all kinds
of weather. Out there we had to put books that we didn't mind destroying
after the tables were forgotten during tornado season or after the bindings
froze and thawed any number of times during a Michigan winter, books
we didn't mind losing to the shoplifters strolling past.

Most of the time we didn't sell very many of these bargain books, just
a few each day. We didn't make very much money on them, just enough,
perhaps, to keep us in toilet paper and ballpoint pens. But once a year our
city sponsors something it calls the Art Fair, and hundreds of thousands of
people come to town looking for cultural bargains. Then we could sell anything, as long as it was priced low enough. I imagined our bargain books—

about farming practices in twelfth-century Syria or listing the Latin names for the insects of Missouri—drifting off to decorate the bookshelves of midwestern villages and suburbs, gathering the particular kind of dust that collects only on books, until someone, probably an heir, put them out for a yard sale twenty or thirty years later, wondering why Dad or Mom ever bought such dull things.

In July 1996, a couple of days before the beginning of the Art Fair, my friend Karl Pohrt, who owned the bookshop, was going through the boxes of books with me so that we could find the ones we wanted to sell out on the street. Karl found it difficult to admit that he may have purchased, however cheaply, a book about a subject so arcane that absolutely no one on earth would ever read it willingly. In this one case, I was usually the hard-nosed one, insisting that if we put the book out for three or four dollars, we might have a chance of selling it. If we kept it on the shelf inside, it might stay there for fifteen years, clogging up precious space that could be used by something just a bit more profitable. It was an argument we had for several years. Karl was right often enough to make me question my judgment.

But on that July day, Karl, usually so generous to unknown academic titles, came across a book whose specificity made even him laugh out loud.

"Here," he said. "There's probably no one in three states who'd read this. Except you, maybe."

He handed me the book: *Pioneer Policing in Southern Alberta: Deane of the Mounties, 1888–1914,* edited by William M. Baker, professor of history at the University of Lethbridge, and published by the Historical Society of Alberta in 1993. The book was a series of police reports written by or submitted to R. Burton Deane, a superintendent of the Royal Northwest Mounted Police during the period when the western prairies of Canada received their first European settlers and then became the provinces of Saskatchewan and Alberta.

I thought my friend Karl might actually be wrong: not even I could be interested in this. I planned to mark it at four dollars for the Art Fair tables.

Upstairs I was building the piles of cheap books we hoped to sell outside. The weather was living up to its clichés: hot and muggy. I was sweating and uncomfortable. It was the time of year I feel most like a foreigner in Michigan, most like someone from the provinces of western Canada. Before I priced *Pioneer Policing in Southern Alberta* and threw it on the pile, I thought I should look up my hometown, Didsbury, in the index.

There was one reference to it, on page 177. The place-name was easy to find. It was the last word on the page: "we went there to Kansas 15 miles s.w. of Didsbury." This meant nothing to me. I'd never heard of a town or region close to where I grew up called Kansas. And I had no context for the quote. The entry began just a couple of short paragraphs above. William Baker, the editor, had labeled it:

A True and Faithful Wife

Constable K. G. Murison, Crime Report (submitted to Deane):
Suicide of Mrs. Mary Findlay of Kansas, 23 October 1907.

I thought this was an interesting coincidence. My great-grandmother, alive around then—I didn't remember the date or condition of her death— was named Mary Finlay, without the *d*. But I had never heard of Kansas. And even though there were many family stories about the pioneering generation, there was certainly no story about a suicide.

Like many Westerners I am proud of my pioneering grandparents. I know that the myths we built about their undaunted courage are at best half-truths, but I also know that there is still some truth in them. The stories of their survival and success are the stories that have been preserved. After all, I am here, living a bookish life none of my grandparents could have imagined. My cousins and second cousins, my aunts and uncles— business owners, plumbers, politicians, police officers, engineers, teachers, preachers, even a few farmers—are still in Alberta, prospering, for the most part, although we have our share of the usual woes.

But I kept reading the police report despite my lack of personal connection to it. A suicide, after all, is usually intriguing.

On the 14th inst I was notified that a Mrs. Findlay had been found in the yard of her house. I notified Dr. Little & then we went there to Kansas 15 miles s.w. of Didsbury.

Constable Murison would almost certainly have gone on horseback. Dr. Little may have ridden in a buggy, although the roads out there in 1907 would have been nothing but mud paths. The weather had probably turned cold already, although I doubt that the ground would have been completely frozen yet. The wind coming down from the mountains fifty miles to the west would have been bitter.

It is easy for me to imagine that landscape. It is the one that formed my sense of how the world should be. For the first eleven years of my life

I lived at the very northwest corner of the North American high plains, close to the place where the dry grasslands intersect the Rocky Mountains to the west and the subarctic forest to the north. That slightly rolling, sparsely forested land, often intersected by small creeks and the coulees they carve, with a band of mountains, perpetually snow covered, rising to the west, has a rich black soil that people of my grandparents' generation had discovered could grow a type of hardy wheat in vast quantities. Range cattle grew fat there, despite the weather. Beneath that land was one of the world's largest supplies of fossil fuels, although most of my family sold off their farms before oil was discovered.

Since Alberta was settled so recently, mostly after the completion of the Canadian Pacific Railway in 1885, the stories of European immigration to Canada and the struggles of homesteading in the West have always seemed much closer to my life than the comparatively older stories I hear about the American West. Although not possessed by the bug of genealogical research, I have ended up with a fair number of documents and photographs, primarily because I expressed more interest in these old stories than most of the relatives of my generation.

I have a photograph of the Finlay family taken in a studio called Abernethy, at 29 High Street in Belfast around 1897, several years before they emigrated. They are all cleanly scrubbed and wearing clothes they would have worn only to church. Even their shoes are clean. The younger children had not yet been born, and Great-Aunt Mary—who had her mother's name just as the firstborn son, William, carried the father's—was still alive, probably about eighteen in the photo. Over the years I had looked at her more than anyone else, trying to imagine her death from tuberculosis just a couple of years later. She looks wide-eyed in the picture, a bit stunned, but she is beautiful. She is the only one smiling. She resembles the pictures of my mother when my mother was young. There is something in her and in the other children pictured—Aunts Sadie (whose given name was Sarah) and Lizzie; Uncles Will, Charles, and James; my grandfather, John, as an eight-year-old—that resembles my own child. Some of their characteristics are immediately recognizable: the jaw line, the shape of the eyebrows, the way the lips are pushed together seriously.

Great-Grandmother Mary is holding a baby, Charles, and is wearing a long black dress. Her hair is pulled back severely, making her look angry. Because of her straight-backed unsmiling presence, I had called her the Wicked Witch of the West.

Finlay Family, Belfast, Ireland, circa 1897

Great-Grandfather William dominates the photograph, squinting into the camera, his big beard looking uncombed and a bit wild, his large, obviously calloused right hand resting dangerously on the armrest of the photographer's chair. All of our stories indicated that the family was poor, but in this photograph they look quite prosperous.

I turned the page of *Pioneer Policing* and started down 178:

Mr. William Findlay said as follows:

William is a common enough name, and I thought there could have been several Williams in 1907 out in that rural district, even though the population density then was something less than one person per square mile. And my great-grandfather's place in the world was a common place. His family's story was like most of the homesteaders' stories.

The Finlays were the last of my ancestors to arrive in Alberta. After a series of bad debts overwhelmed their small vegetable farm in Northern Ireland, they immigrated to Canada in 1904. Even that late they were still able to get 160 acres simply by building a home on the land and clearing one field within three years. Like many of the English and Irish immigrants, filled with hope but also carrying their memories of the pastoral landscapes of the old world, they named their farm. Because they built their house close to a natural spring on the side of a slight rise falling off to the east, they called their place Springhill Farm. Perhaps the name disappeared when they sold the farm. More likely it disappeared during the Depression, when the mortgage officers remembered debts simply by the names of the farms. The beleaguered farmers dropped the names in the hope that they would be forgotten or unfindable. Some were, but the romance of the names never returned.

The Springhill Farm homestead was in an area I had always known as Westcott, a small farming center some fourteen miles west and a bit south of Didsbury. William and Mary Finlay came with nine surviving children. One child had died in infancy, and their oldest child, my Great-Aunt Mary, had died of tuberculosis in Ireland several years before the family left.

Because their second son, my grandfather, John Finlay, died of a brain tumor at the age of thirty-two in 1921, four months before his only child, my mother, was born, certain stories were preserved. My grandmother created an image of her husband for my mother. She selected and described the life of the Irish immigrant farmer until she turned him into a prairie saint. She wrote a book describing his life that she gave to my mother on her thirteenth birthday, on September 5, 1934. It is bound in leather with my mother's name, Joyce M. Finlay, embossed in gold letters on the front. The title is *Your Daddy*. After my mother's death, that book, filled with cracking photographs, poems, and the story—as my grandmother hoped it would be remembered—became part of my library.

In this book about my grandfather, the early life on the prairie is given some of its harshness. My grandmother quickly describes how the first house the family built had burned down during their first winter on the prairie. The family lost three hundred dollars, all of their savings, and everything they owned but a couple of books. Those old primers from northern Irish schools, charred and water-stained, have been a part of my library for many years. I've read with pleasure *Aunt Margery's Maxims,* published by Hodder & Stoughton at 27 Paternoster Row, London, in 1897. The bookplate on the inside cover, from the Rosetta National School, reads:

Presented to Master John Finlay for very superior Answering in the Third Class at the Annual Results Examination, June 1898.

ISSAC HARVEY, PRINCIPAL

The book's cover and the edges of the pages are blackened by the fire that destroyed everything else. When I hold that book, I can quite literally smell the fire in that isolated prairie farmhouse during the fall of 1904.

Although there are hints of trouble in my grandmother's book, I had never seen them. I was glad to own it, but I was overwhelmed by the tedium of her attempt to accent the rosy endurance of this immigrant family she had married into. My grandmother's truth was the one that forgot or erased pain and remembered only joy. She begins her description of the family in Ireland, around a fireside in what most of us would now consider a crofter's shack: "Blessed and interesting is that fireside with its detail of home life into which has been carefully woven care, discipline, schooling and religious training of a family of rollicking boys and girls." I found this sentimentality at best amusing and at worst boring. What is perhaps more unusual is that, like my mother before me, I believed it.

If we had wanted to know information that presented a different side of the family life, we wouldn't have had to look very far. We owned another photograph of the Finlay family, this one taken in Alberta in 1905 or 1906. We seldom looked at it. Like the earlier one, it's a posed and planned family photo, but this time it is not a studio portrait. Here the family sits outside, with a white clapboard wall behind them. The siding matches the siding of the tiny Baptist Church a couple of miles from the farm that is also preserved in a photograph. Unlike the Irish photo, there is no record of the photographer, but it seems likely that an itinerant photographer passed through on a Sunday morning. The picture taking would have been an event, and all the members of the family, this time including the three youngest girls, are obviously dressed in what passed for their finery.

But the look and feel of this later picture is entirely different. Not only do they all look weathered, the way we would expect them to look after working in the wind and under the prairie sun for months on end, but they look leaner. Hungry. William, so daunting in the photo eight or nine years earlier, now looks tired, scruffy, and perhaps a little crazy. He is a man much diminished from the earlier picture. Mary too has changed. Even though she is smiling, her face is sagging. Haggard. Her eyes seem manic and a little frightening. Only the older sons, including my grandfather, and

Finlay family, Westcott, Alberta, Canada, circa 1905

the two oldest daughters look slightly comfortable. The family in this photograph is unmistakably poor. And the picture is unsettling.

In his report Constable Murison puts the statement of Mr. William Findlay in quotation marks. Although he makes the farmer sound a bit like a provincial bureaucrat, I began to imagine the voice, reserved and thick with brogue:

> Mary Findlay, deceased, is my wife. She is 45 years old & Irish. We
> have been in this country three years. My wife never spoke to me
> with regard to taking her life, but she was terribly worried about the
> hard luck we have had in this country. We have been burned out,
> hailed out, & frozen out during our 3 years' residence here.

Like most farming families, we had heard the stories about crop failure. The burned books, the only things to survive the fire, were now comfortably preserved in a closet in my Ann Arbor home. I was becoming less convinced about the idea of coincidence.

> I last saw deceased on the night of the 13th when I went to bed. She
> had been sleeping with the children for the last two weeks so I did not
> know whether she was in bed or not. I woke up about 2 a.m. & saw a

> light burning in the kitchen & I called to my wife to put it out but there
> was no answer, so I got up & looked around but could not see her.

I wondered what the light was. A kerosene lamp? A candle? Homemade
or store-bought? And I was impressed by the syntax of that last sentence,
everything running together in a kind of desperate hurry, the syntax of
grief and, maybe, just maybe, the syntax of self-justification.

In the police report he continues speaking:

> After a while I went & called my neighbour Mr. Alex Robertson &
> we looked together but without result. Next morning we found her
> dead lying just where you see her now.

At this point I no longer had many doubts. Alex Robertson was a name I
knew. The chances of coincidence had disappeared. Alex and his son were
family friends, and my family had kept in touch with them well into my
own childhood. I think I was even taken to their farm when I was very
young.

Constable Murison now quotes Alex Robertson:

> I came over to Mr. Findlay's about 3 o'clock a.m. on the morning of
> ,the 14th inst. & helped look for Mrs. Findlay but could not find her.
> We found her where you see her now. No one has touched her since.

Now the questions started, the ones that could never be answered except
in imagination. Who would have ridden the mile or so over to the Robertson farm? John, my grandfather? He would have been eighteen then.
He would certainly have been helping his father. Did they find Mary's
body when the sun came up? Was it a shadow in the grass that slowly became ominous as the light lifted? Did they cover her body? The younger
children were very young, and wouldn't my grandfather have tried to
protect them?

Constable Murison, the Mountie, continues in his own words:

> We found her body lying about 2 yds from the water closet & in the
> closet I found a bottle of carbonic acid nearly empty.

My father, born in 1920 and an Alberta farm boy until he was released
from essential duty at the end of World War II, remembers the carbolic

acid they used to doctor the animals. They would dilute it heavily, just a splash or two in a pail of water. It still stung his hands when he patted it on saddle sores or the scratches along the legs of horses. They used it on the stumps left after they clipped the cattle's horns.

> I also found a letter in deceased room bidding her children good-bye which I enclose.

Here, just given the layout of prose on the page, I knew what I would soon read. But I didn't jump ahead. I had to read everything.

> Dr. Little performed a post mortem & found that she had been poisoned by carbonic acid & stated that as deceased had stated in her letter, bid good-bye, & also that she would never be seen alive again, there was no doubt that she died by her own hand & therefore no inquest would be necessary.
>   The body was handed over to her husband. Deceased leaves 9 children, 4 of whom are under 12 years old . . .

I stopped for a moment at the ellipsis at the end of the report. Was it part of the original, or had something been cut by the editor? Was it the kind of information—names, perhaps—that would be of interest only to the family? One sentence followed.

> The following is a copy of the letter referred to in above report:

I wasn't sure if this was a direction from the editor or if it had been written by the constable. It seemed to me by then that both of them had a sense of the dramatic that I could trust. I knew I was about to read my great-grandmother's suicide note, and that no one in the family had known about it for two generations. I read it in one rush.

> Sunday night, Oct. 13th, 1907
>
> My dear dear children.
>
> This is likely the last words you will hear of me or from me. I have not much to say only that my life has been blighted with trouble and disappointment. I have been a true and faithful wife. Your father

told me this morning to leave the place because I will not sleep with him. I love my children. God only knows how I love you all. I don't want any more children, but my heart yearns for each of your prosperity and eternal salvation. You all know that your sister Mary has gone to Heaven and [I] want you each one [to] meet her there. Jesus Christ is the way to God. I know I will lose my reward but I know in whom I have believed. If you ever get married study the matter well and never be advised by anyone unless you love the person. To you Sarah & Lizzie, Willie & John I leave to have a mother's care for the younger children. May God bless & provide for them & you all is the prayer of your own mother. Good bye till we meet again.

Although I immediately told Karl and some of my coworkers in the bookshop what I had found in this book we had all been willing to chuckle about a few minutes earlier, part of me still couldn't believe the story. I thought that something of this must have survived in the family history. Although I know enough about them to understand why they chose to hide this story, I couldn't believe the people in my grandparents' generation could be so successful at it. I went home to look in the book my grandmother had written for my mother. In the first chapter I found these sentences, so unremarkable in their sweetness that I had never noticed them before:

This refined and beautiful Mother gave herself to her family most untiringly. After many heartaches and losses by fire, and the hardships of pioneering in a new land, she died on October 13, 1907. This sweet, brown-eyed, rose-tinted Mother just wore out.

Three weeks before I found Professor Baker's book, I had been back to Alberta for the funeral of a paternal uncle. I had driven by the Westcott Road. It heads off toward the mountains from old Highway 2 about fifty miles north of Calgary. It moves up one of the slowly rolling rises in the land, then disappears over the crest. I thought of my Irish ancestors struggling at their Springhill Farm a few miles down that road. I thought how odd it was that no one but me and perhaps one or two of my mother's cousins had thought of that place-name for half a century or more. I didn't take the diversion to see the old place. I wasn't sure I could find it.

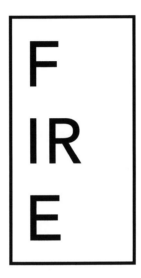

Rhoda Janzen

UNFORGETTABLE BABY

MY NEW STEPSON, LEROY, WAS IN A BAND. He didn't sing, or play, or make it to many rehearsals. But he looked exceptionally stylish in my skinny white jeans. Leroy's career goals included owning a chartreuse Fender Stratocaster and becoming a world-famous rock star. The band would travel in a Dassault Falcon 7X, accompanied by their own videographer. The videographer was son of the youth pastor at the drummer's church.

While Leroy did not write actual songs or produce any music, he did attract a rock-star stream of smitten young women. They called and texted with flattering urgency. I was willing to bake cookies for these young women, many of whom shared insightful texts such as, "OMG, Leroy is INSANELY cute!!!! So random!!!!!"

Who could complain about such an introduction to motherhood? If sixteen-year-olds preferred to text about the cuteness of my stepson, and the related cuteness of Harry Styles, and if they occasionally touched on global themes such as Rihanna's hair, then in the name of marital flexibility I would nod and express interest.

Until I became a stepmom, working in the church nursery was my main exposure to smaller fry. Tots were democratically endearing. It was easy to adore them all: nappers, cuddlers, shin-kickers, smooshers of crackers. Some childless women bravely admit that they just aren't up for the company of kids. I wasn't one of them. I liked kids. They could be bribed a dollar to improvise Irish Riverdance in the philharmonic lobby at intermission. "You have to kick your leg straight out from the hip at least once," I whispered to my niece, extending the dollar.

"Okay."

"Two dollars if you throw in a move called Dog Poop on My Shoe."

"Okay."

My niece's hearty Celtic stylings there in the lobby of the philharmonic strongly suggested a pattern of expectation. Babies were plump; nine-year-olds, tractable. Applying the transitive property of equality, I figured that Leroy and his friends would be likewise endearing. The hyperbole of adolescence: cute, right? Prom anxiety, mohawks, neck tattoos of realistic wolves—what's not to love? "I can do this," I told myself.

In grad school most of my friends had begun families. "Is it true," I asked, "that parenting matures you like nothing else?" "Absolutely," they said. They read de Saussure and conversed about sparkly ponies *at the same time*. They poured out the milk of human kindness. They needed fewer shoes. One friend had developed an eerie sixth sense involving the deployment of Lil Smoky Sausages as a preemptive strike. All this seemed admirable, yet I continued to experience parenting as something to admire from afar, like Mount Rushmore.

Growing up in Mennonite circles, I had often heard a Malthusian argument, recycled by the eugenics movement a century later, though the ladies who affirmed it may have never read Malthus. These dear souls explained that women who chose to remain childless were selfish. They gently suggested that the cheery of heart and healthy of womb had a *moral duty* to reproduce, as if to cancel out the choices of crack moms and careerists who fed their kids frozen waffles. I wasn't looking to rock the Mennonite boat. Never a rebel, I would have been astonished, like the aunties and grandmas, to come across either crackpipes or frozen waffles. Who can explain these things? I never felt called to be a parent, that's all.

Except that it wasn't all.

At age forty-two, I had a son who'd popped into my life like the toaster pastry I never tried. Could I roll with it? Leroy ate no vegetables. He said *I seen*. He made effing six out of seven classes look positively easy. But he would find his way, would he not? All roads lead to broccoli. Besides, Leroy and I liked each other. I breezily introduced home-cooked meals as if they were no big deal, lalala! At first he was suspicious. Soon he was sneaking back into the kitchen to eat seventeen leftover *Rollkuchen*, all at one sitting. Was there projectile vomiting? Sure! But I was privately cheered. Step one, fritters! Step two, roasted cauliflower! Step three, college!

What blindsided me was a curious and unexpected dislike for one of Leroy's friends. This young man, Ari, had been brought up in a single-parent household. For most of his life, his father had been incarcerated. Ari had met him only once, a stranger in an orange jumpsuit. It was Ari's mother who told me this as she pressed into my hands a moist packet of catfish that Ari's younger brother had caught from the Grand Haven pier.

Ari's mother didn't speak English, but I understood the gist of it. She was tsk-tsking over Ari's faults, implying that they could be attributed to the lack of a positive male role model in the home. She had done the best she could. Ari's younger brother, Orlando, now was a fine young man. The catfish represented Orlando's industry, not Ari's, but she thought we might appreciate some fresh catfish. The best way to prepare catfish was to deep-fry them in a crunchy buttermilk batter.

When Leroy first brought his friend home, Ari seemed merely a sociable young man with a heart for music. "*Christian* music," he said hastily, as if worried I might think he preferred secular tunes. It should have been touching to see how Ari clung to his guitar, and how he was always practicing his vocals.

Unlike my new stepson, Ari really was committed to his music. Yet his melancholy tenor put me in mind of a Vegas heartthrob with a suggestive wink—imploring lyrics, airborne panties, tipsy fans. Ari said his songs were about Jesus, but they sounded like crybaby breakup songs to me. We danced in the rain, we stole a kiss! The songs strongly suggested that Jesus, lovestruck and heartbroken, had removed his shirt. And while Our Lord had a ripped set of abs, all the songs sounded the same. If Ari wasn't already singing when we came into the room, he'd grab his guitar and commence an anthem to the soul of romance, an unforgettable baby who'd done him wrong. On these occasions I recalled the prison daddy and the catfish, and I applauded encouragingly. "I love the part about the seagulls!"

Then there was the situation with my pants. I did not love the part about my pants. Is it ever appropriate for an adolescent boy to remark on the fit of a middle-aged woman's jeans? Especially if the woman is your buddy's stepmom? I was trying to interpret Ari's badinage as an outcropping of an uninformed desire to please. Here's a sample. After helping himself to a third or fourth cookie, Ari might cock an eyebrow and say with a playful little smile, "These cookies are so good I'd like to put you in my pocket and take you home!" In a professional setting a remark like that would be instant grounds for a harassment case. But I was a mom now, and my maternal role applied by extension to Leroy's friends. So instead of putting Ari crisply in his place, I described his style to my husband. Mitch shook his head and said, "No. That won't fly. Not in this house." The next time he took the boys fishing, he called Ari out on it.

"Young man's got some issues with his mouth," Mitch reported afterward. "I didn't like the way he was talkin' to the fish."

"He was rude to the fish?"

Mitch jerked an imaginary rod in imitation. "'Hey now, baby, come and suck it like a good girl!'"

"Ew."

Mitch told Ari that he needed to be more respectful. "You can call my wife Dr. Janzen," he said. Ari did, after that. But my bad feeling didn't go away.

Ari attended our church. I asked him why he wasn't performing with the other musicians during worship. There was a whole crowd up there on Sunday mornings.

He sighed deeply. "I wish I could!" A note of wistful longing suggested that this goal was impossibly distant, and therefore sad enough to write a song about.

Our church had an excellent music team. Sister Clara had a set of pipes that could make even Colin Powell shake a tailfeather. Sunday morning service involved things that would have startled the Mennonites of my childhood—sparkler pom-poms; backup crooners; choir outfits themed Bolo Turquoise or Animal Print; a banner-twirling ministry; vigorous djembe solos; and a twitchy hip-hop group who always got a standing O for shooting imaginary AR-15s. There were so many folks up on stage they always reminded me of the one-hit band Chumbawamba. "I get knocked down, I get up again!" Which, come to think of it, would have made a good Pentecostal theme song.

I was new to jiggier forms of worship, and I wasn't sure about the protocol. Couldn't an enormous cadre of performers absorb one more eager tenor? The pastor's wife ran the music ministry. Over the phone I explained that Ari had a great solo voice. Maybe she could audition this gifted young man.

A hesitation cooled the line. Obviously I had made some kind of faux pas. Perhaps newbies weren't allowed to make recommendations on behalf of their son's friends? I thought that's what moms *did*.

The director summoned her tact. "Well now," she said carefully. "The music team is already aware of Ari's gift. I agree, he has a remarkable tenor." Another pause. "But certain circumstances." Her voice trailed off. She tried again. "Ari has made some lifestyle choices that aren't compatible with the standard of moral excellence we expect from the praise and worship team."

"Oh."

"The team is responsible for the tone we set, and we expect all the psalmists to make mature decisions in their personal lives."

"Oh."

I thanked her and hung up. To me this seemed like one of those awkward shaming moments that often attach to faith communities, as if the special mission of religious folks is to make everybody else feel like crap. Repent, sinners! It had never occurred to me that a high school boy would be denied the opportunity to sing just because he copped a buzz once in a while. Or whatever. He was just a kid. What could he be doing that was so bad? Well, as I understood it, it was the job of moms to encourage. Dang it, if I could support my stepson when a football skirmish tore a gauge out of his earlobe, causing it to hang down to his shoulder like a droopy uvula, then surely I could support some sappy songwriting! I doubled down.

Alas, the more I invested, the more I disliked my son's friend. Here was a young songwriter who blew lyrics like bubbles, wobbly and nacreous. My dislike seemed a bizarre overreaction, so I reasoned that I was merely out of my element. Most of the young men I knew were older, see. My college students read Marx, Chomsky, Foucault. They would not appreciate a faded love note found in a bottle, especially when retrieved by a shirtless Lothario on a windswept shore. But of course it was unfair to compare twenty with seventeen. My students wanted to engage with critical inquiry. Ari wanted to strum my pain with his fingers.

It got so that when I heard the telltale strains wafting up the stairs, I'd go lock myself in my study. There I upped the volume on a CD of meditation music leftover from when I had cancer. This CD was titled *Pure Streams: The Soothing Natural Sounds of Water Flowing over Smooth Stones on a Journey to a Faraway Sea*. I'm not a huge fan of music that needs to journey to a faraway sea, but at least it wasn't soulfully unbuttoning its shirt. *Pure Streams* invoked a faint chemo quease, but a long journey over smooth stones was preferable to "Your lips like wine, babeeeee!"

One day Leroy approached me with an air of urgency. There is a time for all things under the sun, and this was the time for Operation Songwriter Rescue. Could Ari stay with us for a couple of months?

"What's wrong with his own home?"

Leroy shook his head significantly. "Not a good scene. Ari's mom's always nagging him to get a job."

"Well, Ari's old enough to work," I said decidedly. We mothers needed to stick together. "Don't lots of kids have part-time jobs?"

"No, you don't understand the situation." Leroy's voice grew hushed. "She wants him to get a *full-time* job!"

"How would Ari get his homework done if he had a full-time job?"

"He don't go to school no more."

"He dropped out of school?" I was trying to stay open-minded, but a teensy cloud of disapproval was darkening the horizon.

Leroy dropped the bomb. "Ari graduated five years ago."

At first I was speechless. Then I gathered my forces. "Okay, so what you're saying is, Ari is *twenty-three* years old, he lives at home, and he doesn't have a job?"

"That's why I thought it would be a good idea if we invited him to stay with us for a while. His mom just doesn't seem to respect the fact that he's an adult."

The poignant idea of the fatherless young songwriter now seemed underwhelming. Ari's strumming had been bad enough when he was seventeen. But now that he was twenty-three, the situation called for high-tech earplugs. My incoming freshmen wrote better poetry at age eighteen! They would never have penned anything as sticky as Ari's lyrics. Yes, okay, new writers might contribute the occasional poem about an ex's sweatshirt. But who among them would produce a chorus such as

> Our love will never fly!
> Summer over, babeeeee,
> Rainclouds in my sky!

One night my husband was shaving his head. It usually took him a good five minutes, so I trapped him at the sink and shared some of my many thoughts on whiny love songs.

"And where *else* would rain clouds be, for heaven's sake?" I demanded at lecture's end. "Do we really need to say that rain clouds are *in the sky*?"

Mitch thoughtfully rinsed his razor. "Why you so het up on that young man?"

"You can't possibly like those songs. Can you?"

He twiddled his hearing aids and grinned. "Don't have to." His tone suggested that the problem could be addressed with a teensy patch of toilet paper, like a nick from the razor. "Ain't no call to keep on about it."

"I *know*. That's what's so weird. I can't figure out why I dislike him so much."

"Honey, you just objectin' to the human condition. Easier to get in agreement with what you can't change."

I sat down abruptly on the toilet lid. Nothing like a tardy epiphany to round out the evening!

Instantly the clichéd lyrics and vampiric need for attention assumed a significance shared by my longing to re-create myself as a good wife, and therefore as a mom. Longing requires what T. S. Eliot called an "objective correlative," a connection between a state of experience and the thing we use to represent that experience. We can't experience desire without projecting it onto something. You could even say that *desire* is the ultimate transitive verb, because it needs a direct object like no other verb in the lexicon. In other words, we're on autopilot. Just as wisteria somehow knows what to do when it sees a pergola, we have a de facto function that trains desire to loop the objective correlative. And if the human imagination has an upward creep, it follows that we cannot thrive unless we find something for our desire to twirl around. I thought of Plato, arguing that *not having* was constitutive of desire. If you could ever possess the ____ of your dreams, you wouldn't desire it anymore, because your desire would then up and itch for something else. On the other hand, if you never possess the _____ of your dreams, you can go on experiencing the full tragic whammy of desire, like Edgar Allan Poe. It's tragic, see, because we can't fix it. It's tragic because we don't *want* to fix it.

The intended object of desire, whether Love Forever True or I Can Do This!, is less interesting than the desire itself. We'll latch onto any convenient prop in order to identify as beings whose every gesture articulates a metonymic longing. Perhaps it's because we can't face the fact that we may be longing for something larger than our own appetites, something larger even than our imaginations. We crave something huge and unseen—an inkling of Oedipal ambivalence if you're Freud, an unknowable patronymic that jump-starts all other signification if you're Lacan, a literal Creator if you're Pascal. And so we come up with an endless series of objects that concretize desire, hoping that, once we possess these objects, the longing will go away.

But desire doesn't work like that. It's not *supposed* to go away. Mick Jagger, ancient seer in leather pants, said it best: we can't get no satisfaction. We were made to long for something elemental, and to experience longing *as* elemental.

Pascal believed there was a God-shaped vacuum in every heart. Was there not also a subtext of reverence in every bad breakup song? The agon of Ari's *not having* implied the larger pain *of not knowing*. I liked this metaphor! Sure, it was flawed. In this poker hand the unattainable girlfriend was the Bitch of Hearts, the cruel cipher of absence who represented a universal truth no woman should have to represent. But didn't all serious seekers deserve some poetic license? Surely I could reframe Ari as the new poster child for doomed desire, a voice crying in the wilderness, a prophet to his generation!

Before I could limn the filiation between rain clouds and man's search for meaning, Ari was arrested for criminal sexual misconduct with a thirteen-year-old. The girl's parents discovered the relationship after a pregnancy scare. They belatedly whisked their daughter out of harm's way. Charges were pressed, statements were taken, a jumpsuit was issued.

Ari insisted he had been the one wronged. His girlfriend's parents hadn't understood the depth of his passion! And thus he achieved something like the object of his desire. He became the star-cross'd lover he had always wanted to be. Could we even believe this shit, how everybody was ganging up on him?

It was richly obvious that Ari meant his indignation and outrage. He was hurt that nobody believed in the authenticity of his vision. Before the case went before the judge, Mitch tried to move Ari to an understanding of the term *statutory rape*. But our young man, in a voice of infinite injury, could repeat only that the thirteen-year-old had truly loved him, and that she loved him still. He bowed his handsome head and shed a tear for all the unfair incursions of the world.

The judge sentenced him to six months, all of which he served in mournful denial.

Leroy left the nest six years ago, and we don't see much of Ari anymore. I caught sight of him once last summer toodling down Lakeshore in a Mercury Montego with a pizza-delivery sign on the roof. It was hot, and the Montego's windows were rolled down. Ari was singing. Even from my car I could see the tilt of his chin, the expressive eyes that couldn't help checking himself out in the rearview. I didn't hear the words. But the song would have heartache, a misty shore, and solitary footprints in the sand. It would pay homage to a beautiful unforgettable baby, a road not taken, a paradise lost. It would be tender, this song, heavy with the weight of all we cannot lift, the one melody we cannot carry.

Mardi Jo Link

SMALL-TOWN MONSTERS

MY INBOX IS BURNING.

The messages arrive day after day after day. It was dozens at first, then hundreds, and by now it must be into the thousands. The messages come from strangers who write to say they are on fire with disbelief, with horror, with rage against the injustice.

I used to wonder if I'd suffocate under the weight of their words.

I used to wonder why so many messages and why to me.

For example.

> She did not stumble, Mary S. assures me. She did not fall down the stairs and clutch at her own crushed windpipe. The jury believed that lie, but Mary S. knows different. Her father prosecuted that case; he's dead now, but Mary S. says it was the thumbs on the hands of Gee-Gee Jackson's lover that made those bruises. Oh my God but Gee-Gee must have been beautiful in that evening gown. Then Robert Bednasek had to go and kill her. And get away with it. There has to be something I can do.

There isn't.

> Joseph K. would never put me through reading all 100,000 words of his entirely factual true crime memoir if he didn't know too much to keep silent. What he wrote will definitely cause permanent destructive damage to the system. But these people have wronged him. They need to come to grips with justice before it's too late. Time is running low. He will be forced to do something rash, like upload his masterpiece to the Internet if I cannot help him.

I cannot.

Waterman is a weird first name. Maybe that's why he did it. Maybe that's why Waterman Philip Stison raped his own niece and, when he found out she was pregnant, committed her to the Reed City Sanitarium. In 1904 families did things like that to each other. Lindsey J. has no idea what happened to Waterman or to his niece, but she lives in Reed City now, so of course she wonders. I am the kind of person who can find out. I am the kind of person who can uncover the best details. And share them with her.

Am I that kind of person? Am I?

At first it was the content of the messages that felt smothering. But then it became their volume. Did this change in my perspective mean I'd become desensitized? The answer to that question bothered me. Because the answer was yes. After a decade writing about crime it was true. I was no longer disturbed by the violence one human was capable of exacting upon another human.

Did W. H. Thacker poison his wife and children before running off with that floozy? Was Michael George really the Comic Book Killer? What did a girl like Lisa Dunn see in a thug like Danny Remeta? Who could have snuck into the garden level of Gambles Department Store to beat Janette Roberson to death? Nobody should be surprised that six of Father Stanislaus Bur's sexual abuse victims committed suicide. All Jane Snow did was pull off I-75 into a Gaylord rest area, so why did she get stabbed twenty-two times? I mean, she had two kids. Did I know there was once a sniper at Lansing's Potter Park Zoo; once a Sault Ste. Marie nurse who sold human organs; once a pretty doctor's wife whose husband overdosed her to death on stolen Demerol? Well, *did* I?

I do now.

Here's the surprising thing about the messages. Reading email I didn't ask for, from people I didn't know, about crimes I'd never heard of, became useful to me. They were a diversion allowing me to avoid thinking too hard about why I write what I write. Why I spend years researching and writing about a family of six shot to death; a nun bludgeoned with a shovel; an oilfield worker dead by his own hand from drugs and the innocent men imprisoned for a murder that wasn't.

The strangers and their emails kept me from obsessing over whether my own writing was really what anyone needed.

It wasn't him—it was his roommate. Thrill-killer John Norman

Collins is doing life in Marquette State Prison, and his pen pal Kristy L. is not saying he's innocent, but he can't be guilty of *all* seven murders can he? The M.O. doesn't fit. Only *some* of those women were strangled with their own clothes. Plus, John has extremely artful penmanship. If I can spare a minute to Google Kristy L., I will see she's an executive at a reputable company for god's sake. If John Norman Collins is innocent, then a terrible wrong needs to be made right. And if I don't believe that, what *do* I believe?

I'll get to what I believe. I promise.

First, I need to tell you what I know.

I know my office is on the second floor of an old Northern Michigan house built in 1897, and the walls are a shade of pink called "blush." I know I had a large pane of beveled glass inserted into the door so that when my sons were small I could get my writing done while still being able to see what they were up to. I know no good can come from unmonitored sons. I know I am a nonfiction writer from good parents who provided me a happy childhood and paid for journalism school. I know every morning when I wake up I look forward to walking into this room and taking my seat on the vintage Steelcase desk chair a defense attorney once gave me as payment for writing services rendered.

I know it swivels.

And I know I have something inside that compels me to chronicle why people conspire against, beat up, betray, and kill each other.

Many authors get fan letters. I get case files and theories on motive and crime scene photos and forensics. I get trial transcripts and police reports and links to newspaper stories. My own father once sent me a link to a *Detroit Free Press* article about a triple homicide in the Upper Peninsula, saying, "Ran across this online. No one we know but think you might find it interesting." I clicked on the light-blue underline because I am nothing if not a dutiful daughter but also because I cannot *not* click.

The article said that Heather, Jody, and Carrie were killed by Kenneth, Garry, and Marietta. Strangulation, then dragging, then an Oldsmobile Bravada with legroom, then two ten-gallon cans of gasoline and some road flares, lit with a Duck Commander cigarette lighter, resulting in a roadside bonfire within sight of the Hiawatha National Forest.

A place my family and I camped once when my brother and I were kids.

My father is right. I do find the article interesting. Frightening, infuriating, pointless, and sad, but also interesting. After years of writing about crime I have become a relentless researcher, a patient interviewer, a meticulous builder of narrative arcs that seek to apply logic to the illogical. I used to think that was why strangers turned my email inbox into a bonfire of the violence Michiganders inflict upon one another.

Now I know that is not why.

Now I know that people reach out to me only when the entity responsible for providing them justice or a simple acknowledgment of their existence shirks their duty.

For the longest time I did not understand that.

Then, something happened. To someone in my family.

And like the crimes in my books, and like the crimes strangers email me about, the crime against my family member had a discovery phase, a backstory, a main narrative, and an ending.

The discovery.

August 2016. A workday afternoon and my landline rings.

By the pause and the now-familiar echoing hiss, I know my mother and my father are on speakerphone. My parents and I talk on the phone all the time, but not like this. This is premeditation. A sign of bad news. My father doesn't say anything, because he has a progressive lung disease and it is hard for him to talk. Even about our family. So it is my mother who does the talking. About someone else in our family.

"They beat him up. And it's pretty bad."

The backstory.

May 2008. One of those optimistic spring evenings known to rescue Michigan from its annual wintertime brutalization. My family member, let's call him Roy L., was buying. I know this only from witness statements and not firsthand. I want to admit right up front that I wasn't there. I wasn't with Roy L. at that cabin, at that party. My parents and much of my extended family still live in the cluster of midsize industrial towns in southeastern Michigan where I grew up. Not me. I got out. I live in the pine-needle-and-sandy-shore postcard that is the pristine, mostly safe, carefree northwestern part of the Lower Peninsula.

So to be clear, I wasn't at that party with Roy L. when, you know, he really could have used me.

Anyway. A couple cases of beer? Sure. A fifth of this, a fifth of that, plus your favorite mixer? No problem. If Roy had cash, then my witty, easy-going, lackadaisical, and outdoorsy relative had friends. Several hours of focused drinking later, Roy L. was coherent enough to fasten a helmet on his head, get himself upright on his new ATV, turn the key, gun the engine, grin at his friends, and squeeze the throttle.

Roy L. was fun like that.

And the ride? Oh dude. It would have been epic.

Except that the helmet was a "brain bucket" no more durable than a party hat. Except that the quad was fuel injected, with tires that ground into the gravel when Roy turned too sharp. Except that the brakes didn't work. Except that his friends, the people he bought all that beer and all that Crown Royal for, well, after my relative survived the accident, after he survived the ambulance ride to the hospital and the helicopter ride to another hospital, after he made it through six hours of cranial surgery, four days in a medically induced coma, and three weeks in a rehabilitation center, after his broken jaw and his broken ribs and his broken eye socket, after Roy L. had to abandon the use of his right eye and put duct tape on the right lens of his glasses because of the double vision, after speech therapy and cognitive therapy and physical therapy and occupational therapy, after being diagnosed with traumatic brain injury with pseudo-bulbar affect, causing daily episodes of uncontrollable weeping, after his medical bills absorbed his net worth and then some, after Medicaid and Supplemental Security Income and food stamps, and—well, after all that, his friends walked away. Didn't even visit him in the hospital. Not once.

Main narrative.

June 2016. We'll move Roy L.'s life forward in time eight years from the day of his accident.

The long-term diagnosis by the neurosurgeon and the neuropsychologist and the family physician and my extended family and me was that the accident killed the part of my relative's brain that housed his alcoholism. He hasn't had a drink since it happened.

Equally clear was that the accident had not killed the part of his brain that was both friendly and responsible for making poor choices. So he took to engaging with any living being who would spare him a minute of their attention. Sometimes this was the happy woman who lived across the street or the understanding man who delivered his mail. But Roy L. was on disability, and because his income was small but his desire for independence large he lived in marginal trailer parks or stayed with marginal acquaintances or lived in a camper in a campground. So more often the beings who could spare him a minute were parolees, drug dealers, aging bikers, hoarders, high school truants, drunks, stoners, and junkies.

Partly because of the brain injury, and partly because that is just who he is, Roy L. is trusting, gullible, and impulsive. Solely because of the brain injury, he cannot work, he cannot drive a car, he cannot remember complex sequences, and he has no depth perception or sustained attention span. He is witty. He is kind. He can cook his own meals and make hot chocolate. He can fish. He can take care of his dog. He can take care of his lawn. His goal in life was to live independently and fish for walleye, so my family bought Roy L. a foreclosed house on a double lot in an industrialized town across the street from the Saginaw River.

My mother painted the walls and planted flowers and sewed him curtains. My father installed gutters and fixed the heating system and fenced in his backyard. I visited (in between my very important writing deadlines and my very important author events), called him on his free government cell phone for the disabled, and sometimes sent him money.

He tried to adjust. He'd ride his bicycle to the community center to work out, or to go to the corner store for groceries, or to refill his prescriptions, or just for fun. He outfitted his lawn tractor with a custom trailer hitch he made himself, so he could tow his rowboat across the street to the boat launch and fish for walleye. After all the surgeries and all the therapy and all the medication trials and all the help from my family, it seemed like Roy L. had learned to live on his own.

And then he met a nineteen-year-old lapse in God's everlasting wisdom named Roger W.

An aside.

Journalism is all about rules. Such as, a story is only as good as your sources. Verification before dissemination, always. And give everyone the opportunity to comment. Usually, journalism's rules and my rules are one and the same, but not this time. This time is different. I'm not being objective, I'm being subjective, and so I'm not using the last names of strangers who've written me about crime because they never asked to be reduced to a metaphor. I'm not using the real name of my relative, because he would call the use of his suffering for my in-print edification a bad trade. Normally, I would use the real names of feckless public officials and heartless police officers with glee and self-congratulation, but in this tale their role is meaningless. Plus, their names would be a clue to my relative's identity, and a chance for trouble to find him anew.

Returning to the narrative.

Police Sergeant Nathan W. says he is glad I called to tell him about my relative's brain injury. Because that really explains some things.

"I just could not understand why he kept letting that small-town monster get under his skin," the sergeant tells me over the phone.

A common side effect of a traumatic brain injury is a loss of impulse control, I explain to Sergeant W. So when Roger W. and his associates ride by Roy L.'s house on their bikes and taunt him, or make jokes about his disabilities, or threaten to harm him, it is going to be difficult if not impossible for Roy L. to ignore them.

Sergeant W.: "Huh."

Roy L. is not some derelict looking to cause problems for police, I add. Roy L. is a homeowner, a citizen, a high school graduate, a former electrician, a father and a grandfather who is loved by his family. He is a middle-aged, mentally and physically handicapped man who just wants to drink hot chocolate, fish for walleye, take his dog for walks, and mow his lawn. There must be something the police can do to help keep him safe.

"There is," Sergeant W. says. "Tell him to call 911."

"He's been doing that. I'm sure if you look at your records, you'll see that he's called several times, and always about Roger W. By the time you send a car, Roger is gone. When officers go to Roger's house, he tells them my relative is just a crazy old man. My concern is that this is going to escalate."

Sgt. W.: "Well, it's his word against Roger's."

Another aside.

My conversation with Sergeant W. took place in August 2016, four days before my parents made their speakerphone telephone call to me. The one telling me my relative had been beaten up. One relevant detail you will not find in any of the police reports: the beating took place on the eve of my parents' sixtieth wedding anniversary.

Returning again to the narrative.

I wish my parents a happy anniversary, hang up the phone, and drive the 157 miles from my house in the northwestern part of the state to Roy L.'s house in the southeast. He opens his front door. I look at his face and begin to cry. This weeping comes on so suddenly I am reminded of something Roy L. now experiences daily. Called "flooding" by brain experts, people with brain injuries often cry or laugh inappropriately. For Roy L. it is almost never laugh, it is almost always cry.

And yet as often as Roy L. cries, he is made uncomfortable by the crying of others. "It's okay," he tells me in a soothing tone. "There were four of them. So they could've got me way worse."

Stay with me through this next part because Roy L.'s recounting of what happened during the assault comes out in a jumble. That is how brain injuries work. That is how violence works, too.

Roy L. had been riding his bike to the store when he heard someone call his name. He stopped, thinking the voice might have come from the owner of the lost and blind Boston terrier he'd found the week before and returned to its owner. But it wasn't the terrier's owner, it was Roger W. He and his younger brother and two other people punched Roy L. in the face, pulled him off his bike, punched him in the face again, broke his duct-taped glasses, threw his shoes into the bushes, and then stood in a circle and kicked him as he curled up in the fetal position in the middle of the street in the middle of the day.

No one came out of their houses or stopped and got out of their cars to help. Roy L. called 911 just like Sgt. W. instructed, and the police came and made a report and took pictures of my relative's face with the cameras attached to their uniforms.

Only after I stop crying does Roy L. mention to me that he has options.

If he wants to have Roger W. prosecuted, there is paperwork for that, and he has to go to the police station and fill it out. I drive him. On the way I study his injuries. My relative's good eye is almost swollen shut, and his jaw, surgically repaired after the ATV accident, is twice its normal size. His cheeks look like raw hamburger. His lip is split open and oozing blood, his eyebrow is cut but starting to scab over, and I can tell his ribs hurt from how tenderly he sits in the passenger seat of my car. By the way his hands shake, I can also tell he is afraid.

It is a colossal inconvenience for the woman behind the bulletproof glass at the police station to stand upright and become bipedal, but after several minutes and a herculean effort that involves a great expelling of air, she manages it. Just. I open my mouth to let out the rage that needs a little oxygen to burn us all, but before I can say anything my relative puts his cool hand on my forearm. He says with miraculous calm that he wants to handle this himself.

So I step back and he steps forward and talks loudly but politely toward the window so the woman will be able to hear him through the glass.

"Roger," he says. "Boston terrier," he says. "Bicycle, glasses, shoes," he says, trying to explain the inexplicable.

The woman has heard all of this before from other people with black eyes and bloody faces, and when Roy L. finishes talking she says nothing in response, but sighs in a way that makes it clear she alone is keeping the earth and all its human detritus in orbit. Then she deposits a clipboard into the narrow slot under the service window. Roy L. fills in the blanks on the paperwork as best he can. His handwriting is nearly illegible.

My smoldering rage and I are sitting silent and trying very hard not to engulf this center of supposed law enforcement. I succeed at this but only by writing elaborate email messages in my mind. I will send them to the mayor, I vow. I will send them to the governor and to the president. Beside me, my beloved relative is trying very hard to do something, too. He is trying not to cry in this public place. He also succeeds. Ours are two very small victories in this otherwise defeated day.

I drive him home.

On the way I ask him to show me where Roger W. lives.

Initially, Roy L. says no. He is both afraid that Roger W. will see us and afraid of what I will do if he does. I remind my relative that Roger W. does not know my car, and I promise him that if we see Roger W. I will drive right on by. I will not get out of my car. I will not destroy my new manicure on Roger W.'s face, and I will not ruin the heels of my best boots on Roger W.'s ass. I will not. I promise.

My relative snickers at this. When he was in fourth grade and I was in sixth grade, a boy in my grade harassed my relative on the school bus. This went on for several weeks without relief from any adult until one day, when school had let out and everyone on our route was lined up to go home, I cut in line behind the boy in my class. When he and I were both on the steps to enter the bus, I grabbed the back of that boy's coat and pulled. Hard enough to make him fall past me and down the bus's steps, backward and onto the sidewalk.

Maybe Roy L. is snickering at this same memory. Or maybe he no longer has this memory because it was killed in the same accident that took away his alcoholism and damaged his brain. Either way, Roy L. directs me to Roger W.'s house. It looks abandoned. Broken windows, a falling-down porch, dirt for a lawn. I do not see any of the W. family, but I do see the rusty numbers nailed to the rotting trim by the side of the pathetic front door.

Back at my relative's house, I take a notebook and pen out of my purse. I ask Roy L. several questions about the attack as if I am interviewing him for one of my books. I hug him, he cries, I cry, but eventually I leave.

To return to the police station.

Once inside I stride toward the window and my eyes shoot two glowing red holes through the bulletproof glass until the woman makes eye contact and asks me what I want.

I want justice for my relative.

I want Roger W. arrested.

I want his mother, Stacey W., and his father, Daniel W., to be held criminally responsible for not monitoring their sons.

I want to build a time machine and travel to May 2008 and go to that party at that cabin and take away those ATV keys from my relative and tell those losers to buy their own booze.

"I was just here with my relative," I say to the woman, like the sane person I still am, barely. "I have additional information to add to his paperwork."

"You are not the victim. So you can't add anything," she replies.

Her monotone is either intentional or caused by the thick glass. I choose the former, and my blood becomes mercury in hell's thermometer. I am ready to do battle with this woman right here and right now. My skin feels singed and my brain is on fire, and so I am wholly unprepared for the thought that boils up next:

This must be how strangers feel right before they send me an email.

The idea is so surprising, it snuffs all the heat and all the flames, and I feel my composure return.

"You can either add this information to his paperwork or you can go get your supervisor," I tell the woman behind the glass, and my voice is like ice.

The woman puts the clipboard through the slot. I take the piece of paper out of my purse, clip it to the clipboard, and send it back through. On it is Roger W.'s name and his address, a detailed description of what he did to my relative and when, along with information about my relative's head injury. I sign it and add my address and my phone numbers.

I stay and watch to make sure the woman adds the paper to Roy L.'s file. It takes her thirty-six minutes to accomplish this. And for the first time in my professional life I am tempted to ask the most arrogant, self-important, and egotistical question there is:

Do you know who I am?

But in this room I am not a relentless researcher. I am not a *New York Times* bestselling author, not a multiple award-winning writer, not a true crime narrator for the Investigation Discovery channel, not the woman who named the killers, caused corrupt people to be fired, and exonerated the innocent, and I am definitely not someone strangers email by the thousands to seek justice.

In this room I am the relative of an assault victim.

Meaning, I am nothing.

And if I feel this helpless, think how helpless Roy L. must feel.

I walk out of the building and get in my car and shut the door and stare at the impenetrable wall of the police station and wonder if cement block would burn. And then I scream as loud as I can for as long as I can.

Is this illegal?

Is screaming inside your own car in a police station parking lot a crime?

I should know the answer to that. I don't. I hope it *is* a crime. And I hope they send an officer out here right now.

I *dare them* to send an officer.

But of course no one comes, and of course I get ahold of myself, and of course I eventually manage to exhale. I take a breath, and then I take another, and it is then that I know.

I was wrong a few minutes before when I thought I knew how all my emailers feel inside.

Because this right here?

This is how they feel.

The ending.

Oh, how I wish this story really had ended here. With Roy L.'s paperwork safely entered into the justice system. With it being just a matter of time before Roger W. got what was coming to him. With me feeling compassion and love and the urge to obtain justice for my relative, but also having a true understanding for my emailers.

But I promised to tell you what I believe, so I better get to it.

According to the Social Security Administration, after he was acquitted for murder, Robert Bednasek was drafted and survived his service in the Pacific theater during World War II. But for reasons not made public, his disability claim was denied. I believe Gee-Gee Jackson knew there was something hinky about Robert Bednasek. I believe she paid attention to these instincts and tried to end the relationship. And I believe Robert Bednasek killed Gee-Gee rather than lose her, that Robert's parents loved him regardless, and that they hired a skilled lawyer.

I believe that Waterman Philip Stison's conviction of ten years in Jackson Prison for incest was excessively lenient. Hospital records state his niece died of postnatal convulsions due to uterine poisoning three days after giving birth to her baby son, who also died. I believe Waterman deserved to spend the rest of his life in prison, instead of enjoying decades of freedom before dying in 1939 and being laid to rest in a cemetery where his wife, Sarah, who died in 1950, would be buried next to him. At least she had eleven years Waterman-free.

I believe John Norman Collins was the co-ed killer and murdered at least six of the seven victims attributed to him. There is a DNA snafu on the seventh, but he could have killed her, too. And I believe that any woman who corresponds with a convicted serial killer needs to do some serious work on her priorities, or on her self-esteem, or both.

I believe Joseph K. and Roy L. were wronged. By everyone. Because here's the real ending. The ending I don't want. The ending probably nobody wants except maybe the devil and Roger W., who to me are one and the same.

My relative's paperwork successfully made its way to the desk of Assistant Prosecutor Margaret A. She decided not to prosecute Roger W., or the three minors, for beating up my relative. She also declined to meet with me to discuss her decision, but said through an intermediary (the prosecutor's "victim's advocate") that she did not believe she could prove the assault in court.

Following Margaret A.'s decision not to prosecute, Roger W. stood in the street in front of my relative's house and sprayed mace at him, rode by my relative's house on the back of his girlfriend's scooter and yelled that he was going to kill my relative, rode by my relative's house on his bike and threw rocks at my relative, and then threatened to kill other members of my relative's extended family. Meaning, I surmise, me.

My relative called 911 after each of these incidents, the police would send a car, send a car, send a car, but by the time officers arrived Roger W. was always long gone.

Recently my parents dialed my landline again. Speakerphone, again. This time it was to inform me that my relative was in jail. My mother explained that Roy L. had learned Roger W.'s phone number, called him, left a message on Roger W.'s answering machine describing what he would do to Roger W. if Roger W. did not leave him alone. Roger W. played the message for the police, the police sent a car to my relative's house, and officers arrested my relative on a charge of using a telephone to make threats.

Since the arrest, I've developed insomnia. When I do sleep, it is to dream of methods of getting justice for my relative. I will crush Roger W.'s windpipe with my thumbs while wearing an evening gown. I will make a citizen's arrest and put Roger W. in a cell with John Norman Collins. I will commit Roger W. to an insane asylum where the doctors will test the drugs they are developing to cure traumatic brain injury. If Roger W.

asks for a spiritual advisor, I will assign him Father Stanislaus Bur. If Roger W. asks for a painkiller, I will prescribe an overdose of stolen Demerol. If Roger W. sends me an email, I will forward his email address to thousands of strangers I just happen to know are on fire with injustice.

Time is running low. If the police do not help my relative, if the assistant prosecutor does not help my relative, if the judge sentences my relative to jail instead of sending Roger W. there, I will be forced to do something rash.

Like send Roger W. an actual letter with an actual invitation to visit me at my actual address.

Or, I could just publish this essay.

Davy Rothbart

AT THE INN

ON A DARE, BONNIE AND I SPENT A NIGHT AT THE ABAN-
doned motel way out Jackson Road. At first it was fun. We lit candles and
traded scary stories. We shined flashlights up from our chins and moaned
ghost sounds. On a bare mattress in one of the dark, wrecked rooms we
made love. Afterward, we lay in silence for a time, our bodies wrapped
close. Then Bonnie said, softly and a little afraid, "Do you hear it?"

I heard nothing. But the fear in her voice blazed shivers down my back.
Bonnie's heart thumped faster against me, and I felt mine clamor in response. A minute crawled by. "I don't hear anything," I said, and half a
beat later there was a sudden female cry out in the courtyard just beyond
our door. Bonnie gasped and lunged up so she was sitting. We waited for
another sound, but there was nothing. The night shifted, and it got cold,
and we both began to get scared for real.

"I'll go and see," I said at last. I tried to act like everything was cool,
but I was light-headed and teary with fear. Out in the courtyard, the black
open doorways of fifty empty rooms stared at me like pirate eyes. In the
center, an old tin slide glowed with moonlight beside a murky half-filled
swimming pool layered with dead leaves.

Alone and crying softly at the edge of the pool sat a young girl, maybe
eleven years old, in a white T-shirt and jeans. She was clearly a girl and
not a ghost, and that spooked me more than anything. I took one step forward. At the gentle sound of my foot on the grass, the girl looked up, saw
me there, and jumped up and dashed off rabbitlike across the courtyard;
all the way down at the far end she slipped through a tear in the fence and
disappeared. I stood out there for an hour, watched and watching. Big rigs
on I-94 howled whale songs into the sad and haunted night.

Rochelle Riley

CAN'T HELP LOVIN' DAT WINTER OF MINE

WE HAVE A HISTORY AROUND THE GLOBE OF DALLIANCES with evil: countries with evil leaders, women with evil men. We cannot resist the seduction of the dangerous, the hurtful, that which floors us yet makes us come back for more.

For me, my poison of choice is Michigan Winter. Our first date left me in tears. I had never experienced anything so brutal, so uncaring of my feelings. He tore into my skin, scarred my feet, and ended my lifelong love of vanilla snow cream.

He was relentless in his pursuit, wooing me with beautiful white fluff that hid until I ran into his arms his theft of all the degrees outside. I remember hearing in my first weeks in his arms that he had other women—and men!—in places Up North and in the Upper Peninsula, places that sounded like underground clubs where things went on you couldn't tell your mother about. How could they endure more than I? Was he that good?

I heard stories of his past exploits, how he'd stolen even more degrees from the temperature in years past, how he'd brought snow that would reach my thighs, storms that killed people. I read about the White Hurricane of 1913 that came in November, if you can believe it, and brought sustained winds across lower Michigan as high as sixty miles per hour, the speed limit on the Lodge (for those of us who speed). News reports detailed how ships still sailed the Great Lakes during that storm, and 235 sailors died on ships that sank in Lake Huron that season.

There were blizzards in 1967 (news eclipsed by the Detroit riots, which for many were the only thing that happened that year, and underwhelming because Detroit got only four inches of snow, so it was more news than reality) and 1978 and 1999.

I learned of the people Michigan Winter killed because their belief that they were stronger was misplaced. I prayed for the people who cannot escape him, stuck in a city and state that imprisons them for months in their homes.

I prayed for myself—someone who could escape him, but has not. He has bruised and beaten me at every turn and everything in me has said, "Run!"

For sixteen years, sixteen seasons, sixteen horrific encounters: "Run!"

And I have not been able to because I am a sucker.

I am not a sucker for Michigan Winter.

I am a sucker for Detroit.

She is more powerful than Michigan Winter. She is more powerful than the call to cities with beaches and year-round sun. She, in the hundreds of years since her birth, has saved the world, provided sanctuary for slaves, built a home for much of the black middle class, showed that grit and determination are attractive, that women look good in gray and black, that working with your hands, that building something lasting is the greatest evidence of the American spirit.

Detroit is my sister. She has taught me about cars, even more than my grandfather, the patriarch of a Ford family in a small North Carolina town who insisted that I learn to change tires and change oil.

She taught me, in person, about the Industrial Revolution and what blue-collar work looks like up close with millions participating.

She taught me how far people are willing to fall into government corruption and what heroes who defy the temptation look like.

She taught me that three decades of American music, the Sound of Young America, were conceived in a little house on a boulevard, seminated by a man with an eight-hundred-dollar loan and a dream. And that man, Berry Gordy, created iconic couplings that would change the way America sang and danced.

She taught me the importance of water and what it's like to live within a day's drive of the largest surface freshwater system on earth. I never knew a moment like standing on the banks of Lake Superior and realizing that it was real, and not a dream. And I never would have known that moment had I not been a sucker for Detroit and stayed sixteen years longer than I was supposed to when I arrived eighteen years ago.

Detroit is my sister, and our lives became intertwined. Our fortunes have risen and fallen together. Telling her story has given me breath and hope.

So I forgive Detroit for using Michigan Winter to gaslight me, for making me feel like I'm not strong enough or courageous enough or appreciative enough when the snow comes and making me see lovely fluff and brilliantly created snowmen and yummy snow cream instead of the pain and discomfort and days and days of wearing everything I own to fend off the torturous chill. I forgive Detroit for making you believe there are degrees outside . . .

. . . when there are no degrees outside.

And you brave it anyway. You endure it anyway—because to continue your sisterhood with your beloved Detroit, you have to accept her brother, her heinous, unfeeling, jiving, conniving, in-cahoots-with-lying-meteorologists-who-convince-you-it's-not-that-bad brother, Michigan Winter.

And you learn to love him like you love any evil man, with the hope that some days will be better than others, and with the knowledge that he will go away. You don't even think about, admit, acknowledge that he always comes back . . . like a lover whose job takes him away for months at a time . . .

You just appreciate the peace.

You just appreciate that he's gone. And you spend months convincing yourself that before he returns, you will gather your strength, you will be prepared, you will become the lioness in winter. You will defeat him. . . .

But he arrives . . . and hope is lost. You pile on the sweaters and coats and boots and prepare for the beating that you endure for your sister.

. . . because you cannot leave her.

Airea D. Matthews

ANIMALIA REPEATING

A PAVLOVIAN ACCOUNT IN PARTS

"Learning will occur if what happens on trial does not match the expectation of the organism."

—*RESCORLA-WAGNER*

News of the George Zimmerman verdict broke while I was visiting my family in New Jersey. As jurors confirmed their not guilty verdicts, my mother murmured, "Bad history repeats." My oldest son sank his head into his hands. My middle son rose from the sofa, adjusted his jersey, and went to the restroom. After about fifteen minutes, I knocked on the bathroom door, only to find him crying on the floor. I kneeled down, sat with him under the sink, and held his hand in mine, careful to guide his head under my chin. His forehead was damp with stray tears. As his slender body gradually calmed, he wondered aloud, "Why do *they* hate me?" I suggested there was no *"they."* There was only fear and spit and tuning forks and hungry dogs and playful rats and people who were trying against all they've been taught to live with other people who were trying against all they've been taught to live . . . we fell asleep on the cold tile that night, lulled by our own racing and circular thoughts.

"The expectation on any given trial is based on the predictive value of all of the stimuli present."

—*RESCORLA-WAGNER*

Before walking to a newly built shopping center in Detroit, I overheard my sons: "We have to be careful. Make sure you take off your hat before we go inside the store. Don't put your hands in your pockets. Hold your arms at your sides where people can see them. Look everybody in the eye.

Pull up your pants. Smile. Smile wide." I wanted to interrupt and tell them they could safely and comfortably move through the world how they'd like. I stopped myself, midgesture, and instead added, "Please come home before dinner."

> *"Extinction refers to the gradual weakening of a conditioned response and results in the behavior decreasing or disappearing."*
> —*RESCORLA-WAGNER*

I genuflected at Mass, stealing fleeting glances of my sons' hands in prayer—tender, unburdened by veins or violence, unscathed. I redirected my attention, prayed whoever feared their black bodies would soon unlearn myth and space and threat. Hopeful, in the meantime, as every lukewarm Catholic tends, that God will keep his children free from danger. Until, of course, the priest's strange homily reminded me of Divinity's less-than-stellar record: "God's own son suffered and died. Let us pray."

> *"In Pavlovian trials, when the bell was presented repeatedly without the presentation of food, the salivation response eventually became extinct."*
> —*RESCORLA-WAGNER*

In *The Love of God and Affliction*, Simone Weil, famous ascetic philosopher, posited: "Affliction causes God to be absent for a time, more absent than a dead man, more absent than light in utter darkness." Her words looped as a skipping reel in my mind on the drive from church. I was nearly convinced until I read: "During this absence there is nothing to love."

My children laughed in the backseat. It was a sweet laughter, divine, even. They were not nothing.

> *"When a conditioned emotional response has been established for one object, is there a transfer?"*
> —*JOHN B. WATSON*

In line at a suburban Target, two sisters stood in front of my son and me discussing their brother's recent misfortune. He stopped his convertible in some Detroit neighborhood after a late-night tire blowout. As best as I could hear, their brother was assaulted and robbed while waiting for a tow. One sister remarked, "I miss Dad's Detroit." I didn't want to know what that meant. I knew what that meant.

Oblivious to the conversation, when my son reached to grab the conveyor belt divider, careful to excuse himself, the sister closest to him jumped in fear and pulled her wallet to her chest. The other sister comforted: "Move up here, _____. Closer to me. Away."

"*The consequences of behavior determine the probability that the behavior will occur again.*"

—B. F. SKINNER

We woke up from the bathroom floor in the middle of that July night, stiff and uncomfortable. My son, eyelids red and swollen as when he was an infant, mumbled something akin to "Thanks, Mom." Before washing his face at the sink and feeling his way through the stock-still darkness toward his bed, he turned to me:

"Mom, do you think what happened to Trayvon could happen again?"

I searched for a way to shatter my cynicism and basic knowledge of how the human animal operates. I thought about dogs and tuning forks, mice and levers, babies and white rats, and delivered what I believed truth: "Son, his murderer was acquitted, which all but guarantees it will absolutely happen again."

He nodded. We parted ways in the hallway. I promised bacon in the morning.

"*I may say that the only differences I expect to see revealed between the behavior of the rat and man (aside from enormous differences of complexity) lie in the field of verbal behavior.*"

—B. F. SKINNER

Another summer and another brown body with smoke rising. This time his name is Michael. My sons are in New Jersey with family, and I am in Michigan. My phone rings.

"Mom, did you see the news?"

"Yes, Son. Very sad. How are you coping?"

"I'm okay. I think I'm feeling numb or maybe nothing. Is that normal?"

"Sure, I'd call that a conditioned response, or a survival strategy. Living is hard and still very beautiful, you know? It's complex."

"I read that Pavlov thing you gave me last year. How do you think the dogs felt?"

"Hungry, confused, terrified, controlled, alive. But every single time, I think those animals still felt something. That's important, you know what I mean?"

"Yeah."

"Yeah."

Fanon, Diasporic Haints, and the Case of Heightened Sensitivity

> *"I came into the world imbued with the will to find a meaning in things . . ."*

Hump days are difficult—situated smack dab in the middle, doubly pressured by the beginning and the end. Perhaps Wednesdays are the dualist's weekday. For reasons beyond my immediate comprehension, strange, existential things that demand inquiry seem to happen on Wednesdays—at least as far as I am concerned.

> *". . . my spirit filled with the desire to attain to the source of the world . . ."*

Last Wednesday was a particularly odd and long day. I'd finished office hours when my former student and friend Haya dropped by to discuss Frantz Fanon's *Black Skin, White Masks* from her postcolonial lit class. Admittedly, I knew embarrassingly little about Fanon and postcolonial literature. But, fortunately for me, Haya has always been more of a teacher than a student. Rapt by her synopsis of his work, I lost track of time as the clock ticked closer to four p.m. Per my tendency, I remembered, at the last minute, my plans with another friend. I invited Haya to join me. Per her tendency, she agreed. Running late, I grabbed my two heavy-laden teaching bags and locked my office. We began the short walk to my car, descanting on the virtues of Fanon's chapter titled "The Fact of Blackness."

". . . and then I found I was an object in the midst of other objects."

We stepped off the curb and noticed a woman, several years past middle age, barreling down Ann Arbor's Maynard Street in a Jeep Grand Cherokee. She slammed her brakes and came to an abrupt stop about five feet from the crosswalk. Visibly perturbed that our crossing had interrupted her speeding, she honked, flailed her arms, and hurled threatening words from the safety of blue steel encasement. To heighten menace, she gradually released her brake in an intentional effort to inch closer to our bodies, as if trying to shoo deer from an intersection. As soon as my heel clicked against the asphalt's median, my left foot less than a centimeter from her tire, she sped away. I yelled in her flight's direction, "You saw us! We're not invisible!"

"Just as I reached the other side, I stumbled, and the movements, the attitudes, the glances of the other fixed me there."

Haya was quiet when we stepped onto the opposite curb. I was still fuming when a much older man balanced by a cane, a witness to the scene, approached us. He looked us up and down, paused, then offered, "We don't yell in Ann Arbor." Haya respectfully asked him to repeat himself because he spoke as a man whispering confessions. He repeated, again, barely above a whisper, "We don't yell in Ann Arbor." Even though I heard him the second time, I asked him to repeat himself once more because I wanted him to hear himself—not that it mattered. He said it again. Haya looked at me with widened eyes as she adjusted her hijab. I countered him before turning away toward the garage elevator, "Congratulations, *you* don't yell! *We* aren't you! Thank God for small mercies."

Then, as now, I don't know if he responded.

"I was told to stay within bounds, to go back where I belonged."

We sat in my car for a short while before I turned the ignition. We needed to gather ourselves, to make some dumb sense of what had just happened. We needed a moment, or a long lifetime, to consider why people act and/or talk without thinking—the privilege of being able to do so.

"Haya, I'm sorry you saw me lose my temper. I suppose the older woman using her car as a weapon wasn't the thing that bothered me most.

It was the older man who thought it was okay to admonish the wrong people—as if my protective response of yelling at a threatening woman was an inappropriate one."

"Yes, totally understandable. But, Dee, did you notice how he looked at my hijab and our brown skin and assumed we weren't from Ann Arbor?"

"I did. We're not. But I agree, how would he know that? And would he have scolded a white woman? And would he have made that assumption of a white man?"

I felt my voice grow hoarse like I'd been shouting down ghosts in a tunnel. A familiar rage crept up the back of my neck; my throat was slowly closing. I turned the ignition, backed out, paid, and exited.

> *"Everything is anticipated, thought out, demonstrated, made the most of. My trembling hands take hold of nothing; the vein has been mined out."*

We ordered tapas at the restaurant while I recounted the event to my friend Derrick. He listened with the sympathetic attention of a fellow sojourner who knew the burden of parsing other people's complicated motivations. He nodded and low sighed. There was nothing new to add. This was nothing new.

> *"From time to time I would like to stop. To state reality is a wearing task. But, when one has taken it into one's head to try to express existence, one runs the risk of finding only the non-existent."*

"It's possible I overreacted," I offered as I dug through my purse trying to find a lozenge for my sore throat. "It's just tiring. It's like walking through life as a ghost and banging pots to let people know you're still here— fighting nothingness, fighting stale air."

Haya posited, "Or maybe, it's what Fanon wrote: 'straddling nothingness and infinity.' Maybe the struggle will always be dual—battling invisibility and hypervisibility."

"Battling being a ghost and a giant."

Ari L. Mokdad

BODY STUDIES

ARABETS

Inspired by Maggie Nelson

1. Suppose I were to begin by saying that my family immigrated to the United States. Say I am an Arab American woman and I am enjoying the luxury of being a first-generation American—all these white luxuries:

    a. Bliss: a white privilege that allows one to ignore the "others."

    b. Tolerance: the ability for the "others" to be around. Allowing the "others" to simultaneously cohabitate and occupy the same space with the white, privileged class.

    c. Normalization: the cohabit for any white person to naturally be recognized by any person, to have power in a class society. To be automatically able to "fit in" to the mass, white, normative culture.

    d. Privilege: not being able to recognize the advantages that being white grants in modern-day society. The invisibility of the struggle to be white.

2. But I am not white. I am Arab American. I hesitate to check the little white box next to "white" on job applications, census information, and on the school entrance questionnaire. It sometimes gives me an advantage. But my skin is tan, my features are dark, I am not truly white. There is no Middle Eastern option; no *I don't assimilate as white* option. I'll often check the box next to "other."

3. My features don't immediately scream *Arab*. I'm often confused for Mexican, Italian, Brazilian, Argentinian, and Greek. It's a strange,

purgatorial feeling: I belong in the world of whiteness, but I am not assimilated.

4. It's not you, it's me, and it's complicated, too.

   a. My father's family immigrated from Lebanon.

   b. My mother's family immigrated from France.

   c. My mom is white.

   d. My father is dark.

   e. I am both and neither of these things.

5. Yet I feel safer as a white female American. It's dangerous to be an Arab American. Just recently, in Ann Arbor, someone threatened to set a woman wearing a hijab on fire. A man, white, ordered her to take off her scarf.

6. Later, this was debunked. But there is still something to be said when an Arab woman feels so threatened she exaggerates a story. What is truly sad, though, is that so many people have used this *one* untrue event to discount other, real, true happenings.

7. Here's what is true: There were more anti-Muslim and anti-Arab crimes last year than in any other year since 2001. According to a report written by the Center for the Study of Hate and Extremism at California State University, San Bernardino, there were about 260 hate crimes in 2015. The report concludes that Arabs, Muslims, and transgender people all witnessed a rise in hate crimes. In 2016, there have already been even more recorded, although the official number has not been released, yet. In Michigan alone, there has been a 50 percent increase in Arabic hate crimes reported since the election.

8. Even though the woman's story was false, the Arab American community has been shaken. Muslim families beg their women not to wear their hijabs, just in case.

9. *No one wants to bury their daughter. Their son. Their mother or father.*

10. Do I speak to my family in Arabic when we are out to eat, or is

English a safer alternative? Do I remove the Arabic protection stone that hangs around my neck like a talisman?

11. I'm exhausted. I don't want to explain my culture to someone who believes that all Arabs are terrorists. Or that I know how to stop ISIS; or that I am the one who caused 9/11; or that I knew where Osama was hiding.

   a. Seriously. These were all real questions.

12. But mostly, I am disappointed. How did we get here?

13. *Here . . .*

14. November 9, 2016: I am confronted by a man wearing a Confederate flag around his neck like a cape. He asks me: "*How does it feel now that Mr. Trump is President? I hope you enjoyed your time here because you are going back to where you came from!*"

15. Where am I going? According to this man, hell. With the gays and blacks, too.

16. *I wish I could trade his words for a bath full of acid to eat my flesh away.* My skin has melted. There are no nerves to feel, no reaction to make. Just a numbness that makes my bones shiver.

17. His words have lingered around *my* neck like a tightly knit shadow.

18. Where do I come from? My family hails from all over the world: some of us are Muslim (although very few), some are Christian, some have abandoned religion a long time ago. We are French, Icelandic, German, Lebanese, and Irish, we are gay and straight and we speak many tongues. Our family dinners look like a United Nations meeting.

19. My grandmother leaves packages of her homemade, delicious food on the counter, waiting for the mailman to come just so she can say hello. Grape leaves, stuffed squash, curried rice, hummus, fattoush, and little pieces of nomura—the rosewater-kissed and soaked-in-honey cousin to baklava. Later, I found out that the mailman was struggling to survive, caring for an ailing mother. He had no time to eat or make food between working two jobs to care for her. My grandmother fed him and his family for years. It didn't matter that he was black. It didn't matter what his religion was. My

grandmother did this because she could. This was one of my first lessons of acceptance.

20. I'd love to go back to where I came from because this world has become cruel and I don't belong *here*. If only I could.

21. In 1979, my father's family fled the Lebanese Civil War. My father will not tell me the stories, but I've heard the whispers and nightmares that haunt my family.

22. *The streets are smeared with blood.*

23. My father's childhood friend was beaten to death by a soldier. The soldier wrote these words: *"Clean your plate if it is touched by a dog, but break it if it's touched by an Al-Akhdam."*

   a. Al-Akhdam: a racially charged and derogatory term that means "servant," which is *usually* used to describe an extremely dark Yemeni person—who is considered to be at the bottom of the "abolished" class ladder.

   b. Al-Akhdam: although the Lebanese are not Yemeni and are not as dark, this term is used to describe the scum of the earth in the Middle East. A worthless and devalued person. A serious insult.

   c. Al-Akhdam: the righteous onslaught of innocent people because your beliefs don't align.

24. Watching innocent people die in front of your face will callous you. You will become a skeleton of abandoned hope, haunted by the shadows that creep at night. These demons will remove your skin, a layer at a time, until your body has unraveled and you have nothing to protect yourself.

25. *You will grow tougher skin with shallowed eyes.*

26. My family hails from the land near the ruins of Baalbek in Lebanon's Beqaa Valley. This land has a deep history. The ruins of Baalbek are a scientific enigma. To this day, scientists, engineers, archeologists, and architects cannot figure out how these stones were transported. Even our modern-day technology is incapable of moving these stones.

27. The Beqaa Valley, the most fertile land of Lebanon, is shadowed by Mount Lebanon. It does not receive much rainfall, but its history is rich in wineries and olive orchards.

28. تقبرني (To'qborni): In English, we have no equivalent of this phrase. It's used often, and it literally means, "You bury me." But it has a more deeply rooted meaning:

    a. *I love you so much that I would rather die, and you must bury me because I cannot imagine a day in my life without you.*

    b. Mothers will often say this to their children to show their deep love.

    c. You could say this to a loved one you don't see often, about whose safety you worry.

    d. It's no surprise we can say I love you in the most morbid way.

29. Every time I enjoy a glass of wine from Château Musar or Château Kefraya, I can taste the beauty of the land in the rich tannins and the strong hints of earth that resemble the smell of fresh mushrooms or a forest floor. Notes of elderberries, sun-soaked cranberries, and even sumac are layered in the dark-red blends of Carignan, Cinsault, Cabernet Sauvignon, and Tempranillo.

30. I let the wine carry me into a deep, red bliss. For a moment, I am there. I can smell the olive trees and the heavenly scent of cedar. I can feel the breeze of the Dead Sea wind rolling over the valley. I can see the villa homes and the gardens rich with figs and lemons. I can taste the land.

31. Most people don't know that sailing and the numerical system were invented by the Phoenicians, the ancestors of the Beqaa Valley, nor that this valley is the oldest producing wine region in the world. It was this valley's grapes that were brought to France and Italy.

32. Due to the war, civil unrest, multiple rulers, and loss of land, the history of wine from this region has been lost, and modern wine history thinks of Lebanon as a "newly emerging" wine region.

33. على راسي ('Ala Rasi): Literally translated as "on my head" in English, but this is not the true meaning of this phrase:

  a. This phrase is used when someone asks for something or demands something like, "Will you give me a hand moving this heavy table?" The response of "'Ala Rasi" would mean "Anything for you."

  b. It can be a sarcastic yes.

  c. Or it could be very sincere yes: "Of course, it has always been *on my mind.*"

  d. This phrase had a lot of value when you asked a neighbor, family member, or friend if they would help you or your family escape the killings.

34. In an article by Daniel Byman and Kenneth Michael Pollack, the authors claim that the Lebanese Civil War began in 1975 and ended in 1990. It killed over 120,000 people. There was an exodus of almost one million people as a result. The war was fought between religious and political groups. The main groups in conflict were the Maronite Christians, Shi'a Muslims, Druze, the Palestinian Liberation Organization, the Israeli army, and the Syrian army.

35. *No one wants to bury their children. Their mothers and fathers.*

36. The Lebanese have been making wine for over eight thousand years. The Temple of Bacchus, the god of wine, is one of the best-preserved temples in the ruins of Baalbek. It has been designated as a world cultural and historical landmark and is protected under this distinction from further destruction. The walls pay homage to the gods of fertility and ask for their help in a bountiful harvest. The gods can be seen in a mosaic bathing and drinking wines that are as beautiful as the Beqaa Valley itself. This temple pre-dates even the oldest vines found in the Mediterranean.

37. But we are just *emerging* in the wine world. It's easy to forget your history when it's destroyed and taken.

38. One day my cousin's friend was confronted by an angry man when she was walking into work. He said, *"You don't belong here, you fucking terrorist,"* and spit on her face. He must have heard her speaking in Arabic as she walked into the pharmacy. Language, you see, is a marker. We are among you.

39. When my father was sixteen, my family fled their home. I was twelve when the Twin Towers came crashing down. These are the tender years where you don't understand your body or what you mean.

40. I feel like a molted snake unsure of its new skin. The tender patches near my heart, eyes, and stomach are raw.

41. I mourn for something I don't understand. I grieve for a piece of me that feels guilty. The person who suffers is the one who turns pride into shame—some days I can't be alive in my skin.

42. For as long as I can remember, and even before, my family has eaten dinner together at my grandmother's house every Saturday. My grandpa and my dad share small shots of cognac (neither of them is Muslim) with big, deep belly laughs. We all cheers to each other before claiming our seats at the table.

43. My grandmother and her sisters have made a big, beautiful, traditional Arabic meal. My favorite childhood dish, lamb spiced rice with roasted almonds, golden raisins, and nuts, is placed right in the center. My grandma, pausing for a second, smiles at me as she pushes it closer to my plate. There are grape leaves rolled with fresh herbs and garden tomatoes next to the bowls of home-brined cracked olives that my grandmother brought from the Beqaa Valley in November. My aunt brings a giant bowl of tabbouleh, my favorite adulthood dish. I quickly snatch it before my father can—I love to get all the lemon juice and olive-oil-soaked bulgur from the bottom. Oval plates of hummus dusted with paprika and pickled turnips. My grandma places chicken roasted in paprika, red pepper, and garlic sauce in front of my grandpa—his favorite.

44. The flavors of my family's land and a piece of our legacy exist in these cherished recipes. These recipes contain the aromas that create a warm Arabic home like the hearty smell of cinnamon, clove, and allspice on the lamb or the caramelized onions, pine nuts, and garlic that get spread across the top of rice. Every smell reveals a specific dish, each prepared for a special occasion or certain time of year. Sometimes, just because it's delicious and it brings a smile to our faces.

45. In sixth grade, my classmates at the Irish Catholic school tell me
    I caused 9/11. That my people caused this. I am bullied, teased, spit
    on, pushed, and mocked—I am not like you. I am no longer able to
    perform white. I have been singled out as the only Arabic kid in the
    school, and this tragedy is my fault.

    a. Oh, you thought I was kidding? *This tragedy is my fault.*

46. When my family arrived in Detroit, my aunt was still a baby. They
    lived in a run-down house underneath the expressway. When I
    drive by that house now on my way to attend classes at Wayne State
    University, I see a boarded window and a beaten-down front door.
    Struggle and despair have seeped into every grain of concrete. This
    is our humble beginning.

47. *How much longer will this house be standing?*

48. *How much longer can we endure?*

49. My family would run out of money that winter and face going
    back to the war. They spoke very little English and had no resources.
    With no help, they saw their future slipping away like sand in an
    hourglass sinking.

50. Then my dad was entered into a high school math competition
    and won. Four thousand dollars gave them peace: the Detroit slums
    were safer than the mountains of Nabatieh.

51. When I was failing math class in sixth grade, my dad sat me at
    the kitchen table explaining concepts and theories I never could
    grasp.

52. My father said: *Math is the universal language. It is powerful.*

53. I am watching the Syrian people of Aleppo being murdered on
    TV on the Arabic news at my grandparents' house. Buildings are
    collapsing, children are crying, mothers are screaming in agony for
    their dead children: *To'qborni, To'qborni!*

54. In college, my math professor reported me to the counseling
    center saying, "*She has a speech impediment that makes her sound
    incompetent and unable to assimilate into the classroom. I am
    recommending that she be contacted for speech therapy classes.*"

55. Translation: I should learn to speak white, midwestern, standard American English—without an accent. I went to counseling not understanding what was wrong with me.

56. The Arabic news tells a different story, one almost unrecognizable from the Western narrative. Here in America, we are more concerned about TV ratings and the latest weight-loss fad than the real news that tears Middle Eastern families apart. Another bombing, more war, orphaned children search for food in rubble. Meanwhile, America cracks open another Bud Light and watches *The Apprentice*. It's no wonder that America has lost empathy. *The news never tells the truth.*

57. I tested out of my required math class when I found out that my white middle-aged math professor was grading my exams and homework differently than those of my white peers. The same answer and work received more credit if you were white.

58. The tension only grew worse when my professor made negative comments about my ethnicity, like: "It's people like that you need to watch out for. They're the ones who steal your jobs away." The professor says these things in class nonchalantly. I feel like I have been dipped into molten lava, naked. I can't control the rage and sadness that begin to crawl out of me—thrashing like a panther with a fresh kill in its teeth.

59. Later, this professor would be dismissed from the university for racial and discriminatory behavior, but his dismissal would not take the images of his piercing darkness behind his eyes away. *Math is ·powerful.*

60. Marcel Khalife, the famous Lebanese folk guitarist and vocalist, performed in Dearborn this December. Arabs from all over the Middle East who now live in Metro Detroit gathered together to listen to songs of peace and love. Some of them burst into tears—but I didn't know why.

61. My heart feels proud to be a part of this culture, to know the dances of my heritage, to be able to sing and perform our stories.

62. *I am an Arab American woman.*

63. I hear the music in my grandmother's basement, beautiful
    Arabic ballads by Marcel Khalife, who's playing the lutelike oud, a
    traditional Arabic instrument. I am just a small child watching as my
    grandmother and her sisters roll grape leaves for dinner and hum
    along. The smells of fresh-picked parsley, green onions, and rinsed
    rice linger in the air. I dance on the tile floor to Khalife's classical
    Arabic music.

64. January 27, 2017: "President" Donald Trump signs an executive
    order banning citizens of Iraq, Syria, Iran, Libya, Somalia, Sudan,
    and Yemen from entering the country for ninety days. The ban also
    halts refugees coming from Syria who were scheduled to enter the
    United States.

65. I cry for reasons I don't understand. I am angry. I throw books
    across the room when I learn that friends are banned from traveling
    back to the United States after visiting family for their winter breaks.
    My blood boils, and it takes all my strength to not punch holes in my
    walls out of rage. I am not okay for several days following this ruling.

66. A strange feeling of unwelcomeness settles like a thick fog on
    a dark night. It creeps slowly, almost unnoticed, until its presence
    leaves a hazy view of what's ahead. It's too late to turn back now that
    this fog has settled. I begin to feel the white box of "other" closing in
    around me with no way to escape.

67. *What is happening?*

68. I am grateful that my grandmother made it back safely from her
    visit to Lebanon before the travel ban was signed. I reflect on how
    lucky I am to have her, the center of our family, here with me.

69. زيتون (Zaituun): The literal translation in English is "fruit of the
    olive tree," but there is so much more rooted in this word:

    a. Zaituun: an Arabic home will always have olives, often
       homemade brined ones on the table, as a symbol of hospitality.
       Feel free to pick them up and eat them, any time of the day.

    b. Zaituun: the word for olive oil. (In colloquial Arabic, it would be
       shortened to zaat.) Olive oil is another item that is always on the
       table when sharing a meal. It is common to add extra olive oil to
       special dishes like kibbeh. Usually, the best olive oil is served for

guests of honor or when there is a celebration. Feel free to pass the olive oil around and apply it vigorously to your meal.

    c. Zaituun: the "fruit of the olive tree" or an olive branch, which is the international symbol for peace. Ironic that olive trees are everywhere in Lebanon, a country that wants to be peaceful and live harmoniously but has seen massive amounts of violence and civil unrest for centuries.

    d. Zaituun: part of my family's livelihood in Lebanon came from harvesting and pressing olives to produce olive oil. Olives have a lot of value and meaning in our home as they provide not only sustenance but also a means to live.

    e. Zaituun: later translated as "paying homage to my family" by opening my first business as an Arab American woman.

70. When I graduated from my undergraduate program with three BA degrees, I decided to move up north to see if my "useless" degrees could get me a job. Michigan was still recovering from the recession, and Detroit had few options that did not involve my parents' home. I figured that if I could get a job out of college, then I might as well live somewhere beautiful that I love.

71. So, I moved to Traverse City, Michigan, in 2013.

72. Despite my family's protest and how they plead with me that I would have a better life if I moved back to Detroit, that I could get a "real" job in the city and make a decent living to pay off my student debt, I decide I just can't do it.

73. I am spoiled. Growing up in Detroit, I have the luxury of exploring different cultures and witness the many beautiful ethnicities scattered throughout the city. Want Thai food at three a.m.? You got it. Feel like an authentic Lebanese mezze meal, just call Al Ameer. Want to see African American art? Well, the DIA just opened a new exhibit, or maybe check out the African American Museum.

74. But this still wasn't enough. I would return to Traverse City, go to work where I felt unvalued, go home and make dinner, do homework, and start the cycle over. Not once interacting with someone of color until I got back to Detroit for graduate school

again.

75. *Against an all-white background, I begin to feel myself fading into a shade I don't want to become.*

76. When I come home I beg my grandmother to show me more recipes that I am not familiar with. I fear that if I do not learn her tricks and understand each recipe, then they will be gone from our legacy when she is gone.

77. February 10, 2016: I wake up in a cold sweat. A terrible nightmare that my grandmother has died and my father has been taken away but no one knows where. My mind races to the demons that adhere to the back of the headboard—they will not leave my mind alone, playing with it like puppetmasters. My chest tightens, and I'm unable to grip reality. In this 4:32 a.m. frenzy, unable to go back to bed, I grab my grandfather's book, the one that has no dust jacket, tattered at the edges and with pages that are more of a brown than cream white now. It is a book of common Arabic phrases, translated into English. This is the book he taught himself English with while he was traveling to America. A relic of my family that I cherish. I decide to write a poem in Arabic. Knowing it can fight the demons back into the emergence of dawn.

78. February 10, 2017: Near my childhood neighborhood, an Iraqi refugee family is being investigated in the middle of the night. Both families, the one that lived upstairs and the one that lived downstairs, are standing in the streets. The front door has a giant dent in it. It's hard to erase the image that it was beaten down by force. The Trump administration appears to be raiding homes for illegal and undocumented Arabic people, although it is not proven that this is true. There is suddenly a stronger police presence in my Dearborn neighborhood, which is known for being a mostly Arabic community.

79. I did not plan to fall in love with a white man from Northern Michigan. But Chien is a good man whose heart is full of love, acceptance, respect, and kindness. "I'm going to marry a woman that moves like you," were his first words to me when he saw me dance at a performance. I ignored him for over a month, rattled by his first sentence to me.

80. The first dinner that Chien came with me to meet my family
    could have been a skit out of *Saturday Night Live*:

[Enter stage right.] *Ari and Chien arrive at Grandmother's house and sit
    down at the dinner table after awkward hellos and introductions.*

Narrator: Saturday Night Club is a Mokdad family tradition. Every Sat-
    urday at seven p.m., the Mokdad family gets together for dinner to
    discuss politics, play card games, and catch up with one another. This
    poor chap over here [points to Chien] has no clue what he is getting
    himself into.

Grandpa: Whachu do? [Looks up from plate full of food at Chien.]

Chien: I'm a merchant marine captain of a catamaran business in Tra-
    verse City. [Looks up from his food and smiles proudly.]

Grandpa: [In Arabic, to Ari's father] What is he doing here?

Ari's Father: [In Arabic] I don't know, some boat thing. Don't worry
    about it—he won't be here long. [Looking directly into Ari's eyes.]

Narrator: You see, they talk in Arabic so Chien has no clue what they are
    saying and Ari can hear it all.

81. Dinner continues, and I am left to listen to my family talk about
    this man I've brought home. Chien devours his plate of food, and
    like all wonderful Arabic hospitality, my grandmother refills Chien's
    plate, wishing him blessings.

82. صحتين (Sahtein): There isn't an exact translation of this Arabic
    blessing, which literally means "two healths." It would be most
    similar to toasting everyone at the table and saying, "To your health!"
    while everyone else chimed in.

    a. A symbol of respect and a blessing that also means "I hope you
       live a long time."

    b. Since you are eating a lot, you must be healthy because only
       healthy people have a good appetite—this one's a little outdated
       in beliefs now because there is a lot of bad food out there that you
       can also eat a lot of, and it would not be good for your health.

    c. An open invitation to come to dinner and eat together again.

    d. The beginning of Chien's slow acceptance into my family through his appreciation of my family's food.

83. *"Math is powerful,"* my father would say. *"It brings order to chaos."* In my mind, I would talk back and say: "But poetry does, too!"

84. My father refuses to acknowledge my existence. Once he finds out about Chien having a son and that I am falling in love with him, everything gets dark. Sometimes the weight of the waves comes crashing down. Often you can surf them to shore; other times, they engulf you.

85. *In the bath full of acid, as your skin begins to melt away, you'll think of your family and loved ones, pleading that this end is a welcome alternative.*

86. How could I ever love a man who has a child out of wedlock? Why would I want to spend my life with a loser? I would have to be the breadwinner my whole life with a man without a degree. How could I, a hardworking, smart young lady not find a better man? *You are a disgrace. You are not my daughter.*

87. *You'll emerge from the ashes with an armor of Kevlar. You will grow thicker skin and a stronger mind.*

88. At a silent auction, I bid on a piece and win. The piece is a hand-cut wood masterpiece of Arabic calligraphy with ornate golden embellishments. It reads in both Arabic and English: "With wealth, a strange land becomes a homeland. But in destitution, even a homeland becomes a strange land."

89. This art means so much to me. It reminds me of my family's humble beginning, but it also reminds me of the constant conflict that is happening in the Middle East and to those of us who feel displaced.

90. Yesterday, Syrian people were murdered through chemical warfare. It's unclear who did this, or why, or what the ultimate outcome will be. Our president responded with more violence, launching fifty-nine missiles because "he was affected by the images of children dying." It seems that opening our borders to those

seeking refuge would have been a far better response.

91. Acceptance is like eating a prickly pear. Impossible at first to enjoy, through its thick, spiny skin, but once you peel back your layers of hate, misunderstanding, or lack of education, there lies a treat filled with juicy salvation.

92. العائلة هي كل شيء: Family is everything.

    You've "made it" in this family.

    Chien is family.

93. Our family becomes more fluid and loses our strict understanding of the idea of family in a traditional sense. I am expanding my family, bringing a new voice to our table, and it's a tongue they don't often get to interact with—whiteness.

94. I like to think that with each dinner, each dish and glass of wine, we are slowly teaching our Northern Michigan community about the beauty of the Mediterranean and offering a different version than the media portrays.

95. I may not be in exile, but I did find refuge in Northern Michigan. I will always love my Detroit city streets, the clamor and hum of the city against the heavy machinery that is always thrashing, the art that graffitis every building, and the culture that bleeds from the cracks of the city. It is possible to be from two places at once. No matter where I'm going, I always feel like I'm coming home.

96. *And* I am still counting. Like the Phoenicians counted stars when they learned to sail. Like the way I count stars now when I sail with Chien on the silver waves of Lake Michigan.

97. *I am an Arab American woman.*

CONTRIBUTORS

MARCIA ALDRICH is the author of the free memoir *Girl Rearing*, published by W. W. Norton. She has been the editor of *Fourth Genre: Explorations in Nonfiction. Companion to an Untold Story* won the AWP Award in Creative Nonfiction. She is the editor of *Waveform: Twenty-First-Century Essays by Women*, published by the University of Georgia Press. Visit her online at Waveformessays.wordpress.com.

FLEDA BROWN's *The Woods Are on Fire: New & Selected Poems* was chosen by Ted Kooser for his University of Nebraska poetry series in 2017. She has nine previous collections of poems. Her work has twice appeared in *The Best American Poetry* and has won a Pushcart Prize, the Felix Pollak Prize, the Philip Levine Prize, and the Great Lakes Colleges Association New Writers Award. She has twice been a finalist for the National Poetry Series. Her memoir, *Driving with Dvorak*, was published in 2010 by the University of Nebraska Press. She is professor emerita at the University of Delaware, where she directed the Poets in the Schools program. She was poet laureate of Delaware from 2001 to 2007. She now lives with her husband, Jerry Beasley, in Traverse City, Michigan, and is on the faculty of the Rainier Writing Workshop, a low-residency MFA program in Tacoma, Washington.

BENJAMIN BUSCH is a writer, filmmaker, and illustrator. He served sixteen years as a Marine Corps infantry officer, deploying twice to Iraq, and portrayed Officer Anthony Colicchio for three seasons on the HBO series *The Wire*. He is the author of the memoir *Dust to Dust* (Ecco), and his essays have appeared in *Harper's*, the *New York Times Magazine*, *River Styx*, *Guernica*, and on NPR. His poems have appeared in *North American Review*, *Prairie Schooner*, *Five Points*, *Epiphany*, *Oberon*, and *Michigan Quarterly Review*, among others. He teaches nonfiction in the Sierra Nevada College MFA program and lives on a farm in Michigan.

JAIMIEN DELP divides her time between Ann Arbor, where she teaches in the English Department Writing Program at the University of Michigan, and Northern Michigan, where she loves spending time with her family along the coastlines and riverbanks. She earned her MFA in poetry from the Helen Zell Writers' Program, where she was the recipient of a Zell Postgraduate Fellowship. Her collection of poems, *Point of Sand,* won the Michigan Writers Cooperative Press Chapbook Contest. Her work has appeared in *Orion, Mid-American Review, Dunes Review, Boardman Review, Traverse Magazine,* and *The Smoking Poet,* among others.

JERRY DENNIS has earned his living as a freelance writer since 1986. In that time he has published a dozen books including *A Walk in the Animal Kingdom, The Windward Shore, The Living Great Lakes,* and *A Place on the Water.* His essays, stories, and poems have appeared in the *New York Times, Smithsonian, Orion, Michigan Quarterly Review, PANK,* and many other publications. He has won the Michigan Author of the Year Award, the Sigurd Olson Nature Writing Award, and the Great Lakes Culture Award, among others. He lives in Northern Michigan. Visit him online at www.jerrydennis.net.

TOI DERRICOTTE's most recent book is *The Undertaker's Daughter.* Her honors include the 2012 Paterson Poetry Prize for Sustained Literary Achievement and the 2012 PEN/Voelcker Award for Poetry. Her poems have appeared in *American Poetry Review,* the *Paris Review,* the *New Yorker,* and *Poetry.* With Cornelius Eady, she cofounded Cave Canem in 1996. She serves on the Academy of American Poets' Board of Chancellors.

RHODA JANZEN is *the New York Times* #1 bestselling author of *Mennonite in a Little Black Dress* (Henry Holt, 2009), a finalist for the Thurber Award for Humor. Janzen's *Mennonite Meets Mr. Right* (Hachette, 2012) was a finalist for the Books for a Better Life Award. She is also the author of *Squeeze the Sponge: The No-Yawn Guide to College Writing* (Flip, 2018), and a collection of poems, *Babel's Stair* (Word, 2006). Janzen teaches English at Hope College in Holland, Michigan.

MARDI JO LINK is the author of five books of nonfiction, including the *New York Times* bestseller *Wicked Takes the Witness Stand*. She studied journalism at Michigan State University and has an MFA from Queens University of Charlotte. Her memoir, *Bootstrapper*, won the *Elle* Reader's Prize, the Bookseller's Choice Award, and was an Indie Next Pick. Academy Award–winning actress Rachel Weisz has optioned the film rights. Mardi lives in Traverse City with her husband and writes a column for her hometown newspaper, the *Traverse City Record-Eagle*.

AIREA D. MATTHEWS is the author of *Simulacra*, winner of the 2016 Yale Series of Younger Poets. Her work has appeared in *Callaloo*, *Best American Poets 2015*, *Harvard Review*, *American Poet*, and elsewhere. She is an assistant professor at Bryn Mawr College, where she directs the Creative Writing Program.

KATHLEEN MCGOOKEY's most recent book is *Heart in a Jar* (White Pine Press). Her work has appeared in journals including *Crazyhorse*, *Denver Quarterly*, *Epoch*, *Field*, *Indiana Review*, *Ploughshares*, *The Prose Poem: An International Journal*, *Prairie Schooner*, *Quarterly West*, *Rhino*, *Seneca Review,* and *West Branch*. She has also published two other books of poems, two chapbooks, and a book of translations of French poet Georges Godeau's prose poems. She has received grants from the Sustainable Arts Foundation and the French Ministry of Foreign Affairs, and lives in Middleville, Michigan, with her family.

JESSICA MESMAN is the author of four books, including the memoir *Love & Salt*, winner of the 2014 Christopher Award for Literature. She founded and directs Sick Pilgrim, a community of artists and seekers who are inspired (or repelled) by Catholicism. Her chronic homesickness now includes missing Northern Michigan.

STEPHANIE MILLS is a longtime bioregionalist and the author of *Epicurean Simplicity* and *In Service of the Wild*, among other books, as well as numerous reviews and articles. Mills has lived in Maple City, Michigan, since 1984. Her most recent work appears on naturechange.org. Visit her online: www.smillswriter.com.

ARI L. MOKDAD is an award-winning published poet and performance artist. Ari's work has appeared at Wayne State University's Open Field Poetry Series and the Jazz Café at the Music Hall in Detroit. Most of Ari's work deals with multiculturalism, nature, body, ethnicity, and place. Currently, Ari is a doctoral student at Wayne State University, where she studies performance art, creative writing, and embodiment rhetoric. She divides her time between Traverse City and her hometown, Detroit.

ANNE-MARIE OOMEN most recently coauthored *The Lake Michigan Mermaid* with Linda Nemec Foster. She has written *Love, Sex, and 4-H* (Next Generation Indie Award for Memoir), *Pulling Down the Barn, House of Fields* (both Michigan Notable Books), *An American Map: Essays,* and a collection of poetry, *Uncoded Woman* (Milkweed Editions). She edited *Looking Over My Shoulder: Reflections on the Twentieth Century* (MCH). She has written seven plays, including the award-winning *Secrets of Luuce Talk Tavern.* She is an instructor at Solstice MFA at Pine Manor College (MA) and Interlochen College of Creative Arts. Visit her at www.anne-marieoomen.com.

W. S. PENN teaches creative writing (nonfiction and fiction) at Michigan State University. His books include *The Absence of Angels, Killing Time with Strangers,* and *This Is the World* (fiction), *All My Sins Are Relatives, Feathering Custer,* and *As We Are Now* (nonfiction), and *Storytelling in the Digital Age.* He currently has two novels on submission by the Speilburg Literary Agency. This essay is from a collection in progress titled *Raising Bean,* written for and dedicated to his granddaughter.

ROCHELLE RILEY, who always works with two phones, is a columnist for the *Detroit Free Press,* where she has been a leading voice for children, education, competent government, and race since 2000. She is author of the new book *The Burden: African Americans and the Enduring Impact of Slavery* (Wayne State University Press, 2018). She received the 2017 Eugene C. Pulliam Editorial Fellowship from the Society of Professional Journalists and the 2017 Ida B. Wells Award from the National Association of Black Journalists for her outstanding efforts to make newsrooms and news coverage more accurately reflect the diversity of the communities they serve. She is a global traveler who has been to 25 countries and counting. She was a 2007–2008 Knight-Wallace Fellow at the University of Michigan. And she was a 2016 inductee into the Michigan Journalism Hall of Fame.

ROBERT ROOT is a professor emeritus of English at Central Michigan University. He is the editor of *"Time by Moments Steals Away": The 1848 Journal of Ruth Douglass,* and, with Jill Burkland, *The Island Within Us: Isle Royale Artists-in-Residence 1991–1998.* His wanderings in Michigan are recorded in *Recovering Ruth: A Biographer's Tale, Postscripts: Retrospections on Time and Place,* and a collection of his WCMU-FM radio essays, *Limited Sight Distance: Essays for Airwaves.* He is also the author of *Happenstance* and *Walking Home Ground: In the Footsteps of Muir, Leopold, and Derleth* and has a work in progress on the entire arc of the Niagara Escarpment. Visit him online at www.rootwriting.com.

DAVY ROTHBART is a bestselling author, Emmy Award–winning film-maker, creator of *Found Magazine,* contributor to public radio's *This American Life,* and author of a book of personal essays, *My Heart Is an Idiot,* and a collection of stories, *The Lone Surfer of Montana, Kansas.* He writes regularly for *GQ* and *Los Angeles Magazine,* and his work has appeared in the *New Yorker,* the *New York Times,* and *The Believer.* His documentary film, *Medora,* about a resilient high-school basketball team in a dwindling Indiana town, aired recently on the acclaimed PBS series "Independent Lens," won a 2014 Emmy Award, and can now be streamed online. Rothbart is also the founder of Washington to Washington, an annual hiking adventure for inner-city kids. He lives between Los Angeles and his hometown of Ann Arbor. Visit him online at foundmagazine.com.

TERESA SCOLLON is the author of *To Embroider the Ground with Prayer*, from Wayne State University Press, and a chapbook from Michigan Writers Cooperative Press. Scollon is a National Endowment for the Arts fellow, and an alumna and former writer-in-residence at Interlochen Arts Academy. She works as an editor, educator, and a consultant in organization development. She teaches at Traverse City's Front Street Writers program for high school students at the TBAISD Career-Tech Center. She is a native of Michigan's Thumb. Visit her online at www.teresascollon.com.

HOLLY WREN SPAULDING is the author of *If August* (Alice Greene & Co., 2017) and numerous chapbooks, letterpress projects, essays, and articles. Her work has appeared in *Michigan Quarterly Review, Witness, The Ecologist, The Nation, Artsy,* the *New York Times,* and elsewhere. Her poem "Blue Whale" will appear as a limited-edition handbound book from Antler Editions in 2018. She teaches creative writing for Interlochen College of Creative Arts and is the founder of Poetry Forge. Visit her online: www.hollywrenspaulding.com.

MICHAEL STEINBERG, the founding editor of the literary journal *The Fourth Genre: Explorations in Nonfiction,* has written, coauthored, and/or edited six books and a stage play. In 2003, *Still Pitching* won the *ForeWord Magazine*/Independent Press Memoir of the Year. An anthology, *The Fourth Genre: Contemporary Writers of/on Creative Nonfiction* (with Robert Root), is in a sixth edition.

ALISON SWAN's poems and essays have appeared in many publications, including her poetry chapbooks, *Before the Snow Moon* and *Dog Heart,* and the recent anthologies *Ghost Fishing: An Eco-Justice Poetry Anthology* and *Here: Women Writing on the Upper Peninsula.* Her book *Fresh Water: Women Writing on the Great Lakes* is a Michigan Notable Book. She's been awarded a Mesa Refuge Fellowship and the Michigan Environmental Council's Petoskey Prize for Grassroots Environmental Leadership. She teaches in the Institute of the Environment and Sustainability at Western Michigan University.

KEITH TAYLOR has published many books over the years—poetry, prose, and translations. His most recent is a collection of poetry, *The Bird-while,* published by Wayne State University Press in 2017. He recently retired from the writing program at the University of Michigan.

JACOB WHEELER is an independent journalist based in Traverse City, Michigan. He edits and publishes the *Glen Arbor Sun* newspaper in Leelanau County, teaches journalism at Northwestern Michigan College, and freelances for publications including *Bridge Magazine* and *Edible Grande Traverse.* Wheeler was born in Denmark and has penned bylines from five continents. His first book, *Between Light and Shadow* (University of Nebraska Press, 2011), narrates and investigates the Guatemalan baby adoption industry and journey.